IT'S ABOUT TIME

IT'S ABOUT TIME

A HISTORY OF
ARCHAEOLOGICAL DATING
IN NORTH AMERICA

Edited by

Stephen E. Nash

THE UNIVERSITY OF UTAH PRESS

Salt Lake City

Library of Congress Cataloging-in-Publication Data

It's about time : a history of archaeological dating in North America /
edited by Stephen E. Nash.
    p. cm.
  Includes bibliographical references and index.
  ISBN 0-87480-621-6 (alk. paper)
    1. Archaeological dating—United States—History. I. Nash,
Stephen Edward, 1964–

CC78.I87 2000
930.1'028'5—dc21
                          99-046316

Contents

Figures

Tables

PART I

Introduction

CHAPTER 1

The Surprisingly Deficient History of Archaeochronology

STEPHEN E. NASH
Department of Anthropology
Field Museum of Natural History

JEFFREY S. DEAN
Laboratory of Tree-Ring Research
The University of Arizona

Time. Astronomers, philosophers, physicists, anthropologists, politicians, geographers, and theologians have pondered the nature and meaning of "Time." Is it linear or cyclical? Is it a dimension, process, or matrix? Is it absolute and measurable, as it seemed to be to Newton and Galileo, or is it relative and defined merely on the basis of statements of coincidence (Silver 1998)? Is it a natural corollary to the second law of thermodynamics, or is it a cultural construct? Is it reversible? Why is it so difficult to describe time without using spatial metaphors (Gell 1992)? Archaeologists have largely excused their discipline of these epistemological and metaphysical questions (Dark 1995:64; Shanks and Tilley 1987:118), yet few will argue that the single most distinguishing characteristic of archaeology within the social sciences is the examination and interpretation of temporal relationships as represented in the archaeological record. Archaeologists elucidate these temporal relationships, and therefore study the passage of time, by applying any one of a suite of absolute and relative dating techniques that may be applicable in a particular research context. This book is about time because it offers critical histories of the development and application of the most important dating techniques relevant to North American archaeology.

ARCHAEOLOGISTS AND CHRONOLOGY

"Chronology," wrote Fay-Cooper Cole in 1934, "is the soul of archaeology" (Cole 1934). The study of temporal relationships was a major focus of North American archaeological research during the first half of the twentieth century, especially after A. E. Douglass of the University of Arizona announced in December 1929 that he had dated, on the common calendar and through tree-ring analysis, some 40 prehistoric Southwestern sites (Douglass 1929; see Nash 1999). Chronology was not always important to archaeologists, however, nor was it the "soul" of early North American archaeology. Indeed, much archaeological research during the first quarter of the twentieth century reveals a surprising indifference to the study of temporal relationships of any kind (cf. Lyman et al. 1997).

American archaeology prior to 1914 focused on artifact classification, description, and typology (Willey and Sabloff 1980). As archaeologists gained control over these realms, they began to experiment with stratigraphic (Kidder 1924, 1958; Nelson 1916, 1918) and seriation (Kroeber 1916a, 1916b; Spier 1917a, 1917b, 1931) analyses developed by their European contemporaries (Browman and Givens 1996; Lyman et al. 1997; Lyman et al. 1998). There is evidence, however, that archaeologists' stimulus to chronological research came not from within their own quarters but rather from their anthropological colleagues. Ethnologist Berthold Laufer offered his understanding of the task at hand in a review of Roland Dixon's (1913) "Some Aspects of North American Archaeology." Laufer wrote: "Chronology is at the root of the matter, being the nerve electrifying the dead body of history. It should be incumbent upon the American archaeologist to establish a chronological basis of the pre-Columbian cultures, and the American ethnologist should make it a point to bring chronology into the life and history of the pre-Columbian Indians" (Laufer 1913:577; see also Sapir 1916).

Despite Laufer's call to arms, many North American archaeologists of the next decade still did not share the interest in chronology demonstrated by Alfred Kroeber, Laufer, Nels Nelson, and Leslie Spier. Clark Wissler of the American Museum of Natural History (AMNH) explained the situation to his colleague Sylvanus Morley as he described debate over the agenda for Neil Judd's 1921 Pueblo Bonito conference:

> Strange to say, there was among anthropologists [archaeologists] in general a considerable indifference and even hostility to the chronological idea. With the waning of [Frederick Ward] Putnam's influence this reaction gathered strength until the whole subject [of chronology] was taboo. The time was, a few years ago, when no one dared mention the fact that

there might be important differences in our dates. Happily the development of anthropology in Europe has brought us to our senses again. We must establish a chronology for the New World and acknowledge our incompetence. Without a true time perspective the data of our subject will be a chaos of facts from which the general reader and even the student will flee as from a pestilence. [letter August 16, 1921]

Several years later, in 1925, Alfred Kroeber commented that "incredible as it may seem, by 1915–1925 so little time perspective had been achieved in archaeology that Wissler and I, in trying to reconstruct the Native American past, could then actually infer more from the [artifact] distributions and typology than from the archaeologists' determinations. Our inferences were not too exact, but they were broader than from those excavations" (quoted in Lyon 1996:5).

Even as late as 1930, after Douglass had "bridged the gap" and dated prehistoric Southwestern sites, the irascible Edgar Lee Hewett of the School of American Research in Santa Fe protested that "the time factors in American [pre]history have received an amount of attention in excess of their importance....Just why chronology should be considered of such vast importance is difficult to understand" (Hewett 1930:156–157). Given the favorable popular and scholarly reaction to Douglass's (1929) accomplishment and the "time factors" he brought to archaeology (Nash 1997a, 1998, 1999), Hewett's stance was decidedly peculiar and out of the archaeological mainstream.

David Browman and Douglas Givens (1996:80) explain that archaeologists' indifference to time and the study of temporal relationships was a result of archaeologists' perception "of such short time depth for habitation of the continent that attention was focused primarily on the identification of archaeological areas as predecessor to the culture areas then being defined." Archaeologists of the period thus assumed that "very little had changed since the first American Indians had arrived" in North America (Browman and Givens 1996:80). David Meltzer (1985:255) similarly argued that archaeologists of that era did not consider cultural change significant unless it was parallel in scope to the Paleolithic-Neolithic transition previously identified in Europe. Whatever the case may be, it is clear that sometime after 1914 (the exact date is debatable) the study of temporal relationships within the archaeological record evolved from rarely attempted serial, or "percentage stratigraphy" (Lyman et al. 1998) analyses, to become a primary framework within which to structure archaeological research in North America. In the five decades prior to the development of the New Archaeology, a period dominated by the culture history paradigm, archaeologists invested a great deal of time, effort, and therefore money, in the elucidation of temporal relationships and the development of local and regional chronologies.

With the advent of the New Archaeology in the late 1950s and 1960s, the nearly exclusive study of spatiotemporal relationships came to be perceived with some disdain. While it is debatable whether culture historians really saw the establishment of local or regional chronologies as an (the only?) end to their research (Lyman et al. 1997; Martin 1971; Piggott 1959; Willey and Sabloff 1980), it *is* true that archaeologists have since expanded their research agendas to include a wider variety of theoretical orientations, such that symbolic, behavioral, evolutionary, and other archaeologies now have significant adherents while culture history for its own sake does not. Given this, and the development of a number of highly technical dating techniques, the details of which are beyond the province of most archaeologists, it is arguable that archaeologists are now prone to take chronology, in the literal sense, for granted. Archaeologists need only submit samples to the appropriate laboratories, obtain dates, apply them to the appropriate components, sites, or regions under study, and *voíla*, a chronology has been obtained. A strict reading of *chronology* requires, of course, a much more active analytical role on the part of the archaeologist, and the rather pessimistic view just presented does not do justice to the many archaeologists who today actively consider the assumptions, ramifications, and implications of archaeological dates and dating (e.g., Smiley and Ahlstrom 1997). Nevertheless, we submit that, in general, archaeologists in the last decade of the twentieth century have less of an appreciation for the intricacies and nuances of chronology development than did some of their predecessors. Though recent publications present overviews (e.g., chapters in Taylor and Aitken 1997), and in some cases, histories (e.g., Browman and Givens 1996; Lyman et al. 1997; Nash 1997a, 1999; Taylor 1985, 1996) of the dating techniques considered herein, we believe it is time to critically evaluate, in one volume, the development and application of the most commonly used archaeological dating techniques in North America. Such evaluations will allow archaeologists to better understand how these techniques have affected the practice of North American archaeology and the interpretation of North American prehistory.

A Brief Note on Nomenclature

Archaeologists today have at their disposal a wide variety of dating techniques with which to gather data to guide or supplement their archaeological analyses. Each technique has unique principles, theories, assumptions, applications, strengths, and limitations. This creates the potential for a considerable amount of confusion not only when dates derived from a particular technique are analyzed but especially when dates produced by different techniques are compared (Dean 1978:224). It therefore behooves the archaeologist-consumer to understand the interpretive vagaries of the dating techniques and the resultant data, and to determine their appropriateness to the task at hand. These vagaries are treated in detail by specialists in the ensuing chapters, and especially in the references cited therein, but several terminological issues must be agreed upon before we may proceed. These have to do with the differences between absolute and relative dating techniques, independent and intrinsic dating techniques, dated and target events, and accuracy, precision, and resolution.

Absolute Versus Relative Dating Techniques

Archaeological dating techniques have traditionally been divided between *absolute*, or those that yield a date on some quantitative calendar or scale, and *relative*, or those that merely allow phenomena to be placed in sequence. Examples of the former include the majority of the techniques considered herein: radiocarbon, tree-ring, obsidian hydration, luminescence, and archaeomagnetic dating are all absolute dating techniques. Examples of the latter include stratigraphy and seriation analyses. In a strict sense, one could argue that "relative dating" is a misnomer, because relative dating techniques do not produce dates at all, but they do measure time (sensu Lyman et al. 1997) and compare temporal relationships.

Colman et al. (1987:315) suggested that the term *absolute* be abandoned altogether and replaced by four categories: numerical-age methods, applied to those that produce results on a ratio scale but that may have uncertainties attached; calibrated-age methods, in which rates of particular processes must be calibrated by independent chronological control; relative-age methods, those that produce sequences of events; and correlated-age methods, those in which age estimates are produced through correlation (or association) with independently dated events. Unfortunately, the categories proposed by Colman et al. (1987:316) are not necessarily mutually exclusive.

While there is no doubt that dendrochronology and historical record analysis are numerical-age methods and that archaeomagnetism, stratigraphy, and seriation are correlated-age methods, it is less than clear whether radiocarbon dating is best characterized as a numerical-age or calibrated-age method, and whether luminescence and obsidian hydration are best characterized as numerical-age, calibrated-age, or relative-age methods.

In spite of their limitations, the terms "absolute" and "relative" will be retained in this volume because they are well established in the literature. The terms proposed by Colman et al. (1987) are used, especially by Charlotte Beck and George Jones (this volume) when increasingly specific characterizations are required.

Independent Versus Intrinsic Dating Techniques

Some archaeologists find it useful to distinguish between *independent* and *intrinsic* (or *dependent*) dating techniques. The former derive dates on the basis of phenomena that are unrelated to human behavior, such as the growth of a tree-ring or the rate of radiometric decay of an isotope. The latter rely on some aspect of human behavior, be it prehistoric ceramic manufacture, hearth firing, or the construction of an archaeological typology, for the derivation of dates or sequences.

Dated Events Versus Target Events

In an analysis of the role of independent dating in archaeology, Jeffrey Dean (1978) differentiated between *dated* events and *target* events. *Dated* events are those that are actually dated by a given chronometric technique in a particular situation. The dated event in archaeomagnetic dating is the last time an iron-rich clay substance was heated above a certain point and then cooled, thus allowing ferromagnetic particles in the clay to realign with magnetic north. In obsidian hydration dating the dated event is the exposure of a freshly fractured surface to the humidity and, to a lesser degree, temperature of the atmosphere. *Target* events, on the other hand, are the actual events and processes that are of interest to the archaeologist, be they site occupation and abandonment, house construction, or the date at which an agricultural field was last used. Dated events and target events do not always coincide, and much of the difficulty inherent in the interpretation of archaeological dates has to do with identifying and reconciling potential differences between the two (Dean 1978).

Accuracy, Precision, and Resolution

All archaeological dating techniques, be they absolute or relative, independent or intrinsic, measure variables. All measurement techniques have associated sources of error, both systematic and random. Understanding the source and nature of error is crucial to the evaluation and interpretation of a date, within its archaeological context, and dating, within an archaeological analysis. This is not the appropriate forum in which to undertake a detailed epistemological and philosophical analysis of variable measurement and its associated difficulties, but we must elucidate the differences between accuracy, precision, and resolution in order to achieve a common vocabulary, especially because the terms are often used uncritically and interchangeably.

Accuracy refers to the relationship between the estimated value of a parameter and its true value. In the vernacular, it refers to how well a technique "hits" the true value in question, be it mass, velocity, density, or a calendar date. Accuracy is a function of systematic error, which results from uncontrolled bias of constant magnitude and direction, such as that resulting from systematic differences in the way individuals collect archaeomagnetic samples (Lange and Murphy 1990) to the well-known and systematic discrepancies between different radiocarbon laboratories (Rozanski et al. 1992).

Precision refers to the reproducibility of a given measurement. One must ask: How close do repeated measurements come to the same value? Because precision is a function of random error, which is intrinsic to the measurement process itself, the true value of the parameter in question is of no consequence to the issue of measurement precision: Dates with lower standard deviations are simply more precise than those with higher standard deviations, no matter where they fall on the quantitative scale in question.

Resolution refers to a dating technique's ability to "show that events occurred during different intervals of time" (Ahlstrom 1985:26) and has two components: scale and assignment. Resolution of scale refers to the nature, or length, of the units into which the time scale of a particular dating technique is divided: calendar years for tree-rings, radiocarbon years for ^{14}C dating, etc. Resolution of assignment refers to the minimum number of units along that scale that is specified by the technique. Tree-ring dating has a resolution of assignment of one unit, or calendar year; radiocarbon dating has a resolution of assignment of variable numbers of units, depending on the precision of the particular assay.

To make profitable use of any dating technique, archaeologists must recognize that different dating techniques offer different levels of accuracy, precision, and resolution, and must, on those bases, select the appropriate technique given the questions being asked and the nature of the archaeological record at a given site.

ARCHAEOLOGISTS, DATING TECHNIQUES, AND GOALS OF THIS VOLUME

Stratigraphic and seriation analyses were first adopted and developed by archaeologists during the 1910s and 1920s. Dendrochronology was developed and applied by archaeologists in the 1910s, 1920s, and 1930s. Radiocarbon dating was introduced to archaeology in 1949 and was widely applied in the 1950s. The bases for archaeomagnetic, obsidian hydration, and luminescence dating were introduced in the 1960s, though the application of each in North American archaeology has followed radically different developmental trajectories. Since then, numerous other dating techniques have been developed in the physical sciences and have been applied to archaeological research (see chapters in Taylor and Aitken 1997; Wintle 1996), though they are beyond the scope of this volume.

This volume is divided into five sections. The first is this introduction. The second offers detailed, if idiosyncratic, examinations of stratigraphic analysis, ceramic dating, and tree-ring dating—the three techniques that have enjoyed the longest application in North American archaeology. Julie K. Stein considers the application of stratigraphic analysis, using European examples for comparative purposes, and illuminates a number of interpretive problems created when archaeologists inappropriately imbue stratigraphic analysis with cultural and typological concepts. Eric Blinman examines ceramic dating with an eye toward the surprisingly high degree of precision and accuracy afforded by what has been traditionally considered a relative dating technique. Stephen E. Nash then examines the interpretive impact of archaeological tree-ring dating, the first absolute dating technique available to North American prehistorians.

The third section offers histories of more highly technical and more recently developed dating techniques. R. E. Taylor offers insights on the impact of radiocarbon dating on archaeological method and theory. Jeffrey L. Eighmy provides an insider's view into the development of archaeomagnetic dating, and Charlotte Beck and George T. Jones discuss the applications and implications of obsidian hydration dating.

James K. Feathers then considers the development and underutilization of luminescence dating.

The two chapters in the fourth section offer words of warning and admonishment, from an archaeologist and a sociologist of science, respectively. Ronald H. Towner considers the sometimes significant discrepancies between historical data and tree-ring dates relevant to Navajo archaeology to warn the archaeologist-consumer of potential pitfalls in the use of apparently reliable chronometric data. If, as Towner demonstrates, there can be such dramatic inconsistencies between these most precise and resolved dating techniques, we are reminded to always critically evaluate statements regarding the prehistoric, and indeed historic, past that are based on less precise, resolved, and possibly less accurate, techniques. Following Towner's insightful, if disconcerting, comments, sociologist of science and technology Jennifer L. Croissant considers the utility of (self-) reflective histories of archaeology and archaeological techniques on the growth and maturation of the discipline.

In the fifth and final section, Nash reflects briefly on the contributions to this volume. He considers the place of dating within archaeology and calls for renewed emphasis on chronology and increased collaboration between archaeologists and specialists in archaeochronology.

CONCLUSION

The development and application of new analytical techniques in North American archaeology has never been simple or straightforward. Serendipity, perseverance, contingency, sociology, politics, economics, and luck have played a role in the development of all archaeological dating techniques, so much so that the current analytical use of any dating technique must be considered, at least in part, a function of its developmental history.

Critical reviews of the eight most important dating techniques in North American archaeology illuminate only a portion of the interesting and significant lessons, anecdotes, and themes in the history of archaeological dating. Comprehensive histories of each technique would fill volumes (e.g., Nash 1999); we hope that the chapter-length critical histories offered herein serve as the impetus for an increasingly sophisticated dialogue on the nature, significance, and interpretive utility of these dating techniques in North American archaeology. As archaeologists venture into the new millennium, we believe it is about time to critically examine the trials, tribulations, and contingencies that have affected the successes and failures of archaeological dating and interpretation in the twentieth century. Once such an understanding is achieved, we are better poised to productively apply these techniques in North American archaeological research in the twenty-first century.

PART II

Layers, Styles, and Rings: Early Approaches to Archaeological Dating

CHAPTER 2

Stratigraphy and Archaeological Dating

JULIE K. STEIN
Department of Anthropology
University of Washington

Stratigraphic dating has been part of archaeological method since Boucher de Perthes and others used it to associate artifacts with extinct Ice Age fauna. Relative-age determination based on the laws of superposition and context is used in all archaeological excavation and is used more frequently than almost every other dating technique. A site may contain hundreds of superimposed layers, plazas, foundation walls, or streets; in every case, stratigraphy is used to interpret the age relationships between artifacts and architecture.

The value of stratigraphic dating in archaeology becomes apparent in two principal ways—in our daily lives and in the classroom. Common sense tells us that when we rustle through our recycling pile to find the memo discarded a month ago. We use it to sort mail lying on our desks or clothing dropped on the floor. Superposition, as a function of gravity, is part of our everyday lives whether or not we are archaeologists.

The value of stratigraphy in archaeology is reinforced further in the classroom, where the principles of stratigraphy are introduced. As students, we learn that stratigraphy and its role in dating were not always part of archaeology. Excavations used to proceed without recording the superpositional arrangement of strata. Now, stratigraphy has gained such importance that it is always noted using terms such as relative dating, intrusion, stratification, and the law of superposition. We learn that archaeology was present at the birth of stratigraphy, when the diluvial-waters hypothesis was challenged and successions of rocks were correlated across great distances, but that stratigraphy was not necessarily considered when palaces, mounds, and villages were first being unearthed. We learn that it became important again when research questions demanded an increasingly finer scale of age determination and relative dating was the answer.

Indeed, in Archaeology 101 we learn that stratigraphy is more than a pile of clothing.

I would go so far as to say that in the classroom, we learn that for archaeologists, stratigraphy is stratigraphic dating. We use stratification to obtain two kinds of information: chronological and contextual. Age is determined by noting the relative position of superimposed artifacts: those on top are younger than those on the bottom. Context is the association of artifacts inferred from formation processes, including deposition, turbation, and human activities. Stratigraphy in archaeology is taught as the fundamental exercise in determining age and context. Very little other than superposition or its disruption is important to archaeological stratigraphy.

Historians of archaeology (Daniel 1950, 1975; Trigger 1989; Willey and Sabloff 1980, 1993) divide the discipline into periods before and after which archaeologists routinely practiced stratigraphic excavation. Stratigraphic dating using superposition can be accomplished in two ways, through stratigraphic excavation and through stratigraphic observation after excavation (Browman and Givens 1996). Stratigraphic excavation is a method of recording the arrangements of artifacts as excavation proceeds, separating artifacts of one layer from artifacts of stratigraphically different layers. Stratigraphic observation after excavation is a method of recording the superpositional relationship of artifacts in the sidewalls of trenches; artifacts are not separated during or (necessarily) after excavation. Although both methods employ stratigraphic dating, only the first is stratigraphic excavation.

Although not emphasized when stratigraphy is taught in the classroom or defined in textbooks, the shift from stratigraphic dating using general superposition in sidewalls to the implementation of stratigraphic excavation was an important event in the discipline of archaeology (Browman and Givens 1996). Heinrich Schliemann (1875) used superposition but did not excavate in stratigraphic layers at Troy. He simply turned to the sidewalls and identified the layer that contained pottery made by Greeks. On the other hand, Kathleen Kenyon kept strata separate during excavation at ancient Jericho but did not use the artifact groups she extracted to date the layers she excavated. Rather, she used references to the reigns of kings (Kenyon 1952). Archaeologists in North America, who were attempting to establish the antiquity of Clovis and Folsom points and cultures, used stratigraphic correlation with extinct Ice Age fauna. They followed the example of their geoscientist colleagues and extracted artifacts and fossils together within each separate layer. Archaeologists who first attempted to establish the antiquity of the mounds in the Eastern Woodlands did not always keep layers separate (e.g., Holmes 1903; Moorehead 1928) but rather collected ceramics from the surface or from excavation units and mixed the artifacts from separate strata. This practice changed as soon as archaeologists discovered that pottery could be used to tell time through seriation (e.g., Gamio 1913; Nelson 1916; Vaillant 1927; see discussion in Woodbury 1960a, 1960b). Stratigraphic dating and stratigraphic excavation are both pivotal concepts in the history of archaeology, even though they are not synonymous.

Archaeologists typically do not learn the important history of stratigraphic dating during the course of their study. Textbooks emphasize that stratigraphy is important for relative dating but rarely offer information on the methods employed for stratigraphy or any other potential uses of stratigraphy. Students do not learn that stratigraphy means different things to different archaeologists and has been inconsistently applied throughout the history of archaeology. They learn only what is important to their discipline today; that stratigraphy is stratigraphic dating. Stratigraphic dating is the oldest of dating methods in the discipline and the most fundamental and pivotal to its historic development, yet the history of stratigraphic analysis is complex and varied, depending on the nature and age of the site being excavated.

I have been asked to explore the history of stratigraphic dating in the field of archaeology. As I have just pointed out, stratigraphy is crucial to sound archaeological interpretation; it has been since the beginning and still is. Rather than just exploring the historical importance of stratigraphic dating, I include a historical review of a slightly larger concept: stratigraphy as a whole. I examine the subtle connotations of the word "stratigraphy" within archaeology, exploring the differences between those using it in highly stratified sites with artifacts that span long periods of time and those using it in urban settings with historic artifacts that often change in rapid succession. Stratigraphic dating has its greatest potential in providing relative ages but is also crucial for correlations across time and space and for interpreting depositional history and site formation processes of any given context. Stratigraphic dating has figured prominently in the history of archaeological dating but remains an underutilized method for most archaeologists.

WHAT IS STRATIGRAPHY AND
STRATIGRAPHIC DATING?

Before the history of stratigraphic dating can be discussed, a definition of stratigraphy is warranted. Two definitions are offered: one from an archaeological perspective, the other from a slightly broader geoscientific perspective. These definitions point explicitly to the fundamental differences between geosciences and some realms of archaeology. These disciplines overlap but are not the same, and their use of stratigraphy reflects the differences.

Archaeological stratigraphy is defined as "the archaeological evaluation of the significance of stratification to determine the temporal sequence of data within stratified deposits by using both the law of superposition and context evaluation" (Sharer and Ashmore 1993:621). Another text offers that "stratigraphy is the study and interpretation of stratified deposits" (e.g., Joukowsky 1980:159).

Stratigraphy is defined in geoscientific contexts as "the science dealing with the description of all rock bodies forming the Earth's crust—sedimentary, igneous, and metamorphic—and their organization into distinctive, useful, mappable units based on their inherent properties or attributes. Stratigraphic procedures include the description, classification, naming, and correlation of these units for the purpose of establishing their relationship in space and their succession in time" (Salvador 1994:137).

The difference between these two definitions is minor but significant. The archaeological definition does not include the formal description, naming, and classification of strata. Rather, the archaeological definition indicates that the primary purpose of stratigraphy is dating and correlation, generally of artifacts and features within strata, and mentions the laws of superposition and context as guides in the analysis of stratigraphy. The geoscientific definition focuses on the description of rocks, their classification, and interpretation. The purpose of stratigraphy for geoscientists is the determination of relationships between strata in space and succession in time. For archaeologists the purpose is the establishment of temporal relationships exclusively.

The reason for this dichotomy is in part historical and in part scalar (Stein 1993). Archaeology is used differently by those who study very old periods (e.g., Paleolithic and Paleoindian) and younger periods (e.g., early agriculturalists, urban settings of complex societies, classical areas, and historic occupations). Archaeologists do not correlate rock units from one site to another and sometimes not from one pit to another. Archaeologists do not describe deposits for the purpose of establishing relationships of the rocks (deposits) across space. Archaeologists are not often concerned with features as large as basins, oceans, volcanoes, or subduction zones (Stein and Linse 1993). Stratigraphy for archaeologists is not focused on spatial correlation. It is focused primarily on time. This focus, therefore, is reflected in the definition of stratigraphy in archaeology. It is essentially superposition and dating. Archaeologists have simply not emphasized description, naming, and classifying.

The History of Archaeological Stratigraphy and Dating

My approach to discussing the history of stratigraphic dating is to contrast those archaeologists who study people living in ancient (Pleistocene/Early Holocene) periods from those who study people living in more recent periods. In North America, there is a striking difference in the use of stratigraphy between these two groups. Stratigraphy is used very differently in the study of ancient hunters and gatherers from the way it is applied to the remains of more recent hunters and gatherers, or village and urban dwellers.

This review charts the history of stratigraphy in North America but must begin with a brief discussion of events in Europe that influenced North Americans substantially.

The Earliest Beginnings of Stratigraphy

Archaeology and the geosciences began together in the eighteenth century when various scholars used stratigraphy to question the biblically based chronology for the age of the Earth (Daniel 1976; Faul and Faul 1983; Grayson 1983; Trigger 1989). Associations among extinct fauna, primitive artifacts, and stratigraphically superimposed layers were sought, but these eighteenth-century scholars were generalists, not specialists. The disciplines that were much later to become separate and distinct entities shared, at this moment, the same history. Archaeology, stratigraphy, paleontology, and geology began simultaneously as earth science.

The European Influences: Steno, Smith, and Lyell

The beginnings of stratigraphy can be traced clearly to a concern with fossils. The first observers of rock sequences were actually drawn to explaining the presence of marine shells in odd places such as the high peaks of the Alps, beneath the city of Rome, and on either side of the English Channel. The fossils demanded the naturalist's attention and explanation. The fossils in question were the remains of shells and large extinct animals, as well as artifacts, though these were not necessarily recognized as such at the time. These items were found in rocks, and when described could often be traced across great distances.

Nicholas Steno is usually credited with being the first stratigrapher (Faul and Faul 1983; Rudwick 1976). In the middle of the seventeenth century, Steno made a number of observations that, taken together, laid the foundation for stratigraphic reasoning. He first noted that the teeth he removed from a shark's carcass were similar to "tongue-stones" found in various rocks in Italy and subsequently demonstrated that "tongue-stones" were really fossil shark teeth and that they had not grown in situ within the rocks (Rudwick 1976:49–53). He also suggested that the shell-bearing strata beneath the site of ancient Rome must be older than the ancient city itself and therefore must be older than 3,000 years. From these observations, Steno reasoned that particles settle in a fluid in proportion to their relative weights or mass. If particles of various sizes were added to a fluid, they would be laid down in discrete, size-sorted layers and would produce horizontal layering or stratification. If an organism, in this case a shark or shellfish, died near the zone of accumulation, its body parts might be found within the sediment. He knew that these particles and shells must have been deposited particle by particle and layer by layer, one on top of another. Therefore, in any given sequence of multiple layers, a lower layer must be older than any overlying layers. This observation, which seems commonsensical, was revolutionary in 1669.

Steno's observations, now in the refined form of three principles, composed the underlying logic for almost all early interpretations of Earth's history:

Law of Superposition. In any succession of strata not severely deformed, the oldest stratum lies at the bottom, with successively younger ones above.

Principle of Original Horizonality. Because sedimentary particles settle from fluids under gravitational influence, stratification originally must be horizontal; steeply inclined strata, therefore, have suffered subsequent disturbance.

Principle of Original Lateral Continuity. Strata originally extended in all directions until they thinned to zero or terminated against the edges of their original area (or basin) of deposition. (Steno 1968:229–231)

These principles did not come to us directly from Steno, however. Only with hindsight can we see that their origins lie there. They developed through the work of at least four influential naturalists.

Abraham Gottlob Werner, a German professor at the Freiberg Mining Academy, was the first to establish the importance of Steno's observations (Conkin and Conkin 1984; Schneer 1969). Werner believed that all the materials visible in the Earth's crust precipitated, in the chemical sense, from a large ocean that originally covered the Earth. This ocean receded gradually to its present size. Precipitation occurred within this ocean, supposedly depositing minerals from above, below, or within, older rocks. The emphasis on the oceanic origin of all rocks and minerals caused this school to be labeled "Neptunists." Notice that Steno's principles concerning particle behavior were borrowed by Neptunists but that superposition was not.

James Hutton, a Scottish contemporary of Werner, offered a contrasting opinion for the origin of rocks (Dean 1992). Using laboratory experiments and field observations, Hutton proposed that igneous rocks were not precipitated in oceans but were instead cooled from molten rock. The emphasis on molten origins of rocks and minerals led to the label "Plutonism" for this school. Hutton also suggested that sedimentary processes observable today were responsible for the deposition of all sedimentary rocks. His method of using observation in the present to infer processes of the past led to his greatest contribution: uniformitarianism, or "the present is the key to the past." He combined uniformitarianism with superposition to argue against the Neptunists. Hutton built on Steno's principles and established the discipline of stratigraphy.

Werner and Hutton were theorists arguing about the origins of rocks, fossils, and stratification from lofty positions in the academy. Stratigraphy was not embraced by a wide audience, however, until a practical application was presented by a civil engineer, William "Strata" Smith. Because he was an engineer, Smith may not have been aware of the dispute between the Neptunists and Plutonists in 1796 (Phillips 1978), but he noticed certain repeating sequences of rocks and fossils in mines of southern England and used them to predict the depths of these layers. The Industrial Revolution (1789–1847) was driving this exploration, and whoever could expose and extract the coal most efficiently made the most profit. Thus, the reading of stratigraphy was born out of necessity rather than theory. In 1815, Smith produced a map and description of strata across England that should be regarded as the world's first example of geologic mapping.

A similar map of strata and fossils was constructed for the Paris Basin, and by 1830, the strata of England, France, and Germany had been named and put into a sequence. In 1833, Charles Lyell published the last volume of his *Principles of Geology*, describing, among other things, the sequence of rocks and fossils throughout Europe. Lyell combined the theories of Hutton with the practical observations of Smith and created the discipline of geology (Lyell 1837).

At the same time that these naturalists and engineers were looking at fossils and layers of rocks, others were searching for the remains of animals living during the Ice Age in association with people making primitive artifacts. There are excellent summaries of these early discoveries (Daniel 1975; Grayson 1983; Trigger 1989), showing that early stratigraphers, like Smith and Lyell, noted the association of fossils, rocks, river gravels, and artifacts. They used superposition and uniformitarianism to establish the antiquity of people as well as to order, in relative time, all past life on Earth. They argued against biblical and catastrophic accounts of Earth's creation.

Prehistoric archaeology in Europe has been influenced strongly by the close connection to geological stratigraphy. The shared beginnings aligned Paleolithic archaeology with geology and paleontology, and there remains to this day a close association between archaeologists studying Paleolithic time periods and their geoscientific colleagues. The earliest of these prehistorians garnered great prestige because, like geology and paleontology, theirs was a science at "the forefront of creating a new vision of the history of the world" (Trigger 1989:101). Paleolithic archaeologists, who excavate caves and sites associated with glacial deposits, still enjoy this scientific status and close association with geosciences (e.g., Bordes 1961, 1968, 1972, 1978; Farrand 1975, 1993; Laville 1976; Laville and Rigaud 1973; Laville et al. 1980; Lumley 1975; Rigaud 1989, Rigaud et al. 1995; Villa 1983). They note changes in fauna, plants, artifacts, oxygen isotopes, and climate and relate them to the changes that geologists have inferred in other regions. They pay more attention to separating units based on physical descriptions of layers than those units based on animal remains, artifacts, and time.

Paleolithic archaeology set new standards for stratigraphic analysis in the mid-nineteenth century, and those standards were maintained through the twentieth century. Many American archaeologists were trained in excavation by these Paleolithic archaeologists and transported their knowledge of stratigraphy back to America.

The European Influences: Schliemann, Kenyon, and Wheeler

The beginnings of stratigraphy in archaeology were also affected by scholars who came to the discipline from an entirely different methodological orientation. They explored the connections between archaeology and historical texts, languages, and classical civilizations (Daniel 1976; Trigger 1989). They collaborated with scholars in disciplines such as ancient history, linguistics, classics, and art history. Excavations of cities in Egypt, Greece, and the Near East led these scholars to exchange information with classicists and historians. Interest in Roman period sites led to texts, not geosciences. The sites in question had walls, foundations, streets, and inscriptions. The texts spoke greater volumes than the artifacts in strata, and the strata were effectively ignored.

Many of these early urban archaeologists drew plans of architecture and trench walls, but they did not pay any attention to these layers while excavating. In 1871, Schliemann identified, after excavation, seven superimposed layers at Troy. Woefully, Wheeler states:

> We may be grateful to Schliemann for plunging his spade into Troy, Tiryns, and Mycenae in the seventies of the last century, because he showed us what a splendid book had in fact been buried there; but he tore it to pieces in snatching it from the earth, and it took us upwards of three-quarters of a century to stick it more or less together again and to read it aright. (Wheeler 1954:43)

The point is that for European urban archaeologists, both before and during the first part of the twentieth century, stratigraphy and superposition were *not* the crucial observations on which dating rested. Historical texts, inscriptions, and known relationships to Egypt and other Near Eastern civilizations provided the foundation for site dating.

As late as 1952, Kenyon summarized the manner in which urban sites occupied within the last 3,000 years had been dated:

> Basically, all such datings go back to the dating systems established by the great empires of the Near East. As the city states and then kingdoms increased in complexity of organization the need for some chronological

basis for records became apparent, and also some method for calculating the seasons.... Therefore a system based on observation of the stars was worked out, and on this system was based the records of the reigns of the kings. Modern scholars have been able to correlate these records with our present calendar within a small margin of error. (Kenyon 1952:23)

Kenyon recognized that dating urban sites from this period is accomplished by using the Egyptian King's List. No mention is made of stratigraphy. She was, nevertheless, aware of the contrasting manner of dating used by other archaeologists. She points out that

For the earlier periods, including the whole of the Paleolithic and Mesolithic periods, such [text-based] methods clearly cannot be employed since at this time there was no contemporary historical record with which stages of development could be correlated. For these periods largely geological evidence has to be employed. Geologists and geochronologists have been able to provide a broad chronological framework for the advance and retreat of the ice-cap during the glacial period. (Kenyon 1952:24)

Browman and Givens (1996:83) suggest that Schliemann, Kenyon, and Wheeler did not excavate the layers separately, however, or collect artifacts within strata separately. Stratigraphic excavation was therefore not yet practiced, even if stratification was described. Superposition was not needed to date the artifacts, and artifacts were the primary target of these turn-of-the-century archaeological interests.

From the influence of Kenyon and Wheeler came a book about stratigraphy, written for these urban archaeologists. Edward Pyddoke (1961) wrote *Stratification for the Archaeologist* because "there are books and reports from which a beginner in archaeology can learn something concerning the identification of antiquities... but there appears to be no publication which will introduce the archaeologist to the great variety of deposits in which antiquities are discovered or to the processes which lead to their becoming buried and preserved" (Pyddoke 1961:13). The book was for those "archaeologists who have no formal training in the natural sciences or whose work keeps them much in museums and libraries" (Pyddoke 1961:13). He summarized the stratigraphic analysis practiced by these early urban archaeologists as follows: "Whilst most archaeologists today are aware that the strata or layers to be seen in the sides of almost any trench cut vertically into the superficial coverings of the earth are no longer generally regarded as simply part of the God-given structure of a created world, there do remain those who are content merely to draw and number these strata without always discovering and understanding the method of their depositing" (Pyddoke 1961:13). Pyddoke was a natural scientist attempting to train archaeologists, from art, classics, history, and ancient studies.

Even from this brief treatment, it is clear that events in Europe significantly influenced archaeologists working in North America.

NORTH AMERICA

In the Americas a similar dichotomy developed between those archaeologists who focused on the oldest periods of prehistory and those who focused on recent, more complex, and usually sedentary, cultures. As might be expected, these groups came to stratigraphy at different times and from different roots. Those who studied the oldest periods of prehistory, in this case the Paleoindian period, maintained close ties with the geosciences (Meltzer 1983). Those who studied more recent periods, especially those in which ceramics were manufactured and used, developed their own techniques for using the contents of strata to tell time (Browman and Givens 1996). These latter used pottery, architecture, art, and ethnography to date sites and correlate them across space. In point of fact, these archaeologists can be divided into two groups: those that used stratigraphic dating in conjunction with seriation and those that use it in conjunction with architectural reconstruction or, more specifically, historical archaeology.

Stratigraphy in Paleoindian Archaeology

Archaeological research seeking the first inhabitants of North and South America went through two phases, only one of which utilized stratigraphic dating. The first archaeologists to construct North American artifact sequences believed that cruder object morphology indicated greater antiquity (Meltzer 1983). The shape of the object was compared to forms found in the Lower Paleolithic of Europe: If the shape was crude, the object was believed to be old. If morphology was sophisticated, then the object was thought to be much younger. This comparative use of culture sequences from Europe did not require the use of stratigraphy or stratigraphic dating; it was, simply, comparative morphology.

The comparative, nonstratigraphic approach was replaced at the turn of the century by the use of stratigraphic criteria to evaluate the ages of sites. In 1912, Aleš Hrdlička (1912; summarized by Meltzer 1983:29) described the requirements necessary to demonstrate that human bones were geologically ancient. "One had to prove 1) that the specimens were found in geologically ancient deposits, 2) that the age of the deposits was confirmed by paleontological remains, 3) that the bones presented evidence of organic as well as inorganic alterations, 4) that the bones showed morphological characteristics referable to an earlier type, and 5) that the human remains were not introduced in later times." These steps required the use of stratigraphy, and without its use, a site was not considered ancient. After 1912, early sites in America were evaluated using geological stratigraphy: association, context, and fossils.

In response to the recommendations of Hrdlička, most North American archaeologists who sought the continent's earliest inhabitants worked closely with geologists who were reconstructing the Ice Age environment or were themselves geologists. For example, Edgar B. Howard (1935) conducted early excavations at Blackwater Draw Locality 1 and the Finley site (Howard 1943), E. H. Sellards excavated numerous sites in Texas and New Mexico (Sellards 1952), Frank Roberts excavated at Lindenmeier (Roberts 1935a). All of these archaeologists carefully described the strata containing bones and artifacts because their research goals were, often explicitly, to establish the stratigraphic position of the artifacts and their association with extinct fauna. Therefore, the reports written by these individuals included descriptions of site stratigraphy and stratigraphic sequences; most of them correlated these strata across a wide region and discussed the significance of soils as indications of periods of landscape stability. All of them used stratigraphic dating and context to arrange artifacts in a temporal sequence.

Kirk Bryan, a Quaternary geologist at Harvard University, strongly influenced archaeologists who studied the Paleoindians by training and encouraging his geology students to look for fossils and artifacts associated with glacial features and to cooperate with their archaeological colleagues (e.g., Bryan 1937). The association of artifacts and extinct fauna thus was as important to Bryan as it was to the archaeologists (Haynes 1990). At the Lindenmeier site, for example, the research into its geologic history began in 1935, at the same time as the archaeological excavations. The geologic history was summarized by Bryan and Ray (1940), and most of the work was completed by Louis Ray as part of his dissertation. The archaeologist investigating

Lindenmeier, Frank H. H. Roberts, thus employed geologically oriented field methods as part of his archaeological research (Roberts 1935a). Bryan encouraged this interaction and instilled in his students a sense of interdisciplinary cooperation that affected the archaeological discipline for decades (see summaries of regional histories in Mandel 1999).

Every Paleoindian or pre-projectile-point Archaic site is scrutinized today in much the same way that Hrdlička recommended: Archaeologists must consider whether the site is found in geologically ancient deposits, with appropriate Pleistocene fossils, with no evidence of intrusions or reversals. Archaeologists searching since the turn of the century for evidence of the earliest people in the Americas used, and are using, stratigraphic excavation and stratigraphic dating designed by the best of the Quaternary geologists (e.g., Kirk Bryan). Their methods were precise, detailed, and well documented.

Some archaeologists today are still heavily invested in establishing the antiquity of people in the Americas (e.g., Dillehay 1989, 1997), and I would point out that these archaeologists remain closely affiliated with geoscientists and geoarchaeologists (e.g., Holliday 1997; Johnson 1995) or are geoscientists themselves (like C. Vance Haynes, Reid Ferring, Rolfe Mandel, and Vance Holliday) and continue to use stratigraphic dating as well as stratigraphic excavation. Even though new highly refined absolute-dating techniques have become standard (see Taylor and Aitken 1997), they continue to rely on the basics of stratigraphic dating.

During this entire period, the techniques for field description and recording of artifact provenience and context have changed little, and therefore require little historical analysis. Equipment used today is different, and samples are collected for a host of analyses that were never dreamed of in 1935. Stratigraphy and stratigraphic dating used by archaeologists studying Paleoindians in the first half of this century, however, are very similar to those used by Paleoindian specialists today, as well as geoscientists. A historical review of stratigraphic dating, therefore, must acknowledge these early advances and the influence of these archaeologists on the discipline as a whole, but there is little reason to chart more recent activities as closely because, aside from the addition of many absolute dating techniques and the refinement of regional sequences and correlations, the use of stratigraphic dating has remained very consistent among those archaeologists studying Paleoindian occupations.

Stratigraphy for North American Archaeologists
Investigating Complex Societies

Archaeologists who investigate complex societies in North America followed a pathway different from those archaeologists who investigated Paleoindians. They did not collaborate with geoscientists or follow the recommendations of Hrdlička after 1912. These archaeologists were attempting to find out whether the living Native Americans were descendants of the Moundbuilders (Trigger 1989; Willey and Sabloff 1993), and stratigraphic excavation was less effective in answering that question. More important in this regard was demonstrating continuity from historical and ethnographic descriptions of living Native Americans to the pre-Contact artifacts found in the ground. Part of the question concerning descendancy was the issue of antiquity of the mounds and other foundations of village settings present on the landscape. These archaeologists did not have texts or king lists to date their strata, nor did they have easily dated historic objects, such as coins, at their disposal.

These archaeologists were scrambling to figure out the antiquity of North America's recent inhabitants, but they could not use the methods of the archaeologists working on Paleoindians, who had extinct fauna and thick strata that could be correlated across large distances. Village sites in the eastern United States were shallow and spread over plowed surfaces; in the west they consisted of architectural structures on the surface with clearly visible pottery scattered over features such as floors and plazas. The early efforts by these urban archaeologists thus did not include the use of stratigraphic methods. Instead, archaeologists such as Cyrus Thomas, William Henry Holmes, and Max Uhle tried to determine the distribution and relative age of various urban cultures via analysis of architecture and pottery styles. They may have recognized that stratified deposits could provide dates based on superposition, but they chose instead to focus on pottery styles and regional distributions of those styles to arrange pottery into rough chronological order. Thus, stratigraphy was not recorded in their excavation notes. Their emphasis was focused toward the kinds of pottery found in each site and in each region.

Seriation

In the Americas, archaeologists interested in complex societies embraced stratigraphy only when the new technique of seriation established beyond a doubt that piles of accumulated pottery could be used to determine the antiquity and age of sites (Browman and Givens 1996; see Blinman this volume). Archaeologists credited with being the first to use stratification and the underlying assumption of the law of superposition are Manual Gamio, Nels Nelson, and A. V. Kidder (Browman and Givens 1996; Trigger 1989; Willey and Sabloff 1993). These archaeologists did not always save all the sherds from every layer, nor did they use only natural levels to group their sherds. They did, however, demonstrate the potential of stratigraphic excavation, and others quickly followed. Seriation ushered the "stratigraphic revolution" (see discussion in Willey and Sabloff 1993:97–108) into North American archaeology (cf. Lyman et al. 1997; Lyman et al. 1998).

North American Archaeological Stratigraphic Terminology

American archaeologists in the 1920s and 1930s who were not involved in Ice Age reconstructions thought they invented archaeological correlation because they came from an anthropological background, had not used stratigraphy in a geoscientific sense, and therefore did not really conceptualize the method they invented as stratigraphy. These new stratigraphers established chronologies using the vertically differentiated frequencies of projectile points or ceramic types. Unlike the archaeologists investigating Paleoindian occupations, these archaeologists did not need a rigorous geoscientific analysis of the strata, just an occasional notation of what was above and what was below the strata in question. For the first time, archaeologists were able to estimate the age of landforms using artifacts.

In the period from 1930 until the development of radiocarbon dating, a reversal in professional consulting therefore occurred—geologists began going to archaeologists for assistance in dating recent landforms (Stein 1987, 1993). Urban archaeologists, armed with seriation, moved into a respected position as purveyors of a separate and distinct discipline, all predicated on the fundamental tenet of Steno and Smith—superposition.

Along with this new technique came new terminology and methods (Heizer 1949). For example, Phillips et al. (1951) describe stratigraphy and their methods of excavation in the Lower Mississippi Valley.

To many archaeologists, stratigraphy necessarily involves a situation in which materials can be segregated on the basis of distinct and separable soil zones. Such is frequently not the case. It frequently happens, as we shall show, that a homogeneous deposit, without observable soil stratification, may be made to yield a stratigraphic record of the utmost value.

Obviously, such an unstratified deposit will have to be excavated by arbitrary levels, to which method the term "metrical stratigraphy" has sometimes been applied in derogation, as opposed to "natural stratigraphy" obtained by peeling stratified layers.... Village site deposits in the [Lower Mississippi] Alluvial Valley rarely exceed 1 to 2 meters in total depth. Ten centimeters was therefore chosen as a unit of depth, convenient for seriating, without presenting serious difficulties in excavating. The first cut... was dug 3 meters square, but on finding that a sufficient yield of sherds could have been obtained from a smaller area, subsequent cuts were made only 2 meters square. Ideally, cuts should be dimensioned to get an adequate sherd sample per level from the smallest possible space, but we could never agree as to just what constituted an adequate sample, and therefore adhered to the convenient 2 meter square throughout. (Phillips et al. 1951:240–241)

Phillips et al. (1951) separated one natural level (i.e., lithostratigraphic unit; see Stein 1987, 1990) into many parts so as to capture the artifacts in small, more highly resolved, levels. The levels were 10 cm thick, a thickness thought to represent the shortest period of time that is meaningful for artifact accumulation and therefore artifact grouping. In these sites, no physical stratification of the sediment was observed, so the archaeologists could not differentiate levels on the basis of physical characteristics. Yet they did not want to miss changes that may have occurred in the artifacts deposited in that one layer. They knew that using arbitrary levels to group artifacts is not traditionally called stratigraphy, because the arbitrary levels do not represent stratification of sedimentological attributes. The archaeologists did recognize, however, that their arbitrary levels are a kind of chronological interpretation based on superposition. What is unusual about their separation was that they believed stratigraphy using arbitrary levels was very different from stratigraphy using natural levels.

Phillips et al. (1951) thought that they invented a new kind of stratigraphy, one based on arbitrary levels. I suggest that the sherds deposited in the sediments are just as stratified as a sequence of physically different layers. The sherds do not defy the law of superposition; they were laid down one atop another, just like sand grains or gravels. The sherds are found in superpositional order. Their analysis is therefore not different from stratigraphy. The process is the same as studying a sequence of different lithological units. John Phillips, Jack Ford, and J. B. Griffin, as well as Manual Gamio, Nels C. Nelson, and Alfred

Vincent Kidder unknowingly reinvented an archaeological stratigraphy using culturally manufactured objects. Their stratigraphic method is analogous to using fossils, magnetic polarity, or chronometric analysis.

The Lower Mississippi Valley archaeological project (Phillips et al. 1951) greatly influenced American archaeology. From the efforts of these archaeologists came many of the basic excavation strategies, terminology, and methodology that have come to be an integral part of American archaeology (Willey and Phillips 1958). The terms "component," "phase," "horizon," and "tradition" were developed to facilitate correlation. What was actually invented, however, was a procedure analogous to the procedures for correlation used in Paleoindian archaeology and geological stratigraphy. Though the archaeologists were not using lithostratigraphy in a strict sense, they relied on stratigraphic relations to guide their analyses.

Phillips et al. (1951) understood these differences and similarities when they first proposed their stratigraphic method:

> The distinction, however, between "stratification," the description of the actual ground situation, and "stratigraphy," [we shall refer to] as applied to the chronological interpretation of the ground situation, whether by "natural" or "metrical" methods, is a useful one and will be maintained here. Under the heading "stratification," we shall refer to soil zones as revealed by trench profiles; under "stratigraphy," the analysis of the excavated material and interpretation of the results. The one is what you find, the other is what you do with it. The separation will serve to bring out the fact that it is possible to have stratigraphy without stratification and vice versa. In line with this distinction, the terms "stratum," "zone," "deposit," etc., will be hereinafter used to refer to the ground stratification, the term "level" being reserved for the arbitrarily excavated unit of "metrical" stratigraphy. (Phillips et al. 1951:241)

Phillips, Ford, and Griffin thus suggested their own stratigraphic code in 1951. "Stratum," "zone," and "deposit" are lithostratigraphic terms based on physical attributes. "Levels" are ethnostratigraphic terms based on artifacts (Stein 1987, 1990, 1992). I wonder what impact a conversation with a geoscientific stratigrapher would have had on their code. Would they have seen the similarity and behaved differently as a result? Perhaps they did talk to stratigraphers, but later archaeologists missed the important difference between stratification and stratigraphic interpretations based on artifacts.

Although Phillips et al. (1951) understood that the observation and description of lithology is different from interpretation of units on the basis of sherds found within levels, the subtle distinction did not carry over to future generations of American archaeologists. Stratigraphy became the extraction of artifacts in ways meaningful to telling time, as well as (though less emphasized) the description of the layering observed in the site. Phillips et al. (1951) focused on artifacts; deposits were essentially ignored. In North American archaeology, for all practitioners except those studying Paleoindians, stratigraphy became associated with artifacts and dating through seriation. Because artifacts were the data of significance, geological stratigraphy was regarded as irrelevant or at least less important.

Harris Matrices

Following the "stratigraphic revolution" and the development of particularistic North American archeological stratigraphic terminology, the next invention to influence stratigraphic dating in North America was the Harris Matrix. American archaeologists were influenced greatly by Edward Harris, the historic archaeologist who first introduced a sophisticated and systematic method for correlating and recording strata in urban settings. Harris (1975, 1977, 1979, 1989) developed the method as part of the Winchester Research Unit in England when he became frustrated by two-dimensional representations of complex superpositional relationships evident in walls, floors, and urban remodeling. The Harris Matrix is a two-dimensional representation of three-dimensional strata encountered during excavation. It allows the recorder to keep track of the relationship between each layer and all the rest of the layers in the site, not simply the strata that appear in one particular profile. Each layer is represented by a rectangle of uniform size. The placement of the rectangles relative to each other corresponds to the temporal (superpositional) ordering of their deposition. The matrix is, therefore, a record of the temporal superposition of all strata in the site.

Edward Harris was influenced by Martin Biddle, the director of the Winchester Research Unit, who in turn was trained by Mortimer Wheeler. In 1950, the standard method of excavation in historical archaeology was the "Wheeler Box Method," using baulks and 10-foot squares (Wheeler 1954). Stratigraphy was preserved in the baulks, so the sequence of architectural construction and collapse could be reconstructed through the systematic inspection of side walls. This method was brought to North American historical archaeology by Ivor

Noel Hume, who, as Director of Archaeology at Colonial Williamsburg, used it to excavate sites with complex stratification in Virginia's eighteenth-century capital from the late 1950s to about 1980 (Brown and Muraca 1993).

The interesting historical fact is that Noel Hume disliked the Wheeler Box Method and argued that one should keep track of all layers and their relationship to each other across the whole site (Noel Hume 1969) but never followed his own advice. At Williamsburg, he excavated each square separately and never recorded any correlations between them. Perhaps the reason for this was that Noel Hume was never motivated to make the attempt, for he had documentary evidence that recorded historical events associated with the site (Noel Hume 1970) and chronology based on the archaeological layers therefore may have seemed irrelevant.

Although growing out of the Wheeler tradition, Harris's suggestions of single-context planning and tabulating of all strata (not just those that intersected the side wall) represented a reaction against the Wheeler technique, and the Noel Hume practice. Wheeler's technique encouraged its users to excavate each "box" or square separately, producing as many stratigraphic sequences as there were excavation units, and therefore permitting excavators to ignore the issue of how they might be related. Harris's methods were designed to facilitate recovery of a single sequence that integrated all the strata occurring in the entire excavation area.

The suggestion of recording every layer as it was excavated was new to historical archaeologists. Previously, they had texts, coins, inscriptions, and documents from which to derive general dates of building and occupation. Harris advocated the use of the matrix for deciphering small-scale temporal events that occurred within the urban setting, such as road building or house remodeling. Instead of looking only at sections (as Schliemann, Wheeler, and Noel Hume did), historical archaeologists were now expected to number and describe each wall, trench, and floor, and place them on a Harris Matrix. Layers could no longer be excavated without carefully recording their exact relationships and could not be considered only as recollections of the excavator. One had to pay attention to details during excavation and to make superpositional assignments as the digging progressed.

In 1983, some urban archaeologists in Europe revised their excavation strategy so much that they found it necessary to publish a Guide to Archaeostratigraphic Classification and Terminology. The guide was followed by a roundtable discussion at the University of Ghent in 1983, the "Workshop for Archaeostratigraphic Classification and Terminology" (ACT workshop). From this group, the periodical *Stratigraphica Archaeologica* presented contributions on classification and terminology, as well as explanations of types of stratigraphic units. The guide and journal generated much comment (Cremeens and Hart 1995; Farrand 1984a, 1984b; Stein 1987, 1990, 1992, 1996) that focused on whether archaeological stratigraphy is different from geological stratigraphy.

Although Harris contrasts his view of stratigraphy with those of the group meeting at Ghent (Brown and Harris 1993), archaeologists who excavate historic urban sites developed a new interest in stratigraphy and stratigraphic dating, stronger by far than that called for by Wheeler and Kenyon and boldly newer than anything suggested by Noel Hume in America. The orientation of these urban archaeologists comes directly from their intellectual history. They were trained in the classics and in history, not the geosciences and anthropology. When they turned toward stratigraphy in 1975, they believed emphatically that the strata in their sites did not relate to geological or seriation-based stratigraphy:

> We do not wish to denigrate in any way the results which geoarchaeologists and other specialists may make to archaeological projects in geological settings. It is simply that...we do not think that these geological methods can be extended to a majority of archaeological sites, which are those stratigraphically fabricated as a by-product of human society. Nor do we think that the theory underlying those methods can be suitably applied to the discipline of archaeological stratigraphy. (Brown and Harris 1993:15)

They believe that the superposition noted by constructing Harris Matrices is different from the superposition that geoscientists use.

Harris is emphatic that the important unit in his archaeostratigraphy is the boundary around the layer, called an interface. It holds the key to the appropriate placement of a rectangle on the page. Harris is correct. No stratigrapher from any discipline would disagree. What Harris does not appreciate is that the act of noting elapsed time in boundaries of layers is not the art of defining a physical stratigraphic unit. Describing the physical unit during excavation and interpreting elapsed time is thus a two-step task; interpretation follows description.

With regard to the first, descriptions of strata were not systematically recorded by archaeologists until quite recently. Field notes may have included the color of an unusual stratum or the shape of a feature, but most excavators did not (and do not today) record the physical attributes of every layer in their sites. They recorded the kinds and densities of artifacts but not the physical descriptions of the strata.

With regard to the second, assigning an age to a stratum requires that an archaeologist determine the age of manufacture of an object in that stratum or the age of an object nearby. This age determination is therefore an interpretation based on association, correlation with other sites, or dates derived by some absolute dating technique. The age of the stratum is therefore inferred from the age of manufacture of an object found within it or from the association of that object with some datable substance. Determining the age of all strata near the object involves an assessment of the relative superpositional relationship of the layers and the object, as well as an assessment of the rate of accumulation. Archaeologists often presume that if one stratum contains an object made during a period from, for example, 1,000 to 800 years ago, the strata above must be younger than 800 years old, and the strata below must be older than 1,000 years. These determinations are based on an inferred rate of accumulation (Ferring 1986). Thus, units of time are interpretations, based on ages of objects, superposition, and rates of accumulation. The interpretation follows description in a two-step procedure.

Perhaps the point is moot that deposit descriptions are different from interpretations of time. In the end Harris constructs a matrix that is correctly drawn and dated relatively using superposition. He does not choose to recognize the task as that involving different steps and therefore believes that the one step (drawing a Harris Matrix based on interfaces) is the end of stratigraphy. The matrix is, either way, important for stratigraphic dating. It improved our ability to record superposition and therefore engage in stratigraphic dating. Archaeostratigraphers with a more geological bent would say that this is just the beginning, however. They would take the matrix and draw boundaries on it in the locations where various kinds of data change in frequency or appear or disappear (see Stein [1992, 1996] for examples of this approach).

When someone new to stratigraphy examines the methods of archaeological stratigraphy proposed in 1975, and followed by Harris and other urban archaeologists, they may not understand why Harris contrasts his stratigraphy so strongly with that of geoscientific stratigraphy. Harris is emphatic that stratigraphy in archaeological sites is different from stratigraphy in either prehistoric sites, where geological forces overwhelm cultural forces, or geological sequences. He calls walls upstanding strata (Harris 1989:48) and denounces any attempt to borrow terminology from geostratigraphic codes or guides. Because Harris emphasizes differences, he implies that geoscientific stratigraphic dating is different from archaeological stratigraphic dating. I think the explanation for this emphasis lies in the history of how historical archaeologists came to use stratigraphy. Historical archaeologists use superposition to arrange site strata in a relative sequence. Although they note superposition, they do not really need it to date their layers within the sites. Only when they wish to date small-scale events that were unaccompanied by textual dates, did they need to excavate walls and floors separately and record their relative superposition. They came independently to call this method stratigraphy and believed it to be different from stratigraphic practice elsewhere.

Some people disagree with Harris (Colcutt 1987; Farrand 1984a, 1984b; Stein 1987, 1990, 1992) and suggest that stratigraphy in historical sites as well as North American prehistoric sites dated by seriation is still stratigraphy and that stratigraphic dating is the same whether used in geosciences or in North American prehistoric, Paleoindian, or historical archaeology. These scholars applaud the invention of the Harris Matrix as a recording and interpretive device because in its fundamental simplicity it demonstrates that superposition works everywhere, just as Steno suggested. Perhaps the best indication of the rapid acceptance of the Harris Matrix is its use by archaeologists who are oriented to prehistory (e.g., Parkington, personal communication 1998, is using them at Elands Bay Cave in South Africa), middens (Stein 1996; Stein et al. 1992; Stucki 1993), Mayan cities (Hammond 1993), and historic sites (see examples in Harris et al. 1993). The matrix is a recording device that is incredibly useful for complicated stratigraphic deposits. No matter what one does with the resulting matrix, the appearance of the Harris Matrix represents an important moment in the history of stratigraphic dating.

Geoarchaeology and Site Formation Processes

At roughly the same time Harris Matrices were introduced to North American archaeology, the fledgling discipline of geoarchaeology began to influence North American archaeologists trained in seriation and who used the terminology of Willey and Phillips (Butzer 1964, 1971; Davidson and Shackley 1976; Gladfelter 1981; Willey

and Phillips 1958). Geoarchaeology thus grew alongside a newly forming emphasis on site formation processes and middle range theory
(Binford 1964, 1977; Schiffer 1972, 1976) that considered the "natural processes" impacting artifacts and cultural strata. Karl Butzer
(1964) and C. Vance Haynes (1964) were perhaps the first and most
influential geoscientists to convince North American prehistoric
archaeologists that an environmental approach was critical to proper
interpretation of the archaeological record. Geoarchaeology was gain-
ing recognition from the prehistoric archaeologist who had not traditionally used geoscientific methods or geoscientific stratigraphy.

Geoarchaeology, and the consideration of stratigraphy as something more than just superposition, actually appears in North American archaeology at two different times, each of which is thought by
some to be the original geoarchaeology. The first was the collaboration revolving around Paleoindians that began at the turn of the century with Hrdlička's recommendations and Kirk Bryan's insistence
(Mandel 1999). The second was the awakening in the 1970s of prehistoric archaeologists who were trained in the tradition of seriation
and who suddenly realized that collaboration with geoscientists was
potentially beneficial (Gladfelter 1981). Obviously the beginning of
the collaboration defined as geoarchaeology occurred at both times,
but the actual term "geoarchaeology" did not appear until the second
(Renfrew 1976).

The interest in geoarchaeology and the impact of it on archaeology
grew in the 1970s when it was associated with the New Archaeology.
The magnitude of this impact is witnessed to by the number of geoscientists who vociferously joined these early discussions and urged prehistoric archaeologists, who were not already using geosciences in the
search for Paleoindian sites, to consider all kinds of geoscientific methods and approaches in their excavations and research (Gladfelter
1977; Hassan 1978, 1979; Herz and Garrison 1997; Rapp 1975; see
also Rapp and Hill 1998; Waters 1992).

Only in the 1970s did geoarchaeologists begin to contribute to stratigraphic dating in a variety of North American archaeological research,
not just those associated with the most ancient remains. The contributions focused on natural and cultural processes that disturb contexts
and on reconstructing paleoenvironmental contexts (Schiffer 1972).
This collaboration came late and did not strongly influence the use of
stratigraphic dating or stratigraphic methods in general. The methods
and terminology in the North American archaeological discipline had

been set and geoarchaeology and new kinds of stratigraphy had to fit within those methods or they would be ignored.

This chain of events is recorded indelibly in archaeological terminology still being taught and used today. Many terms connote an early focus on artifact seriation and a lack of concern for other objects that could not be seriated. For example, the word "matrix" in archaeological parlance refers to "the physical material that surrounds, holds, and supports an artifact" (Sharer and Ashmore 1993:616). Thus, "matrix" is the material that an excavator tries to separate from the artifacts, the material going through the screens. It is observed, some descriptive information, such as color, is recorded, then it is discarded. The term matrix was defined within archaeology when the artifactual perspective dominated the discipline, and remains in this use today. Most archaeologists now realize that the "matrix" can nevertheless reveal abundant information if appropriately analyzed using geoarchaeological methods. Yet many archaeologists still call the material matrix and refuse, perhaps subconsciously, to use the more precise terminology of sediment, soil, and deposit (Stein 1987).

Another example of this artifact-oriented archaeological terminology, one that relates directly to stratigraphic dating, is provided by comparison with geoscientific (stratigraphic) nomenclature. In archaeology, a "component" is an important term for stratigraphic dating, defined as "a manifestation of any given focus at a specific site, a focus being that class of culture exhibiting characteristic peculiarities in the finest analysis of cultural detail" (McKern 1939:308). A simpler definition is that offered by Brian Fagan (1988:575): "a component is an association of all the artifacts from one occupation level at a site." A component is a fundamental unit used for the purpose of correlation (stratigraphic dating) from one site to another. In geoscientific stratigraphy a fundamental exercise is the correlation of units across space. Any class of data that will enlighten the correlation may be selected, be it foraminifera, plants, tephra, or magnetic signals. Using artifacts for such correlations is an analogous procedure. The act of defining components is consistent. The term "artifact" could therefore be inserted into any of the geoscientific codes (Stein 1987, 1990).

"Phase" is another fundamental term used in archaeological stratigraphic dating, defined as "an archaeological unit possessing traits sufficiently characteristic to distinguish it from all other units similarly conceived, whether of the same or other cultures or civilizations, spatially limited to the order of magnitude of a locality or region and chronologically limited to a relatively brief interval of time" (Willey and Phillips 1958:22). Fagan's (1988:504) definition is shorter: "a phase [consists of] similar components from more than one site." Note that to define a phase, one has to collect information about culturally significant artifacts, time, and space. Once the relevant attributes are described, a phase is supposed to be used to correlate the same "people" moving in the same "time," "across different places on the landscape."

The guidelines set forth in geoscientific stratigraphic codes would exclude the phase as an acceptable stratigraphic unit, and many archaeologists agree that phases are indeed problematic entities, as defined (Willey 1985). Archaeologists are aware that the stratigraphic unit "phase" has within its definition a mixture of attributes requiring numerous observations or multiple classification systems that are difficult to define and collate (Rouse 1955). In many regions, the archaeologist familiar with the sites, artifacts, places, and times knows that phases are not easily correlated. The diagnostic cultural traits change in frequency or in manufacturing styles. Phase timing is often demonstrably transgressive across landscapes. The associated fauna, agricultural plants, architectural style, or preferred landforms often do not remain the same from the type site to other sites in the region. The use of phase as a fundamental unit in stratigraphic dating is inherited from the period before geoarchaeologists collaborated in meaningful ways with North American archaeologists.

In geoscientific guides, units are based on physical properties observed in the field (lithostratigraphic units called "formations"), on fossil content (biostratigraphic units called "biozones"), magnetic properties (magnetostratigraphic units called "polarity zones"), or time (chronostratigraphic units called "chronozones"). When following archaeological procedures, however, one relies on different datasets (e.g., lithics, bones, plant remains, ^{14}C dates) to define units usually grouped into one kind of stratigraphic unit that then becomes the type profile for the stratigraphy of a whole site. The stratigraphic units of an archaeological site are described under the section of the site report called "site stratigraphy" as one sequence of units (for example) numbers 1 through 7, or A through M. The stratigraphy of the site is not discussed repeatedly as each type of artifact is presented. Rather, each type of artifact is crammed into one stratigraphic sequence. North American archaeologists who collaborate with geoarchaeologists are beginning to understand this distinction. They are eliminating the use of phase in exchange for the newer, more powerful, stratigraphic correlation techniques and terminology.

What therefore appears to be happening in the last decade is a "closing of the gap" between archaeologists who study Paleoindian sites and those who study hunter-gatherers, early agriculturalists, village dwellers, or historic peoples. An emphasis on geoarchaeology and site formation processes, along with the use of Harris Matrices, demands that everyone pay close attention to context and superposition, which in turn propels North American archaeologists closer to geoscientific stratigraphy and more elaborate concepts of stratigraphic dating.

CONCLUSION

The history of stratigraphic dating in North American archaeology is a long and circuitous narrative involving events in both Europe and North America. Various kinds of archaeologists contributed to this narrative, including European prehistorians and classicists, North American archaeologists searching for the earliest Americans (Paleoindian occupation), prehistorians using seriation of pottery and projectile points, as well as historical archaeologists.

Of greatest interest in this review of stratigraphic dating are the pieces contributed by the North American archaeologists. The earliest of these contributions was made by those investigating the antiquity of people in the Americas. These archaeologists remained close to their geoscientist colleagues, especially Quaternary geoscientists. Beginning at about the turn of the century, they used stratigraphic associations of Ice Age fauna and artifacts to establish antiquity of people in the Americas.

Closely following the earliest effort was the contribution of archaeologists investigating more recent sites, especially sites with pottery. These scholars depended on seriation to date their artifacts and relied on superposition to guide the seriation process. Stratigraphy was intertwined with the methods of artifact seriation to build chronologies for the whole of North America.

Historical archaeology then contributed the Harris Matrix to the improvement of stratigraphic dating and archaeological stratigraphy. This recording device required archaeologists to describe three-dimensional strata in the field, including the superpositional relationship of each across the whole site. Sophisticated sequences of superposition could be constructed using the Harris Matrix, a fact recognized in its adoption by practitioners of Paleolithic, Paleoindian, Mayan, and other archaeologies.

The last major contribution was provided by geoarchaeologists in conjunction with the New Archaeology. As more sites were excavated and detailed research questions asked, the chronologies originally constructed began to show cracks (Willey 1985). Not only were chronologies being criticized but the interpretations made from arti-fact patterns were also being questioned. New Archaeologists pointed to the importance of site formation processes and their ability to destroy patterns set by behavior. They even pointed to examples where the superpositional relationship of artifacts laid down by cul-tural processes had been reversed by natural processes. Culture histo-rians who once focused on building chronologies have now turned toward an expanded conception of stratigraphy, derived from geoar-chaeology, to assist in the reconstruction of deposition and postdepo-sitional alterations.

The different contributions offered by each group are important to understand because archaeologists have had problems in standardizing the stratigraphic nomenclature of the discipline. Attempts on both sides of the Atlantic were made in the 1980s to standardize strati-graphic terminology (Farrand 1984a, 1984b; Gasche and Tunca 1983; Shaw 1970; Stein 1987; 1990), but these attempts have been hampered by the fact that participants do not appreciate that European urban archaeologists, prehistorians, and Americanists all bring different biases to any discussion about stratigraphy and stratigraphic dating. Archaeologists agree that problems exist, but they envision that they have all experienced a different history of stratigraphic dating and believe there are different problems to solve. Nevertheless, the history of stratigraphic dating reveals clearly that the problems are similar, and archaeologists are closer than ever before to achieving some agreement on nomenclature.

Acknowledgments. This manuscript benefited greatly from the comments of Stephen Nash, David Meltzer, Fraser Neiman, an anonymous reviewer, and especially Patty Jo Watson. I wish to thank Stephen Nash for organizing the symposium where we shared these ideas, and for encouraging me to complete this sojourn into the his-tory of archaeology.

CHAPTER 3

The Foundations, Practice, and Limitations of Ceramic Dating in the American Southwest

ERIC BLINMAN
Museum of New Mexico
Office of Archaeological Studies

The identification, description, and interpretation of cultural variation is the focus of archaeological research. Whether variation is viewed synchronically in descriptions and comparisons of different cultural forms, or diachronically as the study of culture change, control of time is an essential element of the discipline. Toward that end, a tremendous amount of effort, money, and intellectual energy has been invested in the development and use of chronological tools and concepts. Ceramic dating is one of these, and in ceramic dating, we have a glorious circularity. We take advantage of an aspect of culture change to provide a temporal framework for the study of culture change. This framework works elegantly and efficiently in the vast majority of cases, but the inherent circularity is never left far behind.

In this discussion, I draw on the culture area I know best, the Southwestern United States. Pottery has been emphasized in the practice of Southwestern archaeology for more than a century, and nearly all developments in ceramic dating have been applied in this context. The relative sufficiency of the Southwest as an example of the development and practice of ceramic dating is also due in part to the luxury of an extensive archaeological record in an arid landscape. The physical structure of sites and their material culture content are preserved with a nearly unparalleled visibility, and the archaeological record is rich but not so rich as to be dominated by confusing overlays of components. On this landscape, 2,000 years of Southwestern culture history have been played out with pottery as both a major part of the artifact inventory and a major tool for archaeological interpretation.

EXPLORATION ARCHAEOLOGY
AND THE IDEA OF CERAMIC CHANGE

In the early exploration of the Southwest, archaeologists such as William H. Holmes (1878, 1886) and Jesse Walter Fewkes (1904) were confronted with ceramic evidence of obvious cultural discontinuities. Abandoned but clearly once-vital settlements were associated with very different pottery than were the ethnographic Pueblo and Navajo Indian communities of the region. Although the potential temporal implications of this variation were recognized from the first, the geographic nature of the variation was so incompletely known that archaeologists were hesitant to embrace ceramic chronologies. This hesitancy was reinforced by strong differences between the contemporary pottery traditions of many of the Indian groups, differences that were expressed over distances of as little as tens of kilometers. Since space and time are strongly correlated in the changing settlement patterns of the prehistoric Southwest, variation in pottery across the landscape could be interpreted as ethnicity, culture change, or both. This ambiguity is reflected in Fewkes's (1904) attempt to document the variation he observed in his 1896–1897 investigations that were centered in east-central Arizona (Figure 3.1). The geographic variation in pottery was real, but what did the complicated pattern mean in terms of time and cultural relations?

Excavations increased in number through the turn of the century, and the archaeological record became better documented and more widely known. These investigations included stratigraphic sequences that strengthened confidence in the interpretation that at least some of the ceramic variation was a record of ceramic change. Nels Nelson's 1913 excavations in the Galisteo Basin provided clear suggestions of change in pottery styles, ultimately confirmed in a stratigraphic sequence at San Cristóbal Pueblo (Nelson 1914). Two years later, Alfred Kidder (1915) proposed a sequence for the prehistoric pottery of the Pajarito Plateau, documenting the ware distinctions that we use today and arranging them in time according to the apparent degradation of their associated ruins.

Kidder's research coincided with Alfred Kroeber's ethnographic fieldwork at Zuni Pueblo during the summer of 1915. Afternoon walks took Kroeber to ancient ruins in the vicinity, and he returned with his pockets full of sherds. Kroeber's sherds documented strong patterns of variation, and his thoughtful and extremely thorough consideration of this variation is a landmark study (Kroeber 1916b). He

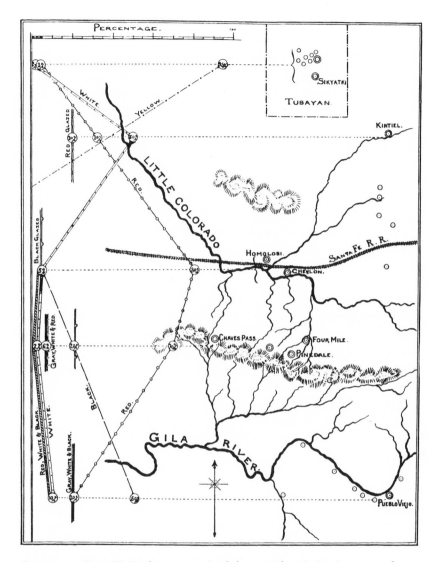

FIGURE 3.1 Jesse W. Fewkes summarized the spatial variation in pottery frequencies that he observed in his 1896–1897 investigations in east-central Arizona (Fewkes 1904:Plate LXX). The frequency curves on the left simultaneously reflect variation in time and cultural tradition.

did not build a ceramic chronology itself so much as he established the conceptual foundations and evidentiary steps necessary for the construction of ceramic chronologies.

The task of executing Kroeber's prescription for ceramic chronology

fell to Leslie Spier, whose study of Zuni area ruins was published in
1917 (Spier 1917b). Combining careful surface collections and observations, stratigraphic excavations that confirmed proposed sequences,
and pottery classification schemes that anticipated temporal change,
Spier laid the foundation for all ceramic chronologies to come. He
took the additional step of applying his dating framework to the study
of changing settlement patterns, a study that has been confirmed and
elaborated in the subsequent years using similar tools and concepts
(Kintigh 1985).

CERAMIC CLASSIFICATION AND THE FABRIC
OF TIME AND SPACE

After Spier's work, the trajectory of Southwestern ceramic studies became inextricably linked with chronology. Initial research and
publication was directed toward filling in geographic and temporal
gaps—documenting the variation in pottery form, fabric, and decora-
tion across the vast expanse of the Southwest. Many researchers contributed toward this end, including Charles A. Amsden (1931), Kenneth
M. Chapman (1921, 1923), Fewkes (1919, 1923), Frederick W. Hodge
(1924), Jean Jeançon (1924), E. F. Schmidt (1928), and Anna O. Shepard (1936). The mass of information being generated prompted Carl E.
Guthe (1927) to advocate standardized approaches to description in an
effort to improve the quality and comparability of the data avalanche.
Standardization efforts focused first on technological attributes, laying
the groundwork for the later balance between technical description and
classification in Southwestern ceramic studies.

Although initial efforts at standardization focused on technology,
the ultimate goal of the ceramists was the development of coherent
taxonomies. Borrowing structures from biological classification systems, wares, series, and types became the vocabulary of Southwestern
ceramic studies (explicated by Harold S. Colton and Lyndon L. Hargrave [Colton and Hargrave 1937]). Types were the basic building
blocks, created by partitioning the continuous variation in many
attributes. This partitioning was not arbitrary, and by the 1930s, most
type definitions were explicitly built from those attributes whose variation correlated with units of time. Series were types arranged in temporal sequences, and wares were series that shared coherent suites of
resources, technology, and function. Broad resource and technological
similarities in pottery were equated with traditions, cultures, or culture
areas, as expressed by Byron Cummings (1936), Winifred and Harold

Gladwin (Gladwin and Gladwin 1934), and Emil Haury (1936), culminating in the current sherd-centric view of ancient Southwestern cultures (Wilson et al. 1997).

What initially had been an effort to describe ceramic variability in whatever terms were convenient became a concerted effort at systematic type descriptions. Harry P. Mera (1931), Lyndon Hargrave (1932, 1935), Colton (Colton and Hargrave 1937), Emil Haury (1930, 1936), W. S. Stallings (1931), and many others carried on the tradition of Kidder and Spier, elaborating, refining, and codifying formal types for all times and all regions of the Southwest. This process continued through the 1950s and 1960s, exemplified by regular regional ceramic conferences and the Museum of Northern Arizona's (MNA's) Ceramic Series under the editorship of Harold S. Colton (Abel 1955; Colton 1952, 1953, 1955, 1956, 1958; Dittert and Peckham 1998).

Meanwhile, through the 1930s, the approach to settlement pattern studies pioneered by Spier was being applied on regional scales. Winifred and Harold Gladwin began systematic surveys of much of the Southwest, capturing snapshots of sites in the form of sherd collections (Gladwin and Gladwin 1928). Many of these snapshots were literally stored as mosaics of sherds glued to boards (Figure 3.2), each encapsulating the temporal and stylistic characteristics of a site. These sherd boards and the other representative sherd collections of the Gila Pueblo Archaeological Foundation ultimately numbered more than 10,000 (Haury 1988:36). Mera (1934, 1935) pursued a similar course in New Mexico and Arizona, using handfuls of carefully selected sherds to characterize sites over broad areas. Both the Gladwin and Mera collections remain tremendously useful today, summarizing in discrete collections the time relations of entire regions. The sensitivity of this research approach is epitomized by Deric Nusbaum's (later Deric O'Bryan) 1930s survey of the La Plata River Valley as part of Earl Morris's (1939) landmark study of the region. Although now scattered among various museums in the Southwest, Nusbaum's collections so effectively capture the variability of the sherd assemblages that 60 years later, they have supported a detailed reconstruction of regional settlement history (Hannaford 1993). Nusbaum's sense of variability and appropriateness was refined enough that in addition to the familiar decorated wares, he collected the undistinguished polished brown sherds that we now know document the pre-Anasazi ceramic tradition in the Southwest (Wilson and Blinman 1994; Wilson et al. 1996).

FIGURE 3.2 An example of a sherd board from investigations of Gila Pueblo in the Red Mesa Valley (Gladwin 1945:Plate XXIII). Use of these sherd boards is described by Emil Haury (1988) in his personal reminiscences of research at the Gila Pueblo Archaeological Foundation.

Following A. E. Douglass's demonstration of the utility of tree-ring dating in 1929, an effort was made to attach the regional pottery sequences to the common calendar. The close interaction between the development of the ceramic and tree-ring chronologies is epitomized by the discovery of the wood samples that linked the undated prehistoric tree-ring sequence with the dated historic sequence. The Third Beam Expedition that recovered the linking specimens targeted specific sites after detailed analysis of pottery types by Lyndon Hargrave (Haury 1931:4–6; Nash 1999). Hargrave identified those pottery types that were not dated by the historic sequence and that were not associated with the floating sequence. The undated pottery types were assumed to fall within the gap between the sequences, and sites with those types were selected for excavation. As a result, beam HH–39 and others were recovered from Whipple Ruin, linking the two tree-ring sequences and establishing the foundation for the absolute chronology currently used in the Southwest (Nash 1997a, 1999).

Much of the ensuing hunt for datable wood in the 1930s was directed toward refining regional phase sequences, but some was explicitly directed toward improving regional calibrations of stylistic change in pottery. This was especially true in the Rio Grande Valley, where relatively few structures and sites proved to be datable either due to the type of wood used or due to the pattern of beam reuse in construction. In these cases, the few possibilities for tree-ring dating were sought to calibrate the much more widely useful potential of ceramic dating (Stallings 1936). As these calibrations became more robust, the modern role of ceramic chronologies was set. Confidently placed in time by tree-ring dates, pottery provided a means of inferring absolute chronology in excavation and nonexcavation contexts where other dating techniques could not be applied. The ultimate compilation of pottery types and tree-ring dates was produced by David A. Breternitz and was published in 1966 (Breternitz 1966). More than thirty years later, Breternitz's compilation remains a valuable starting point for regional studies despite the often coarse resolution of the date and pottery type correspondences.

Through this type of calibration, pottery chronologies could also be extended between regions. The long-distance exchange of pottery provided a means to apply the absolute time scale from better dated areas to areas where tree-ring dating was proving recalcitrant. Often called "cross-dating," this type of chronological information was a major resource for construction of Hohokam chronologies (Gladwin et al. 1938:212–220). Although cross-dating is an inherently weak source of inference due to the generally small samples and the number of assumptions involved, it continues to play a supporting role in the construction and evaluation of Southwestern chronologies (Christenson 1995; Dean 1991:63–66).

THE QUANTITATIVE REVOLUTION

For a few archaeologists, then and since, pottery type classification was sufficient, both as a means of dating sites and as an end in itself for the study of pottery. However, in some cases the level of sophistication in pottery analysis and interpretation took quantum leaps. The most dramatic step was taken in 1945 with the publication of results of the Rainbow Bridge–Monument Valley Expedition by Ralph Beals, George Brainerd, and Watson Smith (Beals et al. 1945). The convergence of pottery typology, ceramic science, statistical sophistication, large, well-documented collections, and tremendous imagination produced a careful and far-ranging study. Relative frequency seriation, stratigraphic confirmation, graphical demonstrations of statistical similarities, and considerations of sample size broke new ground in ceramic chronology. Their work ushered in the modern era of ceramic studies, and their contributions remain ahead of much that is done today.

The foundation of Brainerd's work was the distinction between dating pottery types and dating pottery assemblages (Figure 3.3). The importance of assemblages was implicit in the understandings of ceramists who worked extensively with ceramic collections during the 1950s and 1960s, epitomized by Colton's and others' use of ceramic periods, pottery associations, or ceramic groups. These temporal patterns of ware and type frequencies had far more discriminating power than the interpretation of types as isolated units, overcoming to some extent the loss of resolution inherent in the partitioning of continuous attribute variation into types. Confidence in the validity of dating periods grew with familiarity, and those who worked extensively and intensively in regions developed a breadth and depth of experience that gave them the confidence to date assemblages precisely at a glance. This approach of subjective comparison of collection composition with ideal assemblage composition has continued as the dominant ceramic dating technique through the present day (e.g., Ambler 1985; Blinman 1988b; Goetze and Mills 1993; Heidke 1995; Windes 1977).

While the foundation of Brainerd's work was the assemblage, his legacy also included an explicitly quantitative approach. From the 1950s and accelerating through the 1970s, there was a proliferation of quantitative methods applied to artifact analysis and classification in general (Spaulding 1960). Ceramic dating applications ranged from simple graphical percentage presentations (e.g., Ford 1962; Smith 1971:18–54) through statistical similarity measures between assemblages (Brainerd 1951; Robinson 1951). R. Lee Lyman et al. (1998) provide a detailed discussion of the development of seriation techniques out of descriptions of changing attribute frequencies.

The principles that underlie seriation have been in use since the late nineteenth century (Petrie 1899), but applications increased dramatically as access to the computational power of computers improved (Hole and Shaw 1967; Marquardt 1978). Seriation assumes patterns of regular change in aspects of prehistoric material culture, change that results in measurable increases and decreases in attribute frequencies.

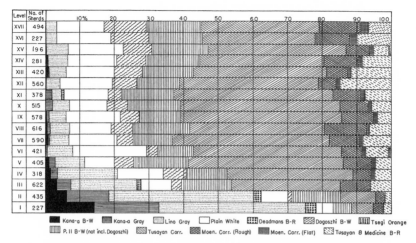

FIGURE 3.3 Pottery type frequencies from the Rainbow Bridge–Monument Valley excavations of the refuse mound at Site RB 551 (Beals et al. 1945: Table 4). This is a percentage stratigraphy presentation (Lyman et al. 1998), and it includes sample sizes for each stratum as a means of assessing the representativeness of the type percentages.

If the assumptions are correct and attributes have been selected properly, collections that have been ordered by the similarities in their attribute patterns will be ordered in an approximation of their temporal sequence. Seriation techniques can be applied to any archaeological data class, but applications to ceramic data are common due to the abundance of pottery in many settings and to the tendency for pottery to carry temporal information.

The quantitative approaches to seriation embraced attributes of design and technology as well as type frequencies (e.g., Steponaitis 1983). Broadening the range of attributes considered in seriations improves potential precision in the same way that the interpretive potential of pottery assemblages is greater than that of considering the temporal implications of individual pottery types. Often termed microseriations, detailed studies of attribute change were applied with success to problems of local and regional chronology (such as De Barros 1982; Leblanc 1975). However, these approaches were "micro" in terms of both attribute scale and geographic applicability, almost to the point of being proprietary. Unlike most of the approaches to typological dating, these carefully developed dating schemes usually were not reused or applied as tools by other researchers. Because of their project-specific subjects and data conventions, microseriations have served as models for the development of other microseriations rather than serving as exportable dating techniques.

The mechanics of creating seriations are incredibly diverse (Marquardt 1978). Over the decades, the similarity coefficients of Brainerd and Robinson have been augmented by many multivariate techniques. Regressions, single or multiple, and time series analyses have been used to exploit both simple and complex changes in attribute states, yielding date estimates for sherds or assemblages (Blinman 1984; Braun 1985; Plog and Hantman 1986). Factor, cluster, and discriminant analyses have been used to simplify more complex patterns of attribute change, and multidimensional scaling has become established as a favorite quantitative approach (Goetze and Mills 1993:113–146; Matson and Lipe 1977; Wallace 1986).

Mean ceramic dating, a method developed in historic archaeology (South 1972), has become a popular seriation technique whose results are expressed in year estimates for assemblages. This technique has been particularly attractive in the Southwest, where tree-ring dates provide such a precise basis for calendric calibration. Mean ceramic dating has been argued to perform effectively in many cases (such as Christenson 1988, 1994, 1995:110–129; Goetze and Mills 1993), but specific results are sensitive to initial assumptions about the production spans of the types (see Sullivan et al. 1995; compare dates for Reserve Black-on-white between Reid et al. 1995 and Wilson 1995). The single calendar year output of mean ceramic date formulas, whether for a single sherd or for a large assemblage, also risks providing a false sense of security in terms of both precision and accuracy. However, a variety of uncertainty estimates are used to qualify results and limit misinterpretation. The greatest limitation of mean ceramic dating is simply that it is ineffective on either end of the time range. If production of the earliest type spans A.D. 550–750 and is assigned a date of A.D. 650 for the calculation formula, then all collections dating earlier than A.D. 650 will be mischaracterized as dating to A.D. 650.

Perhaps the most important trend in ceramic dating is the application of multiple techniques (such as Goetze and Mills 1993; Goff and Reed 1998:26; Heidke 1995). This redundancy compensates for the weaknesses of any particular technique, focuses attention on situations that challenge accepted assumptions, and improves the reliability of the ultimate ceramic date interpretations.

Modern Practice and Constraints

An irony in the recent applications of highly sophisticated multivariate approaches to ceramic chronology has been a tendency of some practitioners to ignore the basic caveats that were laid out in the 1940s. Some of the greatest strengths of the Rainbow Bridge–Monument Valley analyses were serious considerations of sample size and mixture as potentially confounding elements in ceramic dating. These are not trivial concerns, especially the effect of mixture on seriations, but these confounding elements have been given far less consideration than they deserve. But perhaps the most important issue that was minimized in the development and application of seriation techniques is a simple one: whether a seriation result is or is not a chronology is an inference that must be argued (Dunnell 1970; McNutt 1973). In the development of most ceramic dating schemes, too little attention is paid to validation. The best data are usually committed to the calibration process, and subsequently there are only rare demonstrations of reliability or explorations of the conditions under which the technique will fail.

Another rarely acknowledged aspect of archaeological materials in general, and pottery collections in particular, is that our collections behave more like cluster samples than random samples. Vessels are the units of production and are usually the units of use in ceramic-bearing cultures. However, most vessels are recovered from archaeological contexts after breakage and discard, resulting in the sherd as the primary unit of archaeological analysis and interpretation. Each vessel results in many sherds, often 100 or more, that share many attributes. Sherds from a single vessel are not randomly distributed across the horizontal space of an archaeological site, but instead they tend to occur as spatially defined clusters. The cluster can be tight, as in the case of a vessel broken and left in place as primary refuse, or one or more diffuse clusters can result from recycling vessel portions or from various secondary discard practices (Deal 1985). Archaeological collection strategies sample space rather than artifacts, and the overlap between spatially discrete pottery clusters and spatially defined proveniences compromises the independence assumptions that are implicit in both probabilistic and many nonprobabilistic sampling designs. If one sherd from a vessel is recovered during an excavation, spatial clustering results in a higher probability of recovering another sherd from that same vessel than the probability of recovering a sherd from an as yet unencountered vessel.

As a consequence, models of statistical manipulation and inference that rely on assumptions of randomness are at risk of being misapplied to ceramic data. Under the best of circumstances (where refuse deposits have been randomized to a degree by secondary discard practices), variance in pottery collections doesn't begin to approach the expectations of random models until sample sizes reach 600 or more sherds (Figure 3.4). Samples of this size are luxuries in most ceramic dating applications below the level of the component. Where calibrations or applications are based on smaller samples or where collections are from less "randomized" provenience types (such as structure floors), the risks of cluster effects loom larger. Statistical estimates of ceramic dating uncertainty in these circumstances are best viewed as expressions of optimism on the part of the analyst.

Statistical expressions of uncertainty related to ceramic data are most complicated in dating studies where regression analysis is used to first describe and then exploit a relationship between time (conceptually the independent variable) and pottery attributes of interest, such as line width, sherd thickness, or coil height, as the dependent variables (Blinman 1984; Braun 1985; Plog and Hantman 1986). Even in simple description, it is rare that the independent variable, time, is known without error, invalidating the use of traditional least squares (Model I) regression and requiring the use of Model II regression (sensu Sokal and Rohlf 1969:547–555; Thomas 1986a:374–380). This approach is more robust (or "realistic" in that precision decreases while apparent accuracy increases), but results are still subject to bias if error terms are being influenced by cluster effects that raise problems with the necessary assumptions of homoskedasticity, autocorrelation, and normality (Lewis-Beck 1980:26–30). Even when a robust relationship can be demonstrated, the use of that relationship for dating is better characterized as an exercise in inverse calibration or inverse prediction than an exercise in regression (Braun 1985; Sokal and Rohlf 1969:496–498; Thomas 1986a:373–374). Under these circumstances, it should not be surprising that the long-term performance of regression-based ceramic dating techniques tends to degrade from the optimistic thresholds suggested when the techniques are proposed (Christenson and Bender 1994; Plog and Hantman 1986).

Ceramists are doing somewhat better on the subject of mixture in that the confounding effects of mixed assemblages on ceramic dating techniques are obvious to most researchers and are being acknowledged more commonly today than 10 years ago. One multiple regression

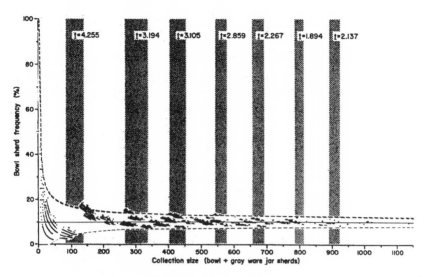

FIGURE 3.4 Variability in bowl sherd frequency as a function of sample size. The frequencies are calculated for all possible combinations of one, two, three, or four proveniences from a single component refuse collection from Site 5MT4479, Dolores area, Colorado (Blinman 1988a:Appendix A). The broken lines define a 95% binomial confidence interval around the bowl sherd frequency for all refuse from the site. Values of t represent the likelihood that the two extreme values within each shaded column could have been derived from random samples of the same population based on a test for the equality of percentages (Sokal and Rohlf 1969:607–610). Critical values of t are 1.96 (p = 0.05), 2.58 (p = 0.01), and 3.29 (p = 0.001). Cluster effects on the bowl sherd frequency values are evident in the scatterplot. In this example, the frequencies calculated from the provenience samples do not behave like simple random samples until sample sizes exceed 600.

approach can deal with mixture problems explicitly but only in well-behaved instances (Kohler and Blinman 1987; Schroedl and Blinman 1989). If temporal patterns of ceramic change can be partitioned into distinctive assemblages, entire collections can be broken down or "unmixed" into the relative contributions of each temporal assemblage to the whole. However, like all numerical seriations, the computer program will produce results but that doesn't mean that the results are correct. In addition to the susceptibility to cluster and sample size problems, colinearity can invalidate multiple regression unmixing results. As a consequence, applications of this technique require considerably more care in development and confirmation than other approaches. Unfortunately, this regression approach is currently the only automated technique that can be used to partition mixed collections, collections that are otherwise an intractable problem with all seriations. Multidimensional scaling is second best in that qualities of the graphical results can warn the researcher that mixing is possible (see discussions in Goetze and Mills 1993:113–146), but multidimensional scaling cannot necessarily resolve the components of the mixture.

In the process of justifying attribute-based studies of ceramic change, the usefulness of pottery typology has been challenged, both for dating and as an element of ceramic studies in general (Plog and Hantman 1986:88–90; Plog 1995:276). Arguments focus on the arbitrary and occasionally inconsistent applications of type distinctions (Fish 1976), as well as on the loss of resolution that results from the coarse partitioning of variation inherent in type definitions. Counter arguments appear to be stronger, especially given the long and persistent history of pottery classification in the Southwest. Although attribute-focused dating techniques do have the potential to improve the precision of ceramic dating over that associated with individual types, that potential has rarely been realized in practice. In one explicit comparison, attribute approaches resulted in no improvement in dating precision over type assemblage approaches (Duff 1996), and attribute-based chronology was abandoned in favor of pottery type-based approaches to dating by the Roosevelt Community Development Study, due in part to the cost of attribute measurement in the face of no gain in either precision or accuracy (Christenson 1995:97). Type assemblages incorporate change in the attributes of many types, creating an approach that is inherently if not explicitly multivariate. What seems to have been lost in the discussion of types versus attributes is that type classification during analysis and interpretation in no way precludes the simultaneous analysis and interpretation of attribute variation. Given the historic success of typological approaches to dating, abandoning typology both compromises regional comparisons and unnecessarily abandons the most broadly reliable source of ceramic dating inferences.

PROSPECTS AND ULTIMATE LIMITATIONS

Despite decades of productive use, ceramic chronologies are coming up against their inherent limitations. Current archaeological problems are demanding greater and greater dating precision and resolution, and ceramic dating is being asked to respond. This need is exposing potentially insoluble problems of sample size, sample quality, and circularity.

All of the ceramic dating techniques assume that the target collection is representative of a "time" along the dimension of temporal variation, but that time can be as short as a pot drop or as long as multiple generations. Pottery collections are by nature clusters of sherds from vessels that were transformed from systemic to archaeological context (see Varien and Mills 1997 for an excellent discussion of sherd accumulations). Most vessels make this transformation through the stochastic process of breakage and discard, and the probability that any particular vessel type will break is dependent on its manner and frequency of use.

As an example, Pueblo I households in the Northern San Juan region may have had standing assemblages of more than 20 vessels, while as few as five may have broken in any single year (Blinman 1988a:143–156; Kohler and Blinman 1987). Within the vessel assemblage, the greatest risk of breakage at the residence would have been felt by small- and medium-sized cooking jars, followed by bowls, large cooking jars, and other forms (Blinman 1988a:159–160; Varien and Mills 1997:166–167). These risks can be modeled and assigned probabilities that would predict the composition of an ideal discard assemblage. At a field house, with different activities and frequencies of those activities, ideal composition would be expected to vary somewhat. In either case, the random element inserts considerable uncertainty about the composition of the discard assemblage in any one year, especially in noncooking vessels.

A nonintense occupation (a few household-years or less) is unlikely to leave a residue of pottery that is representative of the ideal residential discard assemblage. Occupation spans that include multiple household-years improve the likelihood that the residue assemblage will be representative of the ideal. That intensity of occupation can be achieved by several households over a few years or one household over a longer time. Residential sites with an occupation intensity of 10 or more household-years usually will be effectively dated by ceramics since the pottery type assemblage will approach the ideal for the "time." Less intense occupations or seasonal or special-purpose sites will support ceramic dates of less precision and less accuracy because their associated pottery assemblages will be inconsistently representative of the "time" of the occupation.

Quality of archaeological samples also affects potential ceramic dating resolution through the representativeness of the collection. Collections need to maximize sample size while minimizing the potential confounding influence of sherd clusters. Collections with higher risk of including clusters will be subject to higher than expected variances that will in turn constrain some ceramic dating approaches. As the cultural events we would like to date become shorter and shorter in duration, the available sherds become fewer and fewer and are more and more affected by clusters. Sample variance goes up, and the reliability of statistical approaches becomes less certain. Ultimately, we simply cannot reliably date short-term events using either pottery types or attributes. The higher variances will constrain any comparison with calibration datasets where a "time" along the calibration requires that the collection to be dated is a representative sample of the calibration population. Greater dating potential in these cases will lie in techniques such as luminescence that are relatively independent of cultural behavior.

Finally, the only reason that ceramic dating works is that pottery changes in observable aspects of style or technology. However, the nature and rate of change responds to cultural factors rather than to any independent metronome, and not all variation is a record of temporal change. If pottery change is rapid, such as in the densely populated early Pueblo I villages of the Dolores area (Blinman 1984), ceramic dating can be gratifyingly precise (Figure 3.5); but if pottery changes slowly (such as in the more dispersed communities and homesteads after the breakup of the Pueblo I villages), ceramic dating precision is inherently poor, and no amount of cleverness with types, calipers, or statistics can redress the situation. Similarly, if variation in ceramic attributes is responding to cultural differences that are not a time series—such as function or ethnicity—then our seriations based on those attributes will not be chronologies, and we will be at risk for serious misinterpretation.

CONCLUSION

Ceramic dating exploits one aspect of variation in material culture systems. Not all ceramic variation is temporally correlated, but stratigraphy and other dating techniques can easily focus archaeological attention on those aspects of variation that are useful chronological indicators. That has happened in the Southwest over the past century, so that pottery provides the most commonly used organizing framework for the archaeological record of the past 2,000 years. Under the best of conditions, both culturally (through rapid change) and archaeologically

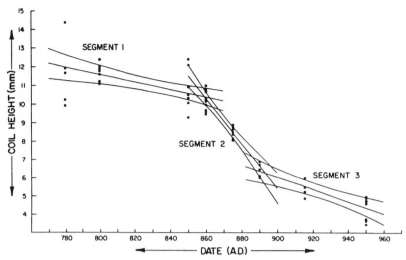

FIGURE 3.5 Variation in "progressive" neckband height in independently dated proveniences from the Dolores area, Colorado (Blinman 1984). Segment 1 coincides with relatively low-density settlement in the valley, and variation in neckband height is ineffective as a dating tool, unable to confidently discriminate differences within an 80-year period. Segment 2 coincides with the rapid development of villages of up to 100 contemporary households (Orcutt 1986; Orcutt et al. 1990). During this period, attribute change is rapid and relatively consistent, supporting fine-grained temporal discriminations of spans as narrow as 20 years. Segment 3 coincides with the breakup of the villages and a return to a low-density settlement pattern. Although still useful for dating, the potential precision of date estimates is much less precise, providing potential discrimination of 60-year periods. In the Dolores case, dating resolution is correlated with the increased social interaction within and among the area villages (distributed along about 15 km of river valley). Attribute-based dating techniques developed for the Dolores Valley do not appear to be directly applicable to contemporary and slightly later communities outside of the Dolores Valley, reflecting the geographic constraints commonly found in microseriation approaches.

(through robust samples), claims of resolution down to 20-year spans are defensible (Ambler 1985; Blinman 1988b). Under poorer conditions of either cultural context or sampling, claims of less than 200-year spans can be irresponsible.

Although there have been calls for the abandonment of pottery typology as an approach to dating and to pottery analysis as a whole (Plog 1995:276), those calls appear to be misplaced. Because pottery analysis and chronology developed simultaneously in the Southwest, the typological basis for pottery classification encodes considerable temporal information. Despite inconsistencies in some implementations of typology, applications of attribute-based dating techniques have yet to prove as useful as typology-based techniques. Attribute-based approaches to chronology will continue to productively exploit specific local potentials for precise dating needs, but regional problems, and many local ones, will continue to be addressed most efficiently through typological approaches to ceramic dating. The solution to the inconsistencies in typological practice noted by Plog (1995) is not the abandonment of typology but increased communication between ceramists, in both contract archaeology and academic settings. This is exemplified by the revival of ceramic conferences at the MNA (Hays-Gilpin and Hartesveldt 1998).

The future of ceramic dating is secure for the very reasons it has prospered over the past century. There is still substantial room to improve both precision and accuracy in many Southwestern regions, but this improvement will be achieved through the patient and careful application of the techniques proposed by Kroeber in the early part of this century. However, at its best, ceramic dating is also approaching theoretical limits of its contribution to chronology, and improving accuracy, precision, and resolution beyond the current state of the art will prove difficult. Accumulations research may improve the quality of ceramic dating by providing a more secure understanding of potentially confounding factors, but the barriers of small samples and clusters will not be overcome easily, if at all. Better tools for dealing with mixtures or long duration components would be a great benefit, but solutions to these problems probably will require advances in statistics rather than advances in archaeological method or theory. Because of these limitations, direct dating techniques such as luminescence may turn out to be the ultimate source of increased accuracy and precision, but even in these cases, traditional ceramic dating will provide the general chronological framework within which these techniques are applied.

Acknowledgments. The ideas presented in this chapter have been strengthened through my collaborations with C. Dean Wilson, H. Wolcott Toll, and many other Southwestern ceramists over the past 20 years. Perhaps most important, however, have been the collaborations with archaeologists whose goals have required precise and accurate chronologies and whose needs drove the development and testing of a series of chronological frameworks for the study of culture change. Foremost among these have been the staff of the Dolores Archaeological Program under the direction of David A. Breternitz and William D. Lipe. Both the content and clarity of this chapter have been improved by critical comments and suggestions from the volume reviewers and from Stephen E. Nash and Dena F. Dincauze. The remaining weaknesses in the chapter reflect my own biases and limitations.

CHAPTER 4

Seven Decades of Archaeological Tree-Ring Dating

STEPHEN E. NASH
Department of Anthropology
Field Museum of Natural History

Dendrochronology, the study of tree-time, is the highly specialized science of assigning accurate calendar dates to annual growth rings in trees (Stokes and Smiley 1968). Since the basic principles of modern dendrochronology were developed by astronomer Andrew Ellicott Douglass during the first three decades of this century, tree-ring dating has been applied to the study of an astonishing number of cultural and natural phenomena in fields as diverse as art history, climatology, forest ecology, geomorphology, hydrology, seismology, and archaeology.

Archaeological tree-ring dating came of age at a time when North American archaeologists concerned themselves primarily with time-space systematics (Lyman et al. 1997; Willey and Sabloff 1980) yet had no absolute and independent dating techniques available to guide their analyses. As a result, archaeologists' predendrochronology assessments of the temporal relations between archaeological phenomena, be they artifacts, architecture, sites, or regions, were based on rudimentary stratigraphic and seriation analyses, as well as educated guesswork. The application of tree-ring dates to archaeological phenomena thus constitutes an incredibly important development in the history of North American archaeology, for it brought chronometry to the archaeologists' analytical repertoire and set the chronological stage for the revolutionary theoretical and methodological developments that followed over the next several decades (Nash 1999).

A full accounting of the history of archaeological tree-ring dating would fill volumes and indeed has not yet been written (see Nash 1997a, 1999 for pre-1950 histories). A summary and review chapter must of necessity consider only a select fraction of the highlights in a narrative spanning seven decades. Treatment here is therefore limited to those episodes that have arguably had the greatest analytical impact on the development of North American archaeology and tends to emphasize earlier developments in the history of archaeological tree-ring dating. This situation exists for two reasons. First, my expertise lies in the earlier application of tree-ring dating to archaeology (Nash 1999). Second, many of the scholars mentioned in the post-1950 history of archaeological tree-ring dating are still active in the discipline and can be consulted for additional perspectives. One theme will become apparent, however: The seeds for much of what we consider to be modern tree-ring research applications were planted, if not actively cultivated, during the halcyon days (Bannister and Robinson 1986) of archaeological tree-ring dating, the 1930s.

Synopsis

Archaeological tree-ring dating developed slowly but surely between 1914 and 1929 (Nash 1999), then blossomed into a full-fledged focus of archaeological research between 1930 and 1942, when the onset of World War II exhausted sources of funding and matériel and drained the pool of young, interested, and able scholars to pursue such research (Nash 1997a, 1999). In 1949 (see Taylor this volume), radiocarbon dating burst on the analytical scene, after which dendrochronology suffered a decade of diminished archaeological attention. Several projects during this period after 1950 nevertheless made significant contributions to archaeological dendrochronology, most notably the Navajo Land Claims Project, the Wetherill Mesa Archaeological Project, and the Synthesis Project at the Laboratory of Tree-Ring Research, University of Arizona. In the late 1960s archaeological tree-ring dating was integrated with questions raised by the New Archaeology and increasingly sophisticated climatological studies. By the 1970s and 1980s, archaeological dendrochronology had matured to the point that archaeologists of many stripes could make use of published data in a host of chronological, behavioral, and ecological studies relevant to the prehistoric and historic past. As we approach the millennium, archaeological tree-ring dating can boast of a sophisticated body of data, method, and theory that, if not holistic or synthetic, nevertheless allows archaeologists with little or no dendrochronological expertise to bolster their analyses with the most accurate and precise chronometric data available in lieu of historic documentation.

ARCHAEOLOGICAL TREE-RING DATING, 1914–1950

The 15-year effort to apply the fledgling science of dendrochronology to archaeological questions began on May 22, 1914,
when Clark Wissler of the AMNH wrote Douglass to ask whether he had
considered using preserved archaeological beams in his tree-ring studies:
"We do not know how old these [Southwestern] ruins are, but I should
be glad to have an opinion from you as to whether it might be possible
to connect up with your modern and dated series of tree specimens [with
wood specimens] from these [prehistoric] ruins by correlating the curves
of growth." Douglass replied that he had not yet considered such a
course of action, but he was enthused by the prospect, and American
Museum archaeologists led by Earl Morris, Nels Nelson, and others subsequently began sending specimens to him in 1916. By 1919 Douglass
had cross-dated the growth-ring patterns found in specimens from Aztec
Ruin, near Farmington, New Mexico, and Pueblo Bonito in Chaco
Canyon, New Mexico, thus demonstrating for the first time and conclusively what archaeologists suspected on the basis of stylistic changes in
ceramic assemblages—that Aztec Ruin was occupied 25 to 50 years
after Pueblo Bonito. American Museum funding for Douglass's research
expired in 1920. One year later, Neil Judd of the Smithsonian Institution, after no small degree of encouragement from Wissler, arranged for
the National Geographic Society to fund Douglass's research through his
long-term research project at Pueblo Bonito. During the 1920s, Douglass
and his associates conducted no fewer than seven "Beam Expeditions"
and a great deal of laboratory research that led ultimately to the discovery of specimen HH–39 and the "bridging of the gap" that allowed
Douglass to assign calendar dates to prehistoric archaeological sites.
(Douglass 1929, 1935; Nash 1997a, 1998, 1999).

Prior to the June 22, 1929, discovery of HH–39 at Whipple Ruin
in Showlow, Arizona, archaeologists had no idea how old the sites
on which they were working actually were. Educated guesses suggested that ruins such as Pecos Pueblo might be 1,000 or 1,500
years old (Kidder 1927, 1936), that the classic occupations of
Chaco Canyon and Mesa Verde might be 2,000 years old, and that
Basketmaker occupations in the San Juan region might be between
3,000 and 4,000 years old (see Baldwin 1938; Cornelius 1938; Kidder 1924; Renaud 1928; Roberts 1935b, 1937). The advent of tree-
ring dating cut these estimates in half and in so doing shocked the
archaeological community, especially Morris and A. V. Kidder, who

had published or pronounced much greater ages for Southwestern archaeological manifestations than were borne out by Douglass's dates. In Kidder's (1936:143) words: "[We] have a sneaking sense of disappointment as the pitiless progress of tree-ring dating hauls the Cliff-dwellers, and with them the Basketmakers, farther and farther away from the cherished B.C.'s."

Despite the reduction in time-scale and attendant interpretive changes required by tree-ring dating, archaeologists were unanimous in their praise of Douglass and their appraisals of his accomplishment. A sample of their letters of congratulation establishes the tenor of the moment:

I have just read your most interesting article in the last [*National*] *Geographic*, which I believe is the most valuable contribution ever made to American archaeology. (J. Charles Kelly, University of New Mexico, November 28, 1929)

With most sincere congratulations on the splendid results which I understand you have achieved and which I am looking forward with the greatest interest to hearing about at the proper time. (A. V. Kidder, Harvard University, November 4, 1929)

I have just finished reading your report of your tree ring study....It not only amazes me, but convinces me that your study is the greatest thing in American archaeology that has ever been done. I feel just as excited over your finds as if I had made them myself!...I am grateful as an archaeologist that you happened into this subject, for it puts that much of our study of the Southwest on a sound basis....I am so excited about the whole thing that I tell everyone around here about you and your discoveries. (Paul Martin, Field Museum of Natural History, December 5, 1929)

Sincerest congratulations on successful closing of [the gap]. Your contribution to archaeological progress in [the] Southwest [is] singularly outstanding. (Jesse Nusbaum, National Park Service, November 19, 1929)

I congratulate you for reaching a happy conclusion in this extremely important task. I consider your discovery one of the most significant in many years and a very remarkable contribution to the archaeology of the SW in particular and also to archaeology in general as it can be applied to other fields as well. (E. B. Renaud, Colorado Museum of Natural History, January 23, 1930)

I wish to congratulate you upon your great achievement in completing the tree ring series for Southwest archaeology. This is to me one of the great scientific achievements of the time and I am sure will always be so regarded. (Clark Wissler, AMNH, December 10, 1929)

These statements foreshadow what Emil Haury (1935:98) later put into print: "It may be stated without equivocation that the tree-ring approach has been the single greatest contribution ever made to American archaeology."

Southwestern archaeologists, especially junior members of the field, were quickly enamored of the interpretive possibilities associated with tree-ring dating; many recognized that prowess in the method might lead to enhanced career opportunities. In January of 1930, less than two months after Douglass published his results, 15 students enrolled in his first course on tree-ring analysis at the University of Arizona. Within two years, three of the top students in that class had been hired to conduct tree-ring dating for archaeological research centers across the Southwest: Emil Haury was hired by the Gila Pueblo Archaeological Foundation in Globe, Arizona; John McGregor was hired by the MNA in Flagstaff; and W. Sidney Stallings was hired by the Laboratory of Anthropology in Santa Fe. Douglass, who was already at retirement age, continued to serve as final arbiter in all dendrochronological matters, but he became less and less directly involved in archaeological tree-ring dating as the decade progressed, though he did collaborate with Morris to extend the central Pueblo tree-ring chronology back to A.D. 11 (Douglass 1936; Morris 1936). Between 1931 and 1942, each of the dating programs established by Douglass's students made a number of significant dendroarchaeological contributions; highlights of their accomplishments warrant review.

The Gila Pueblo Archaeological Foundation

Iconoclast Harold S. Gladwin of the Gila Pueblo Archaeological Foundation offered Emil Haury in May 1931 a salary of $250 per month to conduct archaeological and dendrochronological fieldwork while serving as Assistant Director of Gila Pueblo. Given that the New York Stock Exchange and other financial markets had collapsed eighteen months earlier, it is not surprising that Haury accepted Gladwin's offer. Dendroarchaeologically, the most notable results of Haury's research at Gila Pueblo include the dating of Canyon Creek Ruin (Haury 1934) and the emergence of a rudimentary dendroarchaeological dating theory (Haury 1935).

After conducting an extensive survey of the Sierra Ancha in east-central Arizona in 1930, Haury returned to excavate Canyon Creek Ruin in 1932. Though he was disappointed by the lack of stratified deposits at the site, the dendrochronological results of his research were no less than spectacular. After analyzing three dozen tree-ring cores he had taken from structural elements at Canyon Creek, Haury informed Gladwin that he could identify the sequence, date, and sometimes the season of construction events at Canyon Creek:

> The beam material is all dated and out of it have come some rather interesting results. Cutting dates range from [A.D.] 1326 to 1348. In five rooms the dates of the major beams agreed within each room so that construction dates for them seem practically certain. Summer cuts outnumber those trees on which the last ring is completely formed. The rooms at the ends of the pueblo and those built out in front gave more recent dates than the inner rooms, as would be expected. In the one case where both first and second story rooms dated, the upper one was constructed a dozen or so years later than the lower room. (Haury to Gladwin, August 12, 1932)

Haury's (1934) analysis of Canyon Creek constitutes the first detailed and sophisticated analysis of archaeological tree-ring dates within their architectural contexts and remains a classic study that was arguably three decades ahead of its time. Haury's interpretations were not limited to statements on construction dates and sequences, however, for he offered behavioral inferences regarding the wood-use practices and origins of the inhabitants of Canyon Creek, who had apparently used windfalls as easy sources of construction timber (Haury 1934:19). The heavily scarred surfaces of the major roofing beams indicated that they had been "dragged or rolled for some distance" after cutting (Haury 1934:55). He concluded that prehistoric migrations between A.D. 1327 and 1343 explained the sudden appearance of the cliff dwellings in the area (Haury 1934).

Haury's convincing dendroarchaeological analysis of Canyon Creek Ruin is important because the concurrence between architectural, archaeological, and tree-ring data provided skeptical archaeologists with concrete evidence that analyses of such disparate datasets can produce complementary results. John Otis Brew of the Peabody Museum offered his congratulations:

> Your "Dating" section is superb. I refer this time not to the manner of presentation, which is straightforward and clear, but to the results. It is the most convincing exposition [of tree-ring dates] I have yet encountered. Before I had reached your mention of it in the last sentence I had checked over the dates of 2nd storey, outer, and inner rooms on the ground plan and had found that they came out right. This is truly a beautiful thing, Emil. As you know my skepticism of the validity of tree-ring dating in the hands of a competent analyst has evaporated. (Brew to Haury, April 25, 1934)

By mid-1934, Douglass considered Haury to be the nation's expert in archaeological tree-ring dating; it was therefore to him that archaeologists unskilled in dendrochronology turned for dating and advice. Haury's confidence in this regard is evident in his 1935 article "Tree-Rings: The Archaeologist's Time Piece" (Haury 1935), which considered the differing interpretive utility of cutting and noncutting dates, and offered the first exposition on date clustering as an aid to archaeological interpretation. In this, Haury was again decades ahead of his time.

Haury left Gila Pueblo on good terms in the spring of 1937 to become Head of the Department of Archaeology at the University of Arizona, after which tree-ring studies entered a new phase at Gila Pueblo, one focused on Gladwin's unsuccessful attempts to develop an "objective," read "quantitative," ring-analysis technique (Gladwin 1940a, 1940b, 1947). Gladwin's (1943, 1944, 1945, 1946, 1948) annual harangues and attempts to rewrite Southwestern prehistory will not be considered further here because he was not practicing dendrochronology in the sense of the Douglass method (see Dean [1969a], Nash [1999], and Webb [1983] for detailed treatments). Indeed, his technique for preparing charcoal specimens by sandblasting them guaranteed that he was not examining tree-rings at all. Gladwin's peculiar style and dogmatic personality have attracted much attention in the history of archaeology (e.g., Williams 1991) and detract from the many substantive archaeological and dendrochronological contributions made by Gila Pueblo and its staff over two decades. Gila Pueblo in general, and Gladwin in particular, should be recognized for financially, administratively, and intellectually supporting Haury's dendrochronological contributions between 1930 and 1937, particularly his classic study of Canyon Creek Ruin (Haury 1934) and his seminal contribution to archaeological tree-ring dating theory (Haury 1935). Indeed, Gila Pueblo and Gladwin deserve as much credit in this regard as the National Geographic Society and Neil Judd do for their monetary and analytical support of Douglass's tree-ring research between 1922 and 1929.

The Museum of Northern Arizona

John C. McGregor was hired by the MNA as dendrochronologist and curator of archaeology immediately after he finished Douglass's tree-ring course in the spring of 1930. Under McGregor's aegis, the Museum's archaeological tree-ring dating program focused on the dating of Pueblo I and Pueblo II period sites in the Flagstaff area (McGregor 1938a), the dating of regional ceramic types (Colton and Hargrave 1937; McGregor 1938b), and the dating of the eruption of Sunset Crater (Colton 1945; McGregor 1936), the latter of which forms the focus of attention here (for detailed treatments see Downum 1988; Nash 1999).

In June 1930, MNA staff member Lionel F. Brady (1932) found black-on-white sherds lying on the surface of a buried volcanic ash layer created by the most recent eruption of Sunset Crater northeast of Flagstaff. He logically surmised that people must have been in the Flagstaff area at or near the time of the eruption. When informed of Brady's discovery, Douglass immediately recognized the possibility of a geomorphologic application of dendrochronology: "The possibilities of your discoveries last summer of ruins with volcanic ash in them are tremendously attractive and I am anxious to work that line to the very limit, for it is a most important one" (Douglass to Colton, January 22, 1931). Colton replied that the Sunset Crater problem had become even more interesting because the area appeared to have become more, rather than less, habitable as a result of the eruption. He wrote Douglass: "Our work on the Sunset ash fall has taken another twist. We find that in the area where there was a light fall of ash late Pueblo II and early Pueblo III sites are abundant. Outside of this area of the fall they are scarce. This suggests that the ash made a mulch which made agriculture, by Hopi methods, possible over a limited area.... After the winds stripped the land of ash, putting it into the canyons and the lee side of mesas, the country in late Pueblo III again became uninhabitable" (Colton to Douglass, January 28, 1931).

Dating the eruption of Sunset Crater ultimately proved to be one of the successes of the MNA tree-ring dating program, though it was not an easy task and took 15 years to accomplish. An initial estimate (Colton 1932) placed the eruption between A.D. 700 and 875; a second estimate narrowed the possible range to between A.D. 875 and 910 (McGregor 1936). This estimate was later revised to A.D. 1046 and 1071 (Colton 1945) on the basis of a Gladwin-induced (Gladwin 1943, 1944; see Nash 1999) reanalysis of archaeological data and tree-ring dates from the Flagstaff area. Current evidence and interpretations suggest that there were several eruptions represented in the ash fall area and that the most significant of these occurred in A.D. 1064 and 1066.

The dating of Sunset Crater's last eruption is important from an interpretive standpoint as well as from a chronometric perspective, for it laid a foundation for cultural ecology in the American Southwest. Colton's (1946, 1960) Black Sand hypothesis suggested that the blanket of cinders created by the eruption of Sunset Crater formed a mulch that made the area more, rather than less, favorable for agriculture and that population in the area increased as a result. Though the hypothesis is subject to debate, it represents, with Douglass's identification of the "Great Drought" (Douglass 1929) and the work of Julian Steward (Steward 1937), one of the earliest forays into cultural ecology.

The Laboratory of Anthropology

Douglass had recognized as early as 1927 that tree growth-ring patterns east of the Continental Divide, specifically in the Rio Grande Valley, differed from those found on the Colorado Plateau and the Flagstaff region. Though Jean Jeançon and Oliver Ricketson had collected specimens in the Rio Grande Valley as the First Beam Expedition in 1923, and Kidder had submitted to Douglass samples from Pecos Pueblo throughout the 1920s, Douglass was never comfortable with the cross-dating exhibited in the Rio Grande Valley ring sequences. Indeed, his discomfort was severe enough that he withheld publication of prehistoric dates from Pecos in his *National Geographic* report of 1929 (Douglass 1929). He explained his decision to Kidder in late October of that year:

> It seems to me on the whole that for inclusion in a final list…the Pecos dates should have received a careful comparison with other Rio Grande material. I shall not feel satisfied about the Rio Grande area until it receives a complete chronological study from modern trees back as far as one can go. It has I know many points of similarity to the Flagstaff area

and I believe the dates I sent you are all correct, but in final statement I hold them subject to checking with other Rio Grande material. (Douglass to Kidder, October 28, 1929)

W. Sidney Stallings Jr. was hired by the Laboratory of Anthropology in June 1931, to develop a tree-ring chronology for the Rio Grande Valley, a task that required his full-time effort over the next two years. Once completed (Stallings 1933), a suite of pre- and protohistoric sites east of the Continental Divide was brought into the common-era calendar. Details of the Laboratory's tree-ring research are presented by Nash (1999). I will focus here on the somewhat surprising implications that the Rio Grande chronology has on the historic interpretations of the area, especially when considered in light of interpretations based on documentary and verbal evidence.

Prior to being hired by the Laboratory of Anthropology, Stallings helped his case by collecting tree-ring specimens on his own volition at the Jemez ruins in 1930. Douglass and Stallings worked on these materials in Tucson as administrative details for his position were arranged in Santa Fe. At the end of March 1931, Douglass noted that he was pleased with the "industrious" Stallings, and on June 10, they motored from Tucson to Santa Fe. By late July, Stallings had settled in comfortably and gained the favor of both Kidder, who took a "great shine to Stallings" (Kidder to Douglass, July 6, 1931), and Laboratory director Jesse Nusbaum, who considered Stallings "one of the finest fellows to work with" (Nusbaum to Douglass, July 22, 1931).

On May 15, 1932, Stallings reported to Douglass that he had examined some 1,500 pieces of charcoal and 290 pieces of wood "more or less intensely" and that he now had two significant chronologies. These consisted of a "dated sequence for the Jemez Mountain area back to 1510, with some doubt back to 1436, and a late [i.e., recent] undated sequence of 340 years from the Pueblos of Pecos, San Cristobal, and Quarai." He bridged the gap between the two chronologies on August 8th (Stallings to McGregor, September 20, 1932) and explained to Douglass that the Rio Grande Chronology was well established to A.D. 1200 and that the Pecos Pueblo specimens for which Kidder so desired dates ranged from A.D. 1310 to 1695. He noted that an "intensive drought" occurred in the Rio Grande Valley during the early A.D. 1400s, thereby accounting, in part, for the difficulty in bridging his two major chronologies.

In a brief exchange in November 1932, Stallings and McGregor addressed the differences between their respective chronologies. McGregor inquired in particular whether the Rio Grande chronology indicated a "drought immediately following the Pueblo Indian revolt; that is, during the years [A.D.] 1680–1690," for according to his studies in Flagstaff, a drought occurred in northern Arizona during that decade (McGregor to Stallings, November 14, 1932). Stallings considered the sociopolitical and historical implications of such a drought but replied in the negative.

> There is no good evidence of an extreme drought during this time.... The slightly dry spell during this decade appears to have been scattered locally, and even in such spots was not on the whole extreme. All this is contradictory to the testimony of the Indians following the Re-conquest, but one must bear in mind that this decade was one of social instability around the [Rio Grande] Pueblo population, which would surely affect to some degree their pursuit of agriculture. Further, such testimony was exactly what the Spaniards wanted to hear, and whether completely true or not, it would have been the politic thing to say. (Stallings to McGregor, November 20, 1932)

In the meantime, Stallings submitted a report to Nusbaum on the dating of the "Oldest House in Santa Fe," in which tree-ring dating and archaeological evidence were used to debunk the idea that the "Oldest House" was of pre-Spanish origin:

> Traditionally, the "Oldest House" is supposed to have been built by Indians before the coming of the Spanish, and to have been taken over and used by them. Tradition has it, further, that the house was the residence of the Indian chief of the presumed pre-Spanish pueblo. There is no material evidence to support this view. In the first place, there is no irrefutable evidence, historically or archaeologically, that the site of Santa Fe was occupied by Indians at the time of the founding of the Spanish settlement. The latest historical information, from recently discovered documents in the archives in Mexico City, indicates that Santa Fe was not founded before [A.D.] 1609, and probably in [A.D.] 1610, by the third governor of New Mexico, Pedro de Peralta....Black-on-white sherds can be found in various parts of the city today, and such sherds were picked from the walls of the "Oldest House," but villages in which this type of pottery was made had been abandoned and in a state of ruins well over a century before the discovery of America. Positive evidence that the "Oldest House" is of post-Spanish origin is found in that building itself. In the many places where plaster has fallen away and walls are exposed, adobe brick can be seen. The Pueblo

Indians did not make adobe brick before being taught by the Spaniards, but used a "puddle" method of construction.

The gist of the above evidence is, then, that the "Oldest House" does not date before [A.D.] 1610, and it might well have been built later. If it was first built in the early seventeenth century, there is a good chance that the house was at least partially destroyed during the Pueblo Rebellion of [A.D.] 1680.... It was thought that a study of roof beams might yield data on the antiquity of the house [seven specimens were collected and dated to A.D. 1741–1768].... In summary, there is no foundation except tradition that the "Oldest House" was built in pre-Spanish times. The present roof of the old, lower story was probably built in [A.D.] 1764. Further conclusions [are] not possible until plaster coatings are removed. (Stallings to Nusbaum, March 8, 1933)

He also reported in his paper "Pueblos of Historic Times on the Parajito Plateau, New Mexico," read by a colleague at the American Association for the Advancement of Science [AAAS] meetings in Berkeley, that "our present ideas of the time element involved in the divisions of Rio Grande Pueblo IV culture must be changed" because tree-ring evidence demonstrated that many supposedly prehistoric sites in the Rio Grande Valley had actually been occupied after European contact (Stallings to Nusbaum, September 28, 1934). Stallings's conclusions thus had significant implications for historians, who would have to reconsider Spanish accounts of their relationship to Native American populations in the area.

In early 1936, the Laboratory of Anthropology was in trouble. The Laboratory's financial situation was deteriorating, and the $20,000 budget Stallings submitted to the Rockefeller Foundation for his tree-ring program was cut in half. Stallings enrolled in graduate studies at Yale University in 1937 and continued sporadic tree-ring research for the Laboratory until he joined the military in 1942. Unfortunately, he never published a detailed treatment of the Rio Grande chronology (see Smiley et al. 1953), and the Laboratory of Anthropology Dendro-Archaeology Program's relatively poor publication record stands as the only serious shortcoming in a decade of productive research.

Summary
With Douglass's (1929) announcement of common-era calendar dates for prehistoric southwestern sites, archaeological tree-ring dating

enjoyed a surge of interest and a burst of research activity that has not been matched since. In addition to the dating programs established at Gila Pueblo, the MNA, and the Laboratory of Anthropology, Florence Hawley made significant, if ultimately unsuccessful, attempts to establish tree-ring dating in the American Midwest in the 1930s and 1940s, and James Louis Giddings established archaeological tree-ring dating in Alaska, concurrently (Nash 1997a, 1999).

Once tree-ring chronologies appropriate for archaeological dating have been developed, regardless of region, archaeologists can begin asking increasingly sophisticated questions regarding human ecology, history, sociology, and politics. Archaeologists can begin to make "empirically testable statements" and offer interpretations that, for the first time, can be *proved* correct (Dunnell 1986:29). In general and upon reflection, archaeologists have found that they tended to overestimate the age of ruins in any area to which tree-ring dating has been applied, be it the American Southwest, Alaska, or Europe (see Baillie 1995). Archaeologists trained in the Douglass method of tree-ring dating did more than simply provide dates during this era: Haury began to consider prehistoric wood use behavior and archaeological dating theory; McGregor set the stage for Colton's consideration of human ecology in the Flagstaff area; and Stallings recognized the discord between tree-ring dates and oral and written histories of the Rio Grande Valley (Nash 1999). In short, absolute chronology provided by tree-ring dating in the American Southwest facilitated archaeologists' movement away from two-dimensional culture history toward increasingly sophisticated examinations of culture process.

Given the successes achieved by Haury, McGregor, Stallings, and others during the 1930s, it is indeed curious that by 1942 archaeological tree-ring dating had become, and remains to this day, the exclusive domain of the Laboratory of Tree-Ring Research at the University of Arizona. The exact reasons for the lack of continuity in archaeological tree-ring dating are complex and difficult to pinpoint, though a number of factors are at least partially to blame. American involvement in World War II severely curtailed archaeological research of any kind in North America and drained universities of the men and women who would have become the students who would take archaeological tree-ring dating to the next generation. Haury, McGregor, Stallings, Hawley, and others had moved on to other careers, and Douglass turned 83 years old in 1950. The development of radiocarbon dating in 1949 certainly contributed to the decline in, or at least the failure to resume pre-1942 levels of, archaeological tree ring research activity. Despite these depressed archaeological tree-ring research activities during the late 1940s and early 1950s, tree-ring dating has regained its footing and matured into a productive discipline with its own sophisticated body of principles, methods, and theories.

BACK TO BASICS: TREE-RING DATING AFTER 1950

Shortly after World War II, archaeologically inclined staff at the Laboratory of Tree-Ring Research led by Terah Smiley "inaugurated a program whereby [they] sought to obtain a sample of every tree-ring specimen that had been collected in the Southwest from archaeological sites" (Smiley et al. 1953:4). This program resulted in two significant publications. The first was *A Summary of Tree-Ring Dates from Some Southwestern Archaeological Sites*, in which Smiley (1951) summarized the work of the Laboratory of Tree-Ring Research, the MNA, the Laboratory of Anthropology, and the Gila Pueblo Archaeological Foundation. Smiley (1951) condensed the state of North American archaeological tree-ring dating into a 32-page booklet, with a tabular listing of 5,600 individual dated specimens from 365 southwestern sites. The "Dated By" column in Smiley's (1951:14–25) table includes Haury's initials (EWH) instead of those for Gila Pueblo, but does not include McGregor's (JCM) or Stallings's (WSS) in lieu of the MNA's and the Laboratory of Anthropology's, respectively. Smiley wrote that "this summary [in accordance with the conventions adopted by the First Tree-Ring Conference in 1934] include[s] only those [dates] assigned or checked by a staff member or associate of the Laboratory of Tree-Ring Research" (Smiley 1951:9). Given this criterion, the tree-ring "dates" produced by Gladwin and Gila Pueblo after Haury's departure were, by definition, not listed because they were not considered dendrochronologically sound "dates" in terms of the Douglass method (Nash 1997a, 1999).

The second product of this integration program was Terah Smiley, Stanley Stubbs, and Bryant Bannister's (1953) *A Foundation for the Dating of Some Late Archaeological Sites in the Rio Grande Area, New Mexico*. This document brought closure to Stallings's Rio Grande work for the Laboratory of Anthropology by substantiating his dates and publishing the Rio Grande chronology in full. This document is important also because the authors recognized the need to fully integrate tree-ring dates and their archaeological contexts and therefore published detailed archaeological information for each dated site. In short, they came to recognize that date lists, such as those produced by Douglass (1938), Haury (1938), Hawley (1938), McGregor (1938a), and Stallings (1937), were necessary but not sufficient for use by archaeologist consumers of tree-ring data.

By publication date, these contributions (Smiley 1951; Smiley et al. 1953) are products of the early 1950s. In a very real sense, however, they are products of the 1930s and 1940s, and thus do not constitute original archaeological tree-ring research. Indeed, when compared to the previous two decades, relatively little new dendroarchaeological research was being conducted in the early 1950s, a situation that did not escape Giddings's notice. He wrote the following with regard to Arctic dendrochronology, but his comments apply equally well to archaeological tree-ring dating in any arena during the early 1950s:

> One may well ask why so much of the dendrochronological work begun or suggested for the far north since the middle 1930's is still unfinished. The answer is...the researcher has to explore and collect in many almost inaccessible places, and then to sit endless hours measuring, plotting, and cross-comparing. As a primary discipline, Arctic [or, for that matter, Southwestern] dendrochronology will progress as students learn the fascination of its precision as a research tool, but it cannot be expected to serve at all if it is not given long hours and proper care. (Giddings 1954:25)

The reasons for the diminished archaeological tree-ring research activity in the late 1940s and early 1950s are numerous and complex. Radiocarbon dating was being heralded as an absolute dating technique available to archaeologists working in all times and places relevant to the study of modern humans. Giddings, for one, refused to believe that dendrochronology would relinquish its primacy in archaeological dating to the universally applicable, nuclear-age and high-tech upstart radiocarbon dating: "Some think radiocarbon dating is about to replace the tree-ring method, just as automobiles replaced the horse and buggy. This assumption is doubtful....Even if radiocarbon dating becomes less expensive and more precisely focused, tree-ring dates will still be needed both to verify the general dating and pinpoint the specific" (Giddings 1962:130). Giddings was right, and dendrochronological calibration of the radiocarbon calendar has proved to be a source of much pleasure for archaeologists on both sides of the fence (Taylor et al. 1996). Nevertheless, to believe that the advent of radiocarbon dating did not have a deleterious effect on the market for tree-ring dating would be to ignore the realities of archaeological dating in that period.

The early 1950s were not, however, without their share of new archaeological tree-ring research projects, two of which led to developments that went beyond the scope of tree-ring date production and had substantial implications in tree-ring methodology as well as ramifications for the history of archaeology: the Navajo Land Claims Project and the Wetherill Mesa Archaeological Project.

Scientists at the Laboratory of Tree-Ring Research were asked in 1951 to apply tree-ring dating to the resolution of a land claims dispute between the plaintiff Navajo Tribe and the defendant United States Indian Claims Commission (Stokes and Smiley 1966:2, 1968:viii). Specifically, the Navajo Nation sought to demonstrate that its citizens had at one time occupied areas that were outside the current reservation boundaries (Stokes and Smiley 1963:8). Results of the project were published in four articles (Stokes and Smiley 1963, 1964, 1966, 1969) and led to the production of the now classic, and recently rereleased, text *An Introduction to Tree-Ring Dating* (Stokes and Smiley 1968, 1996). On completion, the Navajo Land Claims Project could count more than 3,000 specimens examined and 1,272 dates produced (Stokes and Smiley 1969).

The Navajo Land Claims Project is important because it legitimized dendrochronology to an audience outside its own relatively narrow scientific community. To be sure, the Douglass method of tree-ring dating had withstood a number of challenges regarding method and theory over the years (see Nash 1999; Webb 1983), but these challenges had come from, and been resolved within, its own sphere of academic and scientific circles. During the litigation phase of the Navajo Land Claims case, the scientific basis for the Douglass method of tree-ring dating was never challenged. The interpretation of individual tree-ring dates and dated sites was, of course, challenged, but the method and theory behind the dates were not.[1] Dendrochronology had arrived as an applied science.

In the late 1950s, the National Geographic Society donated funds to the National Park Service so that the Wetherill Mesa Archaeological Project might address "the problem of reconstructing the prehistoric environment of the [Mesa Verde] area...to provide an understanding of the effects of the environment on the day-to-day lives of the prehistoric population" (Osborne and Nichols 1967:3). This project is significant because it resuscitated two themes that were touched upon, but never played out, early in the history of archaeological dendrochronology: that of dendrochronologist-in-the-field and dendroclimatology, reviewed below.

Douglass recognized the importance of contextual information in archaeological dating during the late 1910s. His students recognized the importance of contextualizing field data as well, especially when they were bombarded with specimens that their archaeologist colleagues expected them to date in the absence of such data. To partially obviate this troublesome situation, Edward T. Hall, a dendrochronologist hired to replace Stallings at the Laboratory of Anthropology, was in 1938 paid $75.00 per month by the Awatovi Expedition to serve as dendrochronologist-in-the-field. Hall oversaw all aspects of collection, evaluation, analysis, and reporting on the Awatovi specimens, and the dating of the site improved dramatically as a result. The dendrochronology of Awatovi has never been published in full, and archaeologists did not again try to fully integrate dendrochronologists in their field research until the Wetherill Mesa Archaeological Project two decades later.

While the dendrochronologist-in-the-field may seem like a minor point in the history of archaeological tree-ring dating, it is important because it demonstrates the productive utility of disciplinary interaction during all phases of an archaeological project. The number of tree-ring dates and the quality of the analysis thereof increase as a result of this interaction. This aspect of the Wetherill Mesa Archaeological Project also led to the development of the 100% sampling procedure. Dendrochronologists decided, just as Douglass had suggested in the late 1910s, that archaeologists, especially in the absence of an on-site dendrochronologist, should collect and submit samples from every wood and charcoal specimen recovered. Though such a procedure is more difficult with some structures, such as a Navajo forked-stick hogan, than others, such as an Anasazi cliff dwelling or a Mogollon pithouse in a damp depositional context, it is nevertheless worth the extra effort (Dean 1996a). All totaled, the Wetherill Mesa Archaeological Project dated 501 out of 1,916 specimens from 10 sites, including Long House, Mug House, Step House, Badger House, and others on Mesa Verde (Nichols and Harlan 1967).

Through increased introspection and a focused return to archaeological fieldwork, tree-ring dating in the 1950s went back to its roots and renewed an allegiance to fieldwork, cross-dating, and chronology development. Gladwin donated Gila Pueblo's tree-ring samples, equipment, and data to California Technical University in Santa Barbara in the early 1950s, after which they were formally transferred to the Laboratory of Tree-Ring Research in 1957. The roundabout donation of the Gila Pueblo material completed the task set forth by Smiley, Stubbs, and Bannister: the Laboratory of Tree-Ring Research now had in their possession "a sample of every tree-ring specimen that had been collected in the Southwest from archaeological sites" (Smiley et al. 1953:4). In many ways, however, their task had just begun.

A Synthesis of Southwestern Dendrochronology

In January of 1963, Bannister submitted to the National Science Foundation a proposal seeking funds to "systematically restudy the...[Laboratory's] collections with the basic aims of checking past work, of obtaining as many new dates and dated sites as possible, of transforming all dates and associated information into a uniform system meaningful to both archaeologists and dendrochronologists...and of recording and publishing the resultant data in an organized and coherent fashion so that a synthesis of Southwestern dendrochronology will be available" (Bannister 1963:3). The Synthesis Project thus had goals similar to the integrative projects of the late 1940s and early 1950s (Smiley 1951; Smiley et al. 1953), but improvements in dendrochronological method suggested that a specimen-up, rather than chronology-down, approach would be more effective. The archaeological site thus became the unit of analysis, and dendrochronologists developed new chronologies for each locale rather than attempting to date all samples using the rather unrefined Central Pueblo and Rio Grande chronologies, as had been done in the past. What was planned as a two- or three-year project soon grew into a 12-year behemoth that examined hundreds of thousands of samples, produced 20,000 dates, dated 1,000 sites, and created numerous local chronologies that improved the prospects for successful Southwestern tree-ring dating in the future. The results were published in 16 "Quadrangle Reports" (Bannister, Dean, and Gell 1966; Bannister, Gell, and Hannah 1966; Bannister, Hannah, and Robinson 1966, 1970; Bannister and Robinson 1971; Bannister, Robinson, and Warren 1967, 1970; Bannister et al. 1968, 1969; Dean 1975; Robinson and Harrill 1974; Robinson and Warren 1971; Robinson et al. 1972, 1973, 1974, 1975) that still serve as the starting point for much archaeological research in the American Southwest.

The Synthesis Project stands in testimony to the persistence and perseverance of Bannister and his staff and should be recognized as one of the major accomplishments, along with the calibration of the radiocarbon time scale, in all aspects of archaeological dating. The entire archaeological tree-ring corpus, already largely the product of one intellectual tradition, was now completely standardized, replicated, integrated, and published. Archaeologists not well versed in the mechanics of tree-ring dating who had access to the Quadrangle Reports were now free to make independent use of tree-ring data in their analyses, be they settlement pattern, demographic, architectural, or stylistic studies. For the first time in the history of tree-ring dating, archaeologists were not held hostage to the benevolence and publication rates of the dendrochronologists: All reliable tree-ring dates were now in the public domain.[2]

Tree-Ring Dating, the New Archaeology, and Beyond

The 1960s were a period of foment in North American archaeology as prehistorians of all stripes began to accept the tenets of a "New Archaeology" that emphasized deductive reasoning, quantitative techniques, the scientific method, and the search for laws of behavior. Where archaeologists of old saw artifacts, trait lists, and cultures, New Archaeologists envisioned technological, sociological, ideological subsystems and prehistoric communities (Martin 1971).

Dendroarchaeologists were not immune to these developments, and in embracing the tenets of the New Archaeology, one dendrochronologist, Jeffrey S. Dean (Dean 1969b, 1970), though he was not a member of the Chicago–New Archaeology "school," joined his archaeological brethren (e.g., Hill 1970a, 1970b; Longacre 1966, 1968) in using archaeological data to reconstruct prehistoric social organization at Betatakin and Kiet Siel in northeastern Arizona. Dean's study marks the first time since Haury's work at Canyon Creek Ruin (Haury 1934) that an archaeologist intensively studied the architectural context of tree-ring dates to make behavioral inferences about the prehistoric population of the site. The tree-ring data at Betatakin suggest that it was built as a unit by a single, if large, group of immigrants in a relatively short period of time. Conversely, the tree-ring data from Kiet Siel suggest that that site was originally occupied by a small group of families who, over a couple of decades, welcomed additional families that added habitation units accordingly. Such radical differences in construction sequence at contemporaneous sites in close proximity to one another were taken to indicate significant differences in social organization at the two sites.

Contributions in archaeological dendrochronology at site and region-wide scales continue to be made, often under the influence of Richard V. N. Ahlstrom, arguably the most dendrochronologically literate non-dendrochronologist working today. Sites recently considered in the literature include Pindi Pueblo (Ahlstrom 1989), Lowry Ruin (Ahlstrom et al. 1985), Walpi Pueblo (Ahlstrom et al. 1978, 1991), Pot Creek Pueblo (Crown 1991), the Johnson Canyon cliff dwellings in Colorado (Harrill and Breternitz 1976), Hubbell Trading Post (Robinson 1985), Acoma Pueblo (Robinson 1990), Canyon Creek Ruin (Graves 1982, 1983), and many others. Studies in the dendrochronology of regions include that of Black Mesa (Smiley and Ahlstrom 1997), though some regional analyses (e.g., Berry 1982) have not gone without vigorous challenge (Dean 1985).

All of the studies listed above have benefited from a body of increasingly sophisticated archaeological tree-ring dating theory that began with Haury's (1935) consideration of the interpretive differences between cutting and noncutting dates, and the definition of date clusters. In keeping with other aspects of archaeological tree-ring dating, no notable improvements in tree-ring dating theory were made in the 1940s and early 1950s. In the late 1950s and early 1960s, such issues were once again considered. Bannister (1962) provides a detailed consideration of the interpretive errors that can occur in archaeological tree-ring dating. William Robinson (1967) builds on Bannister's (1962) work, while Dean (1978) offers a general consideration of terms and concepts relevant to archaeological dating in general and tree-ring dating in particular. Ahlstrom (1985) used an exhaustive site-by-site analysis to examine the nuances of an explicitly dendroarchaeological body of dating theory. These publications have made it easier for archaeologists to independently evaluate tree-ring data from their excavations.

A number of contributions have been made regarding prehistoric wood use behavior (Dean 1996a, 1996b, 1997; Robinson 1967), including long-distance transport of construction beams (Betancourt, Dean, and Hull 1986), periodic harvesting of manipulated tree limbs (Nichols and Smith 1965), and extensive beam reuse and structural repair (Ahlstrom et al. 1991). With regard to dating methods, Stephen Plog (1980), Michael Graves (1991), and Stephen Nash (1997b) made forays into the realm of cutting-date estimation, a topic previously considered by Andrew Douglass (1939) and W. S. Stallings (1940; see also Wroth 1982). The basic methods and mechanics of tree-ring dating have remained essentially unchanged since the mid-1960s, however (Stokes and Smiley 1968).

Cultural Ecology and Dendroclimatology

One final topic, the reconstruction of environmental variables via tree-ring analysis, is essentially tangential to archaeological tree-ring dating, but the two are so inextricably intertwined that any consideration of the history of archaeological tree-ring dating must include a short review of the important elements in cultural ecology and dendroclimatology.

The MNA spent a great deal of time, effort, and therefore money, trying to date the eruption of Sunset Crater because of the obviously significant implications it had for prehistoric populations in the Flagstaff area. Aside from this effort, however, archaeologists through the 1950s largely ignored the possibilities implicit in the climatic study of tree-rings, except in the case of the Great Drought of A.D. 1276–1299.

As early as December of 1928, as Douglass tried to bridge the gap between his 590-year-long undated chronology and his dated chronology that extended back to A.D. 1260, he recognized that "there is [tree-ring and archaeological] evidence . . . that the gap [between these chronologies] represents some great crisis in the history of the Pueblo people" (Douglass to Judd, December 5, 1928). Six months later, in June 1929, Douglass wrote that "the gap period was due to a *great drought* in the late 1200s" (emphasis added) (Douglass to Gilbert Grosvenor, National Geographic Society, June 29, 1929). For the next three decades, the effect, as well as the very existence (Gladwin 1947), of the Great Drought was debated, but most archaeologists were willing to grant the Great Drought some responsibility for the abandonment of the Colorado Plateau. In the late 1950s, Walter W. Taylor (1958:1) questioned "whether the Great Drought affected the Anasazi culture of northeastern Arizona," but ultimately abandoned his "Pueblo Ecology Study" because he could not find sites that would satisfy his archaeologically stringent criteria.

Outside of the archaeological arena, quantitative studies of the relationship between tree-rings and climate came to the fore in the 1950s with the work of Douglass's assistant in climatology, Edmund Schulman. His 1956 book *Dendroclimatic Changes in Semi-Arid America* (Schulman 1956) remains a classic if archaeologically underappreciated contribution to the field. By firmly establishing the quantitative relationship between tree-rings and climate across the American Southwest,

Schulman set the stage for archaeologically related dendroclimatic reconstructions. Schulman's untimely death in 1958 precluded the possibility of additional contributions in this vein for several years.

Physiological ecologist Harold C. Fritts arrived at the Laboratory of Tree-Ring Research in 1960 and soon began to make contributions to dendroclimatology with a dendrophysiological approach rather than one strictly climatological. Fritts (1976) published his *Tree-Rings and Climate* in 1976, though much of its content was beyond the analytical reach of many archaeologists. The following year, Jeffrey S. Dean and William A. Robinson (1977) published *Dendroclimatic Variability in the American Southwest, A.D. 680–1970*, a tome that presented dendroclimatic data in a way that was analytically understandable, and therefore useful, to archaeologists attempting to reconstruct prehistoric behavior. It was, in a sense, dendroclimatology for archaeologists. Using this document, which presented climatological data in numerical form as well as in the form of contour maps of statistical departures from long-term normal precipitation values, archaeologists could begin to examine in greater detail prehistoric relationships between environment and behavior without necessarily having to understand the intricacies of dendroclimatic reconstruction.

Since then, archaeologists have used tree-ring data to reconstruct prehistoric maize yields and storage behavior (Burns 1983), Palmer Drought Severity Indices (Van West 1990), and other climatically relevant variables. Increasingly sophisticated environmental reconstructions have led to increasingly sophisticated models of prehistoric behavior in response to environmental change (Dean et al. 1985; Dean 1988; Dean et al. 1994). These efforts seek to move beyond the "sterile exercise[s] in pattern matching" of old and attempt to develop a "coherent theoretical approach to adaptive culture change" (Ahlstrom et al. 1995:125–126). The annually resolved and precise reconstructions allowed by tree-ring dating have opened doors of archaeological inference that are unattainable in time periods and regions in which dendrochronology cannot be applied.

CONCLUSION

A detailed and complete history of North American archaeological tree-ring dating has yet to be written, but it is clear from partial histories (Nash 1997a, 1999; Robinson 1976) and overviews like this that the narrative is fraught with interesting anecdotes, personalities, and contingencies, and is characterized at once by glorifying successes and agonizing failures. Nevertheless, several themes become clear even in a brief review. First and foremost, the application of tree-ring dating compressed, by as much as 50%, the time scale within which all Southwestern, and by extension North American, prehistory had to be confined. This forced radical changes in archaeologists' interpretations of local and regional culture histories and also induced, slowly but surely, increased reflection on topics and issues such as socioeconomic and political complexity that would not enter the archaeological mainstream for decades. Second, tree-ring dating suggested and facilitated new lines of research in areas such as cultural ecology and the history of the Rio Grande Valley that either had not been considered previously or had been thought to be well understood. Third, many of the applications and extensions of dendroarchaeological research that are common today can find their intellectual ancestors in the halcyon days of tree-ring dating, the 1930s.

After a brief lull in the 1940s and a series of introspective and applied projects in the 1950s and 1960s, dendrochronology entered the modern era with the completion of the Synthesis Project and the standardized production, from one intellectual community, of a published body of data, method, and theory, accessible to archeologists of all stripes. The chronometric precision afforded by the study of tree-rings, in conjunction with the incredible resolution offered by the Southwestern archaeological record, practically insures that the Southwest will continue to serve as a laboratory for the development of North American archaeological method and theory. Nevertheless, tree-ring dating works but is not currently practiced in archaeological situations in Alaska and the Arctic (Giddings 1941; Nash 1999) as well as select situations in the American Midwest (Stahle 1979; Stahle et al. 1985; Stahle and Wolfman 1985), and elsewhere. We must hope that future scholars will build on this work just as dendroarchaeologists have followed the lead of their Southwestern predecessors over seven decades of archaeological tree-ring research in North America.

Acknowledgments: This paper greatly benefited from the comments of Rick Ahlstrom, Bryant Bannister, and Jeff Dean.

PART III

Radiation, Magnetism, Water, and Light: Later Approaches

CHAPTER 5

The Introduction of Radiocarbon Dating

R. E. TAYLOR
Department of Anthropology
University of California, Riverside

The radiocarbon (^{14}C) dating method, now in its fifth decade of general use, continues to be the most widely employed means of inferring chronometric age for late Pleistocene- and Holocene-age materials. Today, we probably would not use the metaphor of the late Frederick Johnson that ^{14}C dating dropped the equivalent of an "atomic bomb" on archaeology in the late 1940s (Johnson 1965:762). However, few would now dispute the suggestion that the introduction of ^{14}C dating into archaeological research has had a profound influence on the way in which prehistoric studies were subsequently conducted. Whether it can be characterized—as does Colin Renfrew (1973) and others (e.g., Taylor 1996)—as "revolutionary" is largely a matter of definition of terms. In this discussion, the questions that we wish to consider are what were some of the effects of the introduction of ^{14}C in North American archaeology and in what ways were these influences manifested.

In the mid-1960s, Glyn Daniel ranked the development of the ^{14}C method in the twentieth century with the discovery of the antiquity of the human species in the nineteenth century (Daniel 1967:266). The mid-nineteenth-century discovery that humankind had lived on this planet much longer than previously suspected had a profound—some would say radical—impact on Western philosophical and theological consciousness and discourse concerning the origin, progress, and destiny of the human species. To rate the influence of ^{14}C dating at the same level of historical significance and import with the acceptance of the temporal connection between extinct fauna and humans, or the acceptance of the view that there were fossil humans, is an evaluation that needs some critical consideration.

EVALUATIONS OF INFLUENCE

In some cases, the task of the historian of science accessing the precise relationship between some event, discovery, or invention on subsequent developments in some area of study is clear and unambiguous. The impact of polymerase chain reaction (PCR) on the study of the human genome has been immediate and obvious. Within a decade, literally thousands of scientists and other investigators for a wide variety of purposes became engaged in the use of the new technology to decode the genetic commands that control the physical development of all living organisms.

However, in many other cases, the actual, direct linkages between some specific discovery and subsequent developments in a discipline or academic field are not at all clear. If the actual discovery process and points of contact between key individuals are not recorded, various factors can influence the nature of the remembered and transmitted "stories" concerning how ideas or concepts originated, developed and influenced other ideas and conclusions. Subsequent developments in the field can influence what parts of the process are recalled, and those that are not. Certain inconvenient facts about what originally occurred may be repressed or forgotten. In some cases, oral narratives quickly develop, are never challenged, and are passed down to subsequent generations of students as historical fact. In some cases, key figures in the development of a technique may forget the exact order of events, and, when asked, will "recreate" their memory of what occurred. The validity of these memory traces can be evaluated only by subsequent research that examines the primary documentation—sometimes decades after the fact.

Several studies have previously undertaken the task of uncovering the precise relationship between the development of the ^{14}C method in the late 1940s and subsequent developments in archaeological method and theory. Gail Gittins, in an unpublished Ph.D. dissertation, undertook a series of interviews with archaeologists and directly addressed the question of the influence of radiocarbon dating on archaeological thought as reflected by the individuals interviewed (Gittins 1984). Gregory Marlowe collected extensive archival materials and examined the relationship between Willard F. Libby and the archaeologists with whom he came into contact during the first phase of the research on the radiocarbon technique in the late 1940s. A portion of this material has been published (Marlowe 1980, 1999). A brief summary of the major events involved in the development of the technique has previously appeared (Taylor 1987:147–170) as well as tentative suggestions concerning the impact of the development of the method on the conduct of archaeology—particularly New World archaeology (Taylor 1978:35–42)—and also as this impact is reflected in the pages of *American Antiquity* (Taylor 1985).

This chapter considers two major aspects of the history of the ^{14}C method: that dealing with the key events in the technical development of the method and that dealing with reactions of members of the archaeological community at different points along that developmental trajectory. Technical elements of the ^{14}C method will be considered in brief outline to provide a time line and context for the reactions of archaeologists as reflected in their use of and attitude toward the method.

RADIOCARBON: THE TECHNIQUE

The basis of the radiocarbon dating method has been widely discussed (e.g., Taylor 1987, 1996, 1997), and there is an extensive literature dealing with various aspects of its application in archaeology (Polach 1988). The natural production of ^{14}C is a secondary effect of cosmic-ray bombardment in the upper atmosphere. Following production, it is rapidly oxidized to form $^{14}CO_2$. In this form, ^{14}C is distributed throughout the Earth's atmosphere by stratospheric winds, and in the process becomes well mixed in the form of a ^{14}C-tagged CO_2 molecule. Most ^{14}C is absorbed in the oceans, while about 2% becomes part of the terrestrial biosphere, primarily by means of the photosynthetic process. Metabolic processes in living organisms maintain the ^{14}C content in living organics in approximate equilibrium with atmospheric ^{14}C concentrations. Once metabolic processes cease, as at the death of an animal or plant, the amount of ^{14}C begins to decrease by radioactive decay—in the case of ^{14}C by beta decay—at a rate measured by the ^{14}C half-life.

The *radiocarbon age* of a sample is based on a measurement of its residual ^{14}C content. For a ^{14}C age to be equivalent to its actual or calendar age at a reasonable level of precision, a set of primary assumptions needs to be satisfied. The most important assumptions are that the concentration of ^{14}C in each carbon reservoir has remained essentially constant over the ^{14}C time scale, that complete and rapid mixing of ^{14}C occurs throughout the various carbon reservoirs on a worldwide basis, and that carbon isotope ratios in samples have not been altered except by ^{14}C decay since the death of an organism. Much of the history of the ^{14}C dating method applications in archaeology involves two types of studies. The first has been and continues to be the documentation of the stratigraphic or geomorphological relationship between a sample on which a ^{14}C age estimate is obtained and the archaeological object, feature, or geological context for which an age determination is desired. The second includes investigations designed to examine and compensate for the effects of violations of the primary assumptions as applied to specific sample types. For example, the violation of the assumption of the constancy of contemporary ^{14}C activity over time requires the *calibration* of ^{14}C age estimates. Calibration involves the adjustment of ^{14}C values to take into account temporal offsets between ^{14}C and solar time.

Radiocarbon age estimates are generally expressed in terms of a set of characteristic parameters that define a *conventional radiocarbon age*. These parameters, introduced in the mid-1970s by Stuiver and Polach (1977) and now widely employed, include the following:

1. The use of 5,568 (±30) years as the defined ^{14}C half-life (even though the actual half-life value is closer to 5,730);
2. The use, directly or indirectly, of an internationally recognized preparation as a contemporary or modern reference standard to define a "zero" ^{14}C age;
3. The use of A.D. 1950 as the zero point from which to count ^{14}C time;
4. A normalization of ^{14}C in all samples to a common ^{13}C/^{12}C(δ^{13}C) value; and
5. An assumption that ^{14}C in all reservoirs has remained constant over the ^{14}C time scale.

In addition, each ^{14}C determination is expected to be accompanied by an expression that provides an estimate of the *experimental* or *analytical uncertainty*. Since statistical constraints associated with the measurement of ^{14}C concentrations in samples is usually the dominant component of the analytical uncertainty, this value is informally referred to as the "statistical error." This "±" term is suffixed to all appropriately documented ^{14}C age estimates and is typically expressed as ± *one standard deviation*. For samples in the age range from 300 years to about 10,000 years, analytical uncertainties at the level of ± 1σ typically range from 40 to 80 years depending on instrumentation and experimental protocols used.

The ^{14}C time scale currently extends from about 300 years to between 40,000–60,000 years. The limitations on the young end of the ^{14}C time scale are a consequence of three factors: significant variability in ^{14}C production rates because of seventeenth-century changes in solar magnetic fields, the effect of the combustion of large quantities of fossil fuels beginning in the late nineteenth century, and the production of artificial ^{14}C ("bomb" ^{14}C) as a result of the detonation of nuclear and thermonuclear devices in the atmosphere, particularly during the period between 1955 and 1963. As a result of the complex interplay of these factors, it is not currently possible, except under very special circumstances, to assign unambiguous ages to materials living less than 300 years by the use of the ^{14}C method.

The maximum ^{14}C ages that can be inferred depend on characteristics of different laboratory instrumentation and experimental configurations. Using relatively large sample sizes, typically not available from archaeological contexts, a few laboratories have the capability to obtain finite ages up to about 70,000 years. With isotopic enrichment—again using relatively large (>15 grams of carbon) amounts of sample material —ages up to 75,000 years have been reported on a small number of samples. While currently not technically feasible, there are efforts now under way to exploit accelerator mass spectrometry (AMS) technology to extend the ^{14}C time scale out to as much as 90,000–100,000 years.

On a world-wide basis, over 140 ^{14}C laboratories have been assigned separate laboratory codes to designate the samples that have been or currently are being processed by these labs. The journal *Radiocarbon* currently lists the codes of 21 United States ^{14}C laboratories, of which four are accelerator-based facilities. Originally, most U.S. ^{14}C laboratories were established to undertake the dating of archaeological samples. This is no longer the case. Currently, most of the U.S. ^{14}C laboratories—both conventional and AMS—are supported by and operate primarily to support nonarchaeological research studies. In the United States, a majority of ^{14}C dates obtained for archaeological purposes are now undertaken in the context of environmental impact report (EIR) activity undertaken as part of cultural resource management (CRM) projects. Such CRM projects are carried out in response to U.S. federal and state legislation that mandates the evaluation and mitigation of the adverse effects of land-modification projects that would impact any aspect of the natural environment. Because of the need for rapid turnaround of samples, most of the ^{14}C analysis for these purposes is undertaken by proprietary ^{14}C facilities. With an increase in building and other economic activity, there is a corresponding increase in the EIR-based studies and thus an increase in the number of ^{14}C analyses undertaken. In contrast to the commercial ^{14}C facilities where most ^{14}C measurements are done, university-based ^{14}C laboratories focus attention on research-oriented projects that require attention to detail and extensive chemical pretreatment of specialized samples.

Regretfully, no comprehensive database of ^{14}C determinations currently exists. The best estimate is that in excess of 150,000 ^{14}C-based age determinations have been obtained over the five-decade history of the method. However, it is difficult to make an informed judgment of the exact number analyzed to date. This is due, in large part, to the large number of ^{14}C values obtained by commercial laboratories for EIR purposes that are not published in the conventional scientific literature. In addition, the advent of AMS technology has also dramatically increased the number of ^{14}C dates processed. In the absence of any comprehensive database, various individual investigators have assembled ^{14}C data for a whole range of different regions and topics.

RADIOCARBON: INITIAL DEVELOPMENT

Reconstructing the events constituting the technical development of the ^{14}C method is much more straightforward than that involving the response of the contemporary and subsequent professional archaeological community. The published record of the development of the method itself is more complete. Also, fortunately, a relatively small number of individuals were involved in the early period of the technical development of the method.

Of the three principals, Willard Frank Libby (1905–1980), James R. Arnold, and Ernest C. Anderson, two, Arnold and Anderson, are still available to interview and to review the documentation of the historical record. Most of the previous treatments of this topic as well as the present discussion have benefited significantly from the information provided by the two principal collaborators with Libby in the development of the method. Libby (Figure 5.1) himself contributed a series of written accounts of his own recollection of events in the development of the method from various perspectives (Libby 1961a, 1965b, 1967, 1970a, 1970b, 1973, 1979a, 1980, 1982). Several individuals, including the author, had an opportunity to review with him some aspects of the history of the development of the method before his death in 1980. The transcripts of two formal interviews are available, one conducted in 1978 by Mary Terrall of the Oral History Program of the University of California, Los Angeles (Libby 1978) and one undertaken the following year by Gregory Marlowe for the American Institute of Physics, Center for the History of Physics (Libby 1979b).

It is fortunate that Libby's principal collaborators in the initial development of the technique—James Arnold (then a Research Associate/Assistant Professor at Chicago) and Ernest Anderson (then Libby's first graduate student at Chicago)—are still active and interested in providing recollections and helpful insights that can be used in developing an accurate record of how ^{14}C dating was developed (e.g.,

<small>Figure</small> 5.1 Willard Frank Libby (1905–1980).

Arnold 1992, 1996). Interestingly, James Arnold's personal background is conducive to his reflecting on the early impact of radiocarbon dating with regard to archaeology.

Although Arnold's father was a corporate attorney by profession, he was particularly knowledgeable in Egyptian archaeology, serving for many years as the American Secretary for the British-based Egypt Exploration Society with responsibility for fund raising (Arnold 1992). In fact, it is through his personal friendship with Ambrose Lansing, then the Curator of the Egyptian collection of the Metropolitan Museum of Art in New York, that the first 10 radiocarbon samples were obtained by Libby's group. This included the first sample (C–1) that was radiocarbon dated—cypress wood from the Saqqara tomb of the Third Dynasty Egyptian King Djoser (Zoser).

James Arnold had grown up in a household where archaeology—at least the Near Eastern variety—was discussed—often and at length (J. R. Arnold, personal communication 1995). In a letter written in 1947, Libby stated that one of the reasons he chose James Arnold as the researcher to be associated with his research on ^{14}C dating was the fact that Arnold, although a physical chemist (his Ph.D. was from Princeton), had "a real interest in Egyptian archaeology" (Libby quoted in Marlowe 1980:1008).

Table 5.1 summarizes the major technical concepts and discoveries instrumental in the process by which the ^{14}C technique was initially developed beginning in the pre–World War II period (modified from Taylor 1987:Fig. 6.1). Libby once observed that it was "difficult to know exactly when the idea [behind radiocarbon dating] was born" (Libby 1967:5–6). He suggested that its beginnings lay in his realization that cosmic-ray ^{14}C production led to "a continuous labeling of the biosphere…which is terminated at death" (Libby 1967:5–6). In an interview conducted a decade later, Libby stated that the origin involved his reading a publication (apparently Korff and Danforth 1939) that reported finding neutrons in the atmosphere: "As soon as I read Korff's paper…that's carbon dating" (Libby 1979b:33, 40).

Libby's first publication outlining the initial consideration that formed the basis of the ^{14}C method was published in the June 1, 1946, issue of *Physical Review* (Libby 1946). In this one-page note, Libby briefly laid out the fundamental idea behind ^{14}C dating: That there should be a difference in the ^{14}C content of fossil carbon and modern carbon. As far as can be determined, the title of the paper, "Radiocarbon from Cosmic Radiation," was the first time "radiocarbon"—a contraction of

TABLE 5.1. Radiocarbon Dating Method: Initial Developments[a]

Date	Researcher	Development
	PRE-WORLD WAR II PERIOD (1933–1940)	
1933	Libby[b]	Screen-wall counter development (not for ^{14}C)
1934	Kurie[b]	Mode of ^{14}C production advanced (cloud chamber)
1939	Korff	Mechanism of formation of natural ^{14}C proposed (cosmic-ray neutron secondaries)
1940	Kamen and Ruben[b]	Slow neutron production of ^{14}C confirmed Long ^{14}C half-life assumed
	MANHATTAN PROJECT PERIOD (1940–1945)	
1940–1945	Kamen	Investigations of ^{14}C half-life[c]
	CHICAGO PERIOD (1945–1954)	
1945–1950	Libby, Anderson, and Arnold	Difference between biomethane (contemporary ^{14}C) and petromethane (fossil ^{14}C)
		Adaption of screen-wall solid carbon counting technology
		Anticoincidence counting
		Contemporary specific activity as function of latitude and carbon reservoir
		Curve of Knowns
		Measurement of unknowns
		First date list [Chicago I] (1950)
		Subsequent date lists [Chicago I–V] (1951–1954)

a = Revised from Taylor (1978; 1987) with assistance of Gregory Marlowe (personal communication 1997).

b = At University of California Berkeley.

c = See Table 1 and footnote 2 in Engelkemeir et al. (1949) and footnotes 2 and 3 for Table 4 in Libby (1955:35).

"radioactive carbon"—appeared in print. This paper was the first of 40 publications that Libby and his collaborators would publish on some aspect of ^{14}C dating (Berger and Libby 1981). It was also Libby's first publication since his appointment in October 1945 as a Professor in the Department of Chemistry and Institute for Nuclear Studies (now the Enrico Fermi Institute for Nuclear Studies) at the University of Chicago. He was then, at the age of 36, the youngest full professor at Chicago.

Since most of the important initial discoveries that established the basic validity of the ^{14}C method were developed in Libby's laboratory in Room 217 of Jones Hall at the University of Chicago, this period has been labeled in Table 5.1 as the "Chicago Period." It began with the *Physical Review* note (June 1946), which will be considered here as the birth event for radiocarbon dating. It concluded in September 1950 with the publication of the first radiocarbon "date list" (Arnold and Libby 1950). Over this approximately four-year period, James Arnold and Ernst Anderson, jointly and separately,[1] undertook the series of experiments that demonstrated the essential validity of Libby's model of how radiocarbon dating should work.[2] The first paper explicitly stating that the method was being developed to provide "ages of various carbonaceous [carbon-containing] materials in the range of 1,000 to 30,000 years" (Anderson et al. 1947a) appeared in May 1947. The first "radiocarbon date" on the wood from the tomb of Djoser (Zoser) was calculated in Libby's laboratory by James Arnold on July 12, 1948 (J. R. Arnold and E. C. Anderson, personal communications 1996) and published in March 1949 (Libby et al. 1949).[3]

The capstone of these experiments was the completion of measurements of the first "Curve of Knowns," a suite of seven ^{14}C measurements on a series of six known-age samples spanning a period from about A.D. 600 to 2700 B.C. This provided the first conclusive evidence of a consistent relationship between ^{14}C activity and chronological age in carbonaceous materials—at least over the last 5,000 years—to a precision, at that time, of about ±10%. This paper, which Arnold would later characterize as "the big one" for ^{14}C dating (Arnold 1981), appeared in late December 1949 in *Science* (Arnold and Libby 1949).

By the time this paper was published, the Chicago laboratory had been measuring, for almost a year, the first series of unknown-age samples. The compilation of the first radiocarbon date list was completed in mimeograph form on January 1, 1950, with a supplement dated in April.[4] A number of the values that appeared in the mimeograph report were subsequently modified, and these revised values appeared in a booklet published by the University of Chicago Institute for Nuclear Studies dated September 1, 1950. This booklet contained 148 radiocarbon age determinations and carried a notation in the preface that the "list itself is not for publication in its present form, though the dates themselves may be quoted freely" (Arnold and Libby 1950). The text of this booklet, with some modifications,[5] constituted the first published Chicago date list (Chicago I), which appeared in February 1951 (Arnold and Libby 1951). This inaugurated the custom of radiocarbon laboratories publishing their ^{14}C values in the form of "date lists." Table 5.2 summarizes the disciplinary and geographic distribution of this first set of ^{14}C determinations.

Almost two-thirds of them were on archaeology-related samples, and the vast majority were from sites in the United States.

The appearance of the first set of ^{14}C determinations inaugurated what Colin Renfrew would later call the "first radiocarbon revolution" (Renfrew 1973:48–68). The geologically late beginning of the postglacial

TABLE 5.2. Initial Chicago Radiocarbon Determinations: Discipline and Region

Total N = 148[a]

Region	Archaeology	Discipline Geology	Other[b]	
Western Eurasia (Near East)	11	–	–	[8%]
Western Europe	3	7	–	[7%]
England	4	9	–	[9%]
United States	48	37	2	[58%]
Mesoamerica (Mexico)	15	–	–	[10%]
South America (Peru, Chile)	11	–	1	[8%]
	92 [62%]	53 [36%]	3 [2%]	

a = Based on Arnold and Libby (1950).
b = Maize, tree rings, guano.

period (Two Creeks at 11,400 B.P.), the first effort to provide a chronometric framework for Paleoindian materials (Lubbock Lake Folsom initially at about 9900 B.P.),[6] and the surprising antiquity of agriculture and sedentary village societies in Southwestern Asia (Jarmo at about 5260–6700 B.P. and Jericho at 7800–8200 B.P.) are examples of major unanticipated results of the first set of ^{14}C measurements. Radiocarbon determinations were also quickly brought to bear on the problem of correlating the Maya Long Count and Western Calendar (Libby 1954b).[7]

The subsequent history of radiocarbon dating (Table 5.3) has been divided into three generations of basic and applied research (Taylor 1996, 1997). Each generation is distinguished partly by the type of detection technology employed, and in part, on understandings about the relationship between radiocarbon and "real" (solar) time. The first generation of archaeological ¹⁴C applications—Renfrew's "First Radiocarbon Revolution"—spans more than two decades (1946–1970). Midway through that period, the great scientific contribution of radiocarbon dating, not only to archaeology but also to geology and geophysics, was recognized with the awarding of the 1960 Nobel Prize in Chemistry to Libby (Libby 1961a, 1961b).[8] Second-generation ¹⁴C studies were fully under way by the early 1970s with the documentation of the degree of divergence of ¹⁴C time from solar time—the ¹⁴C "secular variation" phenomenon—requiring, in some cases, the need to "calibrate" ¹⁴C data (Olsson 1970). The result was Renfrew's "Second Radiocarbon Revolution" (Renfrew 1973).[9] The "Third Radiocarbon Revolution" is associated with the advent of AMS in the late 1970s (Linick et al. 1989; Muller 1977), the extension of the calibrated ¹⁴C time

TABLE 5.3. Radiocarbon Dating Method: Post-Chicago Developement[a]

Period	Generation	Characteristics
1946–1970	I	"First Radiocarbon Revolution" (Renfrew)
		Critical experiments demonstrating essential validity of Libby's model of ¹⁴C dating using solid carbon counting
		Replacement of solid carbon counting (gas and liquid scintillation)
		Libby's Nobel Prize in Chemistry (1960)
1970–1977	II	"Second Radiocarbon Revolution" (Renfrew)
		Secular variation phenomena documented (long- and short-term [de Vries effects])
1977–	III	"Third Radiocarbon Revolution"
		Development of accelerator mass spectrometry (AMS)
		Extension of the calibrated ¹⁴C scale into the late Pleistocene/detailed characterization of Holocene ¹⁴C time spectrum

a = Based on Taylor (1996).

scale into the late Pleistocene, and a more detailed characterization of the Holocene ¹⁴C time spectrum (Taylor et al. 1996).

RADIOCARBON: INITIAL REACTIONS OF ARCHAEOLOGISTS

The first report of the ¹⁴C method to appear in *American Antiquity* was completed in October 1947 at a time when the extent of the essential literature on ¹⁴C dating consisted of two publications: Libby's note in the *Physical Review* predicting a difference in ¹⁴C activity in modern and fossil carbon (Libby 1946) and the first results of the actual measurement of that difference (Anderson et al. 1947a). The author of the report was Robert S. Merrill, then a second-year graduate student in the Department of Anthropology at the University of Chicago (Merrill 1947). The article owed its existence to the interest of Robert Redfield, then the departmental chair, in the development of the ¹⁴C method (J. R. Arnold, personal communication 1997).[10] It might be suggested that Redfield was interested in ¹⁴C dating because he realized that it would, by association, draw attention to the Chicago Department of Anthropology. Some years earlier, Fay-Cooper Cole had brought Florence Hawley to Chicago to work on tree-ring dating.

Redfield had directed Merrill to prepare the report because he was, at that time, the department's only student with a background in chemistry (Sol Tax, personal communication 1985). This background consisted of course work in chemistry while a Chicago undergraduate and employment in a toxicology laboratory during World War II (R. S. Merrill, personal communication 1985). Merrill concluded his brief overview of Libby's conceptualization of the method by stating "this is the theory." He thought the method to be "very promising" but noted that it had "several technical problems which must be solved before the method [when established] can be extensively used for dating archaeological sites" (Merrill 1948:282–283).

Four months before the Merrill paper was published (Merrill 1948), Libby was asked to make a presentation at a "Supper Conference" in New York in January 1948 hosted by the Viking Fund for Anthropological Research (now the Wenner-Gren Foundation).[11] In inviting Libby to make this presentation, the Director of Research for the Viking Fund, Paul Fejos, M.D., cautioned Libby that the "section of your talk dealing with physical chemistry should be on a popular level as most of the anthropologists have little or no training in natural sciences" (Fejos to Libby, November 17, 1947, quoted in Marlowe 1980:1008). Libby was motivated to accept the invitation because the

Viking Fund had provided him with the first extramural funding supporting his radiocarbon research.[12]

Libby's lecture was attended by about 30 individuals including anthropologists, archaeologists, and at least one geologist, the Yale Pleistocene geologist Richard Foster Flint. Despite Fejos's request for a popular-level presentation, Libby's talk was highly technical. What exactly happened at the conclusion of his remarks has been variously reported. According to Fejos's biographer (Dodds 1973), at the end of Libby's talk, the audience remained silent until Flint reportedly said, "Well, if you people [the archaeologists and anthropologists?] are not interested in this, I am.... If you don't want anything dated, I am for it, and would like to send some material" (Dodds 1973:101). However, a tape of this meeting reviewed by Gregory Marlowe (personal communication 1997) records not silence but an immediate question from a member of the audience.

James Arnold, who was present at the meeting, recalls the remark by Flint. His recollection is that the comment was directed at the archaeologists present (J. R. Arnold, personal communication 1997). One possible explanation is that while several archaeologists did understand Libby's presentation, most did not, and the few who did were uncertain about the status of the technique as it stood at that time. This was the view of Frederick Johnson, who attended this meeting, even though he himself was well informed and familiar with the current situation (F. Johnson, personal communication 1987).

Another possible partial explanation for the reaction of some or most of the archaeologists present as reflected in the comment of Flint might have had something to do with the relatively large sample sizes required at this point in the development of the technique—in the range of 1–2 *pounds* of carbon. The reason was that, at that time, it would have been necessary to artificially enrich samples to measure their ^{14}C concentrations, a time-consuming and expensive procedure. The instrument being used in Libby's laboratory for the measurement of ^{14}C was, at this time, still very unreliable (J. R. Arnold, personal communication 1997). Fortunately, these problems would soon be overcome with the continued improvement in the reliability in the instrumentation (see footnote 2 for details of the technical problems). But this was still many months away.

When Libby's counting technology was finally developed to the point where it could be used on a routine basis, sample size requirements were reduced down into the range of several ounces of wood (30–60 grams). However, even at this level, most archaeologists, and particu-

larly those charged with the curation of museum collections, typically
still would not have had charcoal or other organic samples in their collections. The practice of most archaeologists up to the introduction of
¹⁴C dating was to discard rather than collect charcoal samples in the
field. Even if other organic samples were collected, there was a reluc-
tance to turn them over for destruction. Libby later commented on this
problem when he noted that "[t]hose museum dogs were not going to
give it to a bunch of physical chemists to burn up, no way" (Libby
1979b:43). On the other hand, geologists more often would have access
to much larger collections of charcoal or wood and would not hesitate
to have them destroyed (J. R. Arnold, personal communication 1987).[13]

As a result of the Viking Fund meeting, there apparently was a
recognition by many archaeologists that it would take special efforts to
secure well-documented samples large enough to accommodate the
sample size requirements of the counting technology then available. To
accomplish this, the Executive Board of the then newly reorganized
American Anthropological Association (AAA) in February 1948 was
solicited to appoint a committee with a somewhat redundant title:
"Committee on Radioactive Carbon 14" or as it was more typically
termed, the "Committee on Carbon 14." This group originally consisted of Frederick Johnson (R. S. Peabody Foundation) as chairman,
Donald Collier (Field Museum of Natural History, Chicago), and
Froelich Rainey (University of Pennsylvania Museum). The next
month, the Geological Society of America (GSA) appointed Richard
Foster Flint to represent geological interests, and the committee
became a joint undertaking of both organizations (Johnson 1951:2;
Libby 1952a:v). The selection and documentation of the series of
known-age samples used in the first "Curve of Knowns" were collected under the auspices of this committee.

By the time the known-age samples began to arrive in Libby's laboratory, Anderson and Arnold had been able to get the very recalcitrant
and touchy counting instrument to operate—at least some of the time.
The process of measuring known-age samples took most of 1949 to
accomplish. The historical or dendrochronological age of the samples
provided a fixed reference point against which the measured ¹⁴C age
was compared. With fortunately few exceptions,[14] the radiocarbon
ages of these samples were generally—within counting statistics—in
agreement with the known-age samples.

By the middle of 1949, as first results from known-age samples were
becoming available, it had become clear to Libby that his model of how

^{14}C dating *might* work had been, in broad outline, essentially confirmed. The success with the first suite of known-age samples was the occasion for presentations to larger audiences of anthropologists and archaeologists—by Arnold in a paper delivered at a meeting for the Society for American Archaeology (SAA) in May 1949 (see *American Antiquity* 15:171) and by Libby in September at the XXIX International Congress of Americanists held at the AMNH in New York (Bushnell 1961).

By this time, Libby had sufficient confidence in the technique that he began to move into what he called the "great unknown periods of prehistory." Because there were no fixed temporal points with which the ^{14}C values could be directly compared, Libby and Arnold hoped that validation would be accomplished by the degree of "internal consistency from a wide variety of samples and in a wide variety of problems" (Arnold and Libby 1949:680).

The same strategy used to secure the known-age materials was employed in obtaining unknown-age samples—namely, by assembling a group of collaborators (Table 5.4). The membership of this group, selected officially by the AAA/GSA committee, was announced in the pages of *American Antiquity* in July 1949 by James Griffin, one of the collaborators (Griffin 1949). Ten collaborators were named initially; four were added during the next year. Each collaborator was responsible for obtaining samples relevant to a particular region or chronological issue (Arnold and Libby 1949:680; Johnson 1951). Libby later described himself as an "amateur archaeologist" (Libby in Olsson 1970:107), presumably as a result of his involvement with his collaborators and the nature of most of the samples measured at Chicago. Frederick Johnson, by far the most active member of the team of archaeologists collaborating with Libby, noted that the group was "bombarded by an impressive number of letters, photographs of excavations and samples, drawings, affidavits and other documents, all of which were to prove or disprove the validity of the method or to try and convince us that a date on a particular sample was going to solve many of the problems of the universe" (Johnson 1965:763).

During the period of the Chicago laboratory's routine dating operation—essentially from about March 1949 until early 1954 (when Libby was appointed by President Eisenhower as a Commissioner of the U.S. Atomic Energy Commission [predecessor of the current U.S. Department of Energy])—^{14}C values on more than 500 samples were obtained. As was true of the initial set of 148 samples (Table 5.2), about two-thirds of these determinations were also on samples of

TABLE 5.4. Principal Collaborators in Collecting Unknown-Age Samples for Chicago Radiocarbon Study[a]

Region	Collaborators
Mesopotamia and Western Asia [b]	R. J. Braidwood, T. Jacoben, Richard A. Parker, and Saul Weinberg
Western Europe[c]	H. L. Movius, Jr., E. S. Deevey, Jr., and R. F. Flint
United States and Canada[d]	E. S. Deevey, Jr., R. F. Flint, J. B. Griffin, R. F. Heizer, F. Johnson, F. H. H. Roberts, and W. S. Webb
Mexico and Central America	H. de Terra
South America	J. B. Bird

a = Based on Libby (1955:76–140). In addition to the areas with specific collaborators, there were also tree-ring samples and samples from other areas including Japan, Africa, Hawaii, Australia, and Manchuria.

b = Samples from Egypt, Turkey, Iraq, Syria, Iran, Palestine, Afghanistan, and Lebanon.

c = Samples from France, Germany, Denmark, Ireland, England, Netherlands, and Iceland.

d = Samples from New England and Canada; New York State; Illinois, Indiana, Iowa, Kentucky, Michigan, Ohio, Pennsylvania, and Kansas, Alabama, North Carolina, South Carolina, and West Virginia; Louisiana, Mississippi, Missouri, Nebraska, Georgia, and Texas; Arizona, California, Colorado and New Mexico; Nevada, Oregon, Utah, and Washington; Minnesota, Wisconsin, and Wyoming; South Dakota; Alaska.

archaeological significance, most of which had been submitted by or through the collaborators.[15]

INFLUENCE ON THE CONDUCT
OF ARCHAEOLOGICAL RESEARCH

The most obvious impact of the ^{14}C method on the conduct of archaeological studies over the last five decades has been the availability of a chronometric or fixed-rate temporal scale of worldwide applicability that has provided archaeologists and other late Quaternary specialists with a common frame of temporal reference for the terminal

Pleistocene and Holocene. In the words of the distinguished University of California Berkeley African prehistorian J. Desmond Clark, without the ^{14}C time scale, prehistorians would still be "foundering in a sea of imprecisions sometimes bred of inspired guesswork but more often of imaginative speculation" (Clark 1979:7).

Some have argued that *worldwide temporal comparability* has been as important a characteristic of the ^{14}C time scale as was the degree of accuracy of the method in assigning age to samples. Fortunately, the temporal framework provided by ^{14}C data itself turned out to be amazingly accurate given the number of assumptions that had to hold to rather narrow ranges (Taylor 1987:143). This view can still be supported even in light of the increasingly complex, systematic differences between "real time" and "^{14}C time" that have been intensively and systematically studied over the last two decades (Taylor et al. 1996).

Several acute observers (Dean 1978:226; Willey and Phillips 1958:44) have previously noted another important aspect and outgrowth of the availability of the ^{14}C time scale. This is that ^{14}C age estimates provide a means of deriving chronological relationships totally and completely independent of assumptions about cultural processes and totally unrelated to any type of manipulation of strictly archaeological materials. In this context, it has been argued that when pressure to derive chronology primarily from the analyses of artifact data was released, inferences about the evolution of human behavior based on variations in environmental, ecological, or technological factors could be aggressively pursued employing an independent chronological framework (Clark 1984). As Austin Long has commented, cultural chronology was now time based rather than event or artifact based (A. Long, personal communication 1998).

Over the years, several rather specific suggestions as to the influence of the advent of ^{14}C-based chronometry in archaeological research have been advanced. Three of these will be briefly described and commentary offered: one is concerned with a major change in theoretical orientation and two with methodological approaches.

RISE OF THE "NEW ARCHAEOLOGY"

Lewis Binford has reflected that ^{14}C chronology "has certainly changed the activities of archaeologists, so that now, in many ways for the first time, they direct their methodological investments toward theory building rather than towards chronology building" (Binford quoted in Gittins 1984:238). The suggestion that there is a relationship between developments associated with the rise of the "New Archaeology" in the 1970s and the prior advent of ^{14}C chronometry derives, in part, from the observation that the advent of ^{14}C radically shifted the means by which archaeologists approached the development of their chronologies. Once chronology was not the dominant problem that it had been in the pre-^{14}C era of archaeology, the argument is that archaeologists could then redirect their energies in different directions. In the words of Binford, one of these directions was "theory building."

A full understanding of the relationship between the development of the ^{14}C method and the emergence of the "New Archaeology" or Process School within American archaeology must await more forthcoming and explicit statements from those most directly involved in the development of theoretical perspectives in archaeology. Since he was a leading proponent, the comment of Binford, as stated above, is important, but it provides only a point of departure for further examination. The first set of radiocarbon dates became available in 1950. The "New Archaeology" is viewed as having its origins in the late 1950s and early 1960s with applications of cultural evolutionary and systems theory (Willey and Sabloff 1980:188). What needs to be examined is the North American archaeological literature of the 1950–1960 period. To what degree do archaeologists active during this period think of ^{14}C dating as relieving them from the task of "chronology building"? Any analysis of this question must examine in detail both the published materials and contemporary correspondence of the principals. Retrospective reflections need to be scrutinized carefully. It also would be instructive to compare and contrast the reactions of archaeologists working in the U.S. Southwest when dendrochronology was introduced (see Nash 1997a, 1999, this volume)

WIDESPREAD USE OF STATISTICS

David Hurst Thomas (1978:232) suggested that professional archaeologists became aware of statistical theory and statistical thinking largely as a consequence of having to deal with the concept of "standard deviation" in the use of radiocarbon data:

> This technique [radiocarbon dating] precipitated a true revolution in archaeological procedure. . . . But a price was involved. Archaeologists quickly discovered that radiocarbon dates are not really precise statements of age at all. [^{14}C] determinations are only *estimates* of antiquity, and the degree of estimation is encapsuled in the "plus-minus" factor appended to each radiocarbon date. While recognizing the sensational potential of being able to date lumps of charcoal, archaeologists were initially puzzled by this

plus-minus factor. In fact, I'd wager that in the 1950s, not one archaeologist in 100 had the foggiest notion what a "standard deviation" really was. Here was the catch: if you're going to use radiocarbon dates, then you damn well better learn about standard deviations. (Thomas 1978:232)

The observation that archaeologists are often not clear about the meaning or implications of "standard deviations" when citing and using ^{14}C age determinations can be supported by examining many archaeological reports published in the 1950s and 1960s. This is despite the excellent paper by Albert Spaulding (Spaulding 1958) who explained the statistically correct way to compare differences in ^{14}C age estimates in light of the fact that each value had a one-sigma standard deviation as an integral part of the age expression. As is the case with the suggestion of the relationship between the "New Archaeology" and the ^{14}C method, support for the suggestions of Thomas with regard to the use of statistics in archaeology and the development of ^{14}C dating is a proposition to be tested with data yet to be collected.

IMPROVEMENT IN ARCHAEOLOGICAL FIELD METHODS

The late Frederick Johnson argued that the advent of ^{14}C dating inadvertently led to an improvement in archaeological field methods in North American archaeology in the years immediately following World War II (Johnson 1965:764). In his view, the purpose of greater attention to field data recording that he suggests was first introduced in the 1950s, was to determine more precisely the association of samples with archaeological levels. He argued that, in some cases, the initial motivation to improve these field techniques was to demonstrate that a given ^{14}C age estimate was in error because it could not apply to the artifact or site context that was purportedly "dated" by the ^{14}C age value.

An excellent example of this process involves the reaction to the first ^{14}C measurement on a sample intended to date the Folsom horizon in North America. The sample was initially described as charcoal from a fire pit situated *below* bison bones and artifacts collected by H. J. Cook in 1933 at the Folsom site in New Mexico (Arnold and Libby 1950). The Chicago ^{14}C age assigned to this sample (C–377) was 4283 ± 250 B.P. (an average of two determinations) which generated the comment "surprisingly young" (Arnold and Libby 1950:10). Cook revisited the Folsom site in June 1950 and determined that the "sample had been taken from a hearth in the fill of a secondary channel which had cut through the original deposit of bison bone and artifacts" (Roberts 1951:116). In the first formal publication of the results (Arnold and Libby 1951:116), C–377 was listed as charcoal from a "hearth in secondary channel of later date than bison and artifact deposit." A ¹⁴C value of 9883 ± 350 B.P. (C–558) was subsequently obtained on burned bison bone (Libby 1951:293) from what was interpreted as the Folsom horizon at Lubbock Lake, Texas, and has been widely cited as the first date on Paleoindian materials (see footnote 6).

Results obtained from dating methods such as ¹⁴C have, in a number of cases, stimulated archaeologists to revisit sites to reexamine apparently anomalous dates or to recollect samples with a better knowledge of the issues that must be addressed to insure that the chronological information provided by the dating methods can be effectively used.

CONCLUSION

The impact of ¹⁴C dating on the conduct of archaeological research has been, in some aspects, clear and explicit, and in others, more subtle and indirect. Most obvious is the fact that ¹⁴C data provide a common, worldwide, chronometric scale for the entire late Quaternary, the foundation on which a majority of the prehistoric chronologies for the last 40,000–50,000 years in many regions of the world are, directly or indirectly, constructed.

While sometimes not currently stressed or appreciated, almost 50 years after its introduction, the role of ¹⁴C data on the conduct and outcome of archaeological research—at least for those concerned with empirically documenting the validity of their assertions about the past —continues to be both pervasive and persuasive.

Acknowledgments. The author wishes to thank James Arnold and Ernest Anderson for their invaluable assistance in providing information on the early history of radiocarbon dating. The comments of Austin Long and Stephen Nash very much improved the manuscript. Information provided by Gregory Marlowe is also very much appreciated. However, it should be made clear that none of these individuals are responsible for any errors of fact or misinterpretation contained in this account. The author wishes to thank the Gabrielle O. Vierra Memorial Fund for support of his research. This is contribution 97/7 of the Institute of Geophysics and Planetary Physics, University of California, Riverside.

CHAPTER 6

Thirty Years of Archaeomagnetic Dating

JEFFREY L. EIGHMY
Department of Anthropology
Colorado State University

Archaeomagnetism is a dating method that attempts to establish the age of some archaeological features by comparing the magnetization recorded and preserved in the features with known temporal changes in the geomagnetic field. Thus, the physical basis of archaeomagnetic (AM) dating has two basic components: the direction and intensity of the geomagnetic field changes over time and some features of archaeological interest record ancient geomagnetic field values. With good knowledge of the field changes in the prehistoric past, archaeomagnetists can estimate the age of archaeological features containing the preserved geomagnetic readings. While the geomagnetic field changes in both direction and intensity, most AM dating focuses on directional changes, and geomagnetic directions are preserved for archaeologists in two important types of features—in situ features of burned earth and in situ aquatic sediments. When burned earthen features cool in the geomagnetic field, ferrous material in the feature is magnetized (called thermoremnant magnetism [TRM]) in the direction of the earth's magnetic field, and, similarly, as sediments accumulate, magnetized, clay-sized grains rotate in the direction of the geomagnetic field, resulting in weakly magnetized sediments (called detrital remnant magnetism [DRM]). While both burned features and sediments will record magnetic directions, most AM dating in North America focuses on the thermoremnant magnetism of burned features. Carefully collected samples of burned features are taken to labs where magnetometers are used to detect the magnetic direction. (For detailed discussions of field and laboratory processes see Aitken 1990; Sternberg 1997; Tarling 1991.)

Most of the laboratory equipment and protocols for measuring the magnetic direction locked in AM samples have been developed by geophysicists in their studies of ancient geomagnetism recorded in igneous and sedimentary rocks (Tarling 1983). These geological studies are usually subsumed in the field of paleomagnetism, and the principles of paleomagnetism and archaeomagnetism are very similar. The special concern of archaeomagnetists has been discovering how the Earth's magnetic field changed in the prehistoric period. This problem has been solved by North American researchers by finding magnetized features of known age (i.e., those that are closely associated with other, absolutely dated features) and using them as control samples to construct master records of secular change in the geomagnetic field (DuBois 1989; LaBelle and Eighmy 1997; Sternberg 1989). Secular change or variation involves those changes in the direction of the geomagnetic field that occur over several decades to several millennia. Once these master records have been established, AM samples of unknown age can be dated by comparing their magnetic directions against the master curve.

The two basic components of the physical basis to archaeomagnetism, secular change in the geomagnetic field and thermoremnant magnetism, have been known to science for about 300 years. As early as 1691, Robert Boyle reported that fired materials will often retain a magnetization that is parallel to the ambient magnetic field, and a year later Edmund Halley actually described secular change in the geomagnetic field (Boyle 1691; Halley 1692). However, it was not until after 1930 that the French geophysicist Emile Thellier and his students effectively put these two ideas together to make AM dating operational (Thellier and Thellier 1951). By 1960, Thellier and others had perfected collecting techniques, laboratory equipment, and sample cleaning methods to the point that many AM dates were determined for Europe, Japan, and the Soviet Union (Aitken 1961; Burlatskaya and Petrova 1961; Cook and Belshé 1958; Roquet 1954; Watanabe 1959). While some American scientists also understood the potential of applying the secular change in the geomagnetic field and thermoremnant magnetism to AM dating during the 1930s, they did not exploit the opportunity. Geophysicists at the Carnegie Institute of Washington, while actively pursuing secular variation studies and despite working with archaeologists, failed to participate in developing the technique, leaving that up to European and Asian scientists (Wolfman 1990c:318–319).

ARCHAEOMAGNETISM MOVES TO NORTH AMERICA

It was not until the early 1960s, therefore, that archaeomagnetism was really introduced in North American archaeology. In 1963, geophysicist Robert DuBois began exploring the method as a means to further his paleomagnetic studies of geomagnetism (Figure 6.1). As is true of most paleomagnetists who work in archaeomagnetism, DuBois's initial interest in archaeology was to use it to estimate the age of burned features at archaeological sites as a way to date the magnetic parameters stored in the thermoremnant magnetism of these features. However, the potential for using the secular variation records as tools for estimating the age of unburned features was not lost on DuBois or archaeologists of the U.S. Southwest. In a few short years, between about 1963 and 1967, DuBois had measured and assigned independent dates to enough samples that he understood secular change in the Southwest for the past 2,000 years in a remarkably accurate way (DuBois and Watanabe 1965; Weaver 1967) (Figure 6.2). As told by D. Wolfman (1990c:323), in 1963 the British geophysicist Norman Watkins left collecting molds with several Southwestern archaeologists while on a trip to the United States. Upon Watkins's return to Great Britain, samples collected with these molds were sent to DuBois who, by this time, was collecting his own samples and working on secular variation in the U.S. Southwest with Japanese paleomagnetist Naomi Watanabe (DuBois and Watanabe 1965; Watanabe and DuBois 1965). By 1967, DuBois had built a secular variation curve that fairly accurately depicted geomagnetic change for the U.S. Southwest and was using it to date archaeological sites in the area. For example, in 1967 Emil Haury felt that AM dates provided by DuBois for the site of Snaketown confirmed his hypothesis about the early development of irrigation-based village life in the Sonoran Desert (Haury 1976:331–333).

Also in 1967, DuBois moved to the University of Oklahoma, where he continued his interest in archaeomagnetism. There he was joined by archaeologist Dan Wolfman, then a graduate student at the University of Colorado. For six years, DuBois and Wolfman were supported by the Anthropology Program of the National Science Foundation to continue studying the possibility of applying paleomagnetic principles to AM dating in the U.S. Southwest, Central America, and Andean South America. Wolfman was crucial to this effort because he had field experience in both the Southwest and Mexico. As an undergraduate at the University of Oklahoma, I was hired to collect AM samples from sites all over the midwestern and southwestern portions of the United States. This opportunity was my introduction to archaeomagnetism.

In 1973, Wolfman finished a Ph.D. dissertation analyzing the

FIGURE 6.1 Robert L. DuBois, Canyon de Chelly, 1971 (J. L. Eighmy photograph).

chronology of Mesoamerica, using archaeomagnetism as a central element in the reevaluation (Wolfman 1973), and he moved to Arkansas. From his base in Arkansas, and after 1988, in New Mexico, he continued to conduct AM research, publishing independently dated pole positions and AM dates for the Midwest and Southwest of the United States and for Central and South America (e.g., Wolfman 1990a, 1990b;

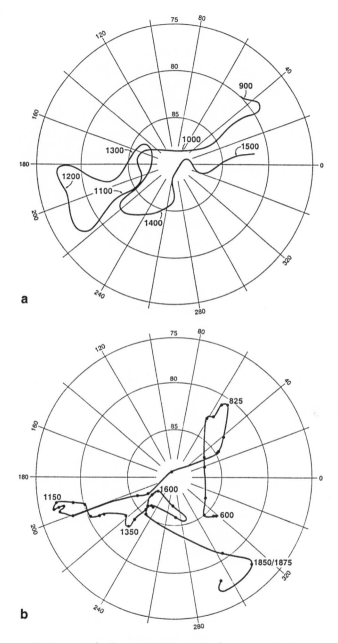

FIGURE 6.2 DuBois's Early Curve/SWCV595. Early version (DuBois 1975) of the DuBois Southwest master curve (a) and a recent version (LaBelle and Eighmy 1997) of the curve based on a different set of independently dated paleopole locations (b).

Wolfman and Dodson 1986, 1987) until his untimely death in 1994 (Schaafsma and Schaafsma 1996; Sternberg 1996). Although initially disillusioned with my prospects in archaeomagnetism, I returned to this area of research in 1977 after finishing an ethnoarchaeological dissertation at the University of Arizona. In collaboration with University of Arizona paleomagnetist Robert Butler, his student Robert Sternberg, and fellow archaeology student Randy McGuire, I collected and measured a small series of AM samples from Southwestern sites. With these samples, we were able to confirm that the DuBois reference curve did seem to produce dates well within the range of archaeologically expected dates (Eighmy et al. 1980). Based on these promising results, Sternberg and I have continued research in North American archaeomagnetism (e.g., Eighmy and Sternberg 1990).

During the late 1970s and early 1980s, some of the archaeologists who had welcomed the initial efforts of DuBois to collect samples and date their sites began to express considerable dissatisfaction with the technique. It appears that this dissatisfaction stemmed from two sources. The first was the fact that DuBois believed and told archaeologists that archaeomagnetism often could produce dates with precisions in the 10–35 year range. DuBois promoted the small precisions because he believed that AM dating precision was determined primarily by the rate of change in the magnetic field direction and the precision with which AM direction can be determined. Since he felt that the magnetic field moved at a rate of about 1° in 10 years and since AM directions could often be determined with precision of radius between 1° and 3.5°, it follows that AM dates could be determined with precisions between 10 and 35 years. Archaeologists came to expect accurate dates at this level of precision. While DuBois did report dates of this precision, they often seemed inaccurate, with reversed relative order to that established in the archaeological context. Thus, archaeologists lost confidence in the technique. The real problem was, of course, that AM precision is less than the theoretical minimum calculated from the current rate of change in the field and sampling precision. Imprecision is greater because the field often changes direction at much slower rates; rates of 1° in 30 or 40 years are not uncommon (LaBelle and Eighmy 1997:434). Imprecision is greater because the field often reverses direction so that it loops back on itself making it impossible to decide the age of firing with any great precision. Finally, imprecision is added to AM dates because prehistoric field changes are not known exactly, and the curve imprecision compounds the sample date imprecision.

The other source of dissatisfaction with the technique as promoted by DuBois in the 1970s was the fact that he did not report results completely or in a timely manner. In many of these cases, where DuBois was still studying secular variation in order to construct a master curve, he simply could not date AM samples nor could he report results in a timely manner. As a result, archaeologists often failed to appreciate the fact that DuBois did not know whether his Southwest master curve was valid outside the immediate Southwest, and result reporting would have to wait a fuller assessment. However, DuBois was slow to report dates even in the Southwest where he had a curve. DuBois often delayed years before reporting laboratory results, usually after repeated inquiries from impatient archaeologists. The results, themselves, were just date interpretations in a letter or phone conversation. He did not attempt to show archaeologists how these dates were derived. DuBois did not provide the laboratory data on sample magnetization or calculated paleopole locations, the master curve against which the samples were dated, or the control data used in constructing the master curve.

One important milestone at the end of this period was the fact that Sternberg (1982) finished the first dissertation devoted to archaeomagnetism in North America. Sternberg's research and the resulting dissertation are important for a couple of reasons. In the first place, Sternberg established the first well-documented secular variation curve for the United States. While DuBois (1975, 1989) established the first curve and published summary depictions of that curve, he never published the ages of the independently dated paleopole positions (called virtual geomagnetic poles [VGPs]) used to construct that curve, believing that with a large enough set of control samples one did not need to know the age of specific samples more precisely than ± 150–225 years (DuBois 1989:23–24). As a result, prior to Sternberg's dissertation it was difficult to evaluate the accuracy and precision of DuBois's depiction of geomagnetic secular variation. Secondly, as is mentioned below, in the dissertation Sternberg detailed quantitative methods for both curve construction and sample dating.

INCORPORATION OF ARCHAEOMAGNETISM INTO ARCHAEOLOGICAL RESEARCH

For all practical purposes, archaeomagnetism is only 30 years old in North America. In that time, it has been possible to observe significant advances in the use of the technique by archaeologists. While the study of rock magnetism and paleomagnetism has also advanced during these 30 years, the focus of the rest of these comments will be on how the technique has been incorporated into North American archaeological research. This incorporation process can be discussed in the context of four major changes: increases in the number of archaeological collectors and AM labs, increases in the number of AM samples and dates, standardization of AM reporting, and an increase in the type of problems addressed by AM methods.

Increases in the Number of Collectors and Labs

In the early years, one of the main limitations of AM dating was the number of trained collectors. When DuBois began processing samples in the mid-1960s, there were probably no more than four people in North America who could collect samples. He and Wolfman undoubtedly collected most of the earliest samples and constructed all the available collecting molds themselves. The molds had to be precisely machined to fit laboratory measuring devices. At that time, there was only one lab in North America, DuBois's lab at Arizona and then Oklahoma, that was actively interested in archaeological applications. At the time that Sternberg learned field collection procedures in 1975, there were probably only five or six other people capable of collecting in the Southwest and probably another five or six archaeologists trained by Wolfman in the Midwest. At that time, there were probably no more the 15 sets of collecting molds in existence in North America, and there were only two labs capable of and interested in measuring AM samples: DuBois's lab in Oklahoma and Robert Butler's lab at Arizona. In the intervening 20 years, the number of competent collectors in North America has increased to 50 or 60, the number of labs to four, and the number of sets of collecting molds to 50.

I have personally trained approximately 30 archaeologists, many of whom are still active in the field. Samples can be sent to the lab established by Wolfman in the Office of Archaeological Studies in the Museum of New Mexico, to Sternberg's lab at Franklin and Marshall College, to the Archaeometric Lab at Colorado State University (CSU), and to the Archaeomagnetic Program at the University of Arizona. Wulf Gose at the University of Texas, Austin, has collected and dated samples from the Southern Plains (Gose 1993); this development is significant because Gose's research is being initiated by an archaeomagnetist/geophysicist outside the DuBois/Wolfman/Eighmy/Sternberg tradition. The estimate of 50 collecting sets is harder to document because many individuals have made their own molds. However, the CSU Lab has sent out about 150 individual molds, usually in sets of six to eight. Thus, the CSU Lab has introduced about 15 to 25 sets of collecting molds from that lab alone.

Archaeomagnetic field collection is a complicated and tedious process, and archaeologists have tended to solve the problem for large excavation projects in one of two ways. Either AM technicians are brought in for the collections on a consulting basis, or crew members are trained in AM procedures and assigned the task of collecting samples. In either case, and unlike most other dating techniques, AM collection has to be considered in the budgeting phase of field projects in order to insure that sufficient resources are allotted to this phase of archaeomagnetism. It is undoubtedly the case that logistic and financial problems associated with obtaining competent field collectors, when needed, has inhibited the full utilization of the technique.

Increase in the Number of Samples and Dates

The 30 years since the North American introduction of the technique have witnessed a strong surge in the number of samples collected and the number of samples processed at these labs. Exact figures on the number of samples collected and processed would be hard to develop. Because many samples are collected and never processed, estimating the number of samples collected will be nearly impossible. While estimates of the number of samples processed will be more accurate and easier to obtain than the number of samples collected, these data from the various labs have not been gathered. It can be reported that the annual number of samples processed from the CSU lab is just under 100 samples down from about 175 in the mid-1980s. To the CSU figures can be added estimates of the processing at other labs (Figure 6.3). DuBois's labs began processing samples in the early 1960s, and he reported processing samples from some 2,000 features by about 1985, an average of about 100 samples per year (DuBois 1989:19, 32). Wolfman and his associates, either in Arkansas or New Mexico, have regularly processed samples since about 1973. The University of Arizona lab has processed samples nearly continuously since 1975. Sternberg, too, has processed samples since about 1983. Roughly, it can be estimated that, currently, at least 275 samples are being processed each year in North America (Figure 6.3).

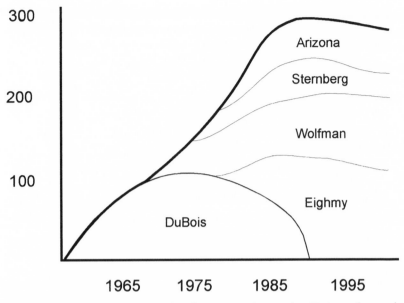

FIGURE 6.3 Annual processing of archaeomagnetic samples. Estimated growth in the number of archaeomagnetic samples processed in North America annually, 1965 through 1995. Named areas in the figure indicate the activity of various researchers and labs.

Standardization of Reporting

Since an AM date is a temporal interpretation about the likely date of the magnetization of an archaeological feature based on the current understanding of how the magnetic field changed (i.e., the current master curve) and since our understanding of the field will change as master curves are updated through additional research, it is essential that the data about the magnetization of samples be published so that the age of the magnetization can be reinterpreted if and when master curves are revised. Indeed, these data regarding sample magnetization are more important than the current date interpretations. The date interpretations can change if the master curve changes, but magnetization data derived from laboratory processing will not change. For these reasons and as more and more labs and archaeomagnetists entered the field, data reporting became more standardized. In 1980, North American archaeomagnetists met to agree on data reporting standards (Eighmy 1980). They agreed that an adequate AM lab report to archaeologists should include the following information:

1. Collecting site location in latitude and longitude,

2. Number of specimens collected from a feature,
3. Number of specimens used in the final results,
4. Demagnetization level used in final cleaning process,
5. Sample mean inclination (I),
6. Sample mean declination (D),
7. Size in degrees of the 95% confidence interval in estimating the mean I and D a_{95}),
8. Latitude of the vgp (paleolatitude),
9. Longitude of the vgp (paleolongitude), and
10. Errors in estimating the paleolatitude and paleolongitude (dp and dm).

Archaeomagnetists routinely now report these data to archaeologists along with the current age estimate of the sample. Unfortunately, there is somewhat less uniformity in the AM data that archaeologists, in turn, chose to include in their research reports. In many cases, none of the basic lab data are reported; instead, reports include only the current date interpretation. Currently, there is no mechanism for reporting AM dates directly from labs, for example, in an annual data list.

Increase in the Number of Problems Being Addressed

Originally, North American archaeomagnetism focused almost exclusively on problems of directional and intensity dating. The objectives of this research focus tended to be either the development of master records of secular variation in the direction and intensity of the field in the Southwest (DuBois and Watanabe 1965; Watanabe and DuBois 1965) or the absolute dating of archaeological features in the Southwest.

While interest among North American archaeomagnetists in the problem of Southwest curve construction (Eighmy 1991; Eighmy et al. 1990; LaBelle and Eighmy 1997; Sternberg and McGuire 1990b) and dating Southwest prehistory remains high, we see, today, the study of secular variation moving outside the U.S. Southwest (Eighmy et al. 1993; Kean et al. 1997; Wolfman 1990a, 1990b) and dating applications moving beyond attempts to estimate the age of burned features. Sternberg (1997) has observed that the objectives of AM dating research now include efforts to assess the productivity of archaeomagnetism (Eighmy and Mitchell 1994; Sternberg et al. 1991), to apply archaeomagnetism to regional chronometric problems (Dean 1991; Deaver and Ciolek-Torrello 1995; Eighmy and McGuire 1989; Wolfman 1990b), and to date sediments (Eighmy and Howard 1991). Wolfman (1990c:344) long argued that even when absolute dates are not possible, archaeomag-netists can provide precise information on the relative age of features, and several examples of the possibility of relative AM dating have been published by North American archaeomagnetists (Eighmy and Davis 1997; Eighmy and Hathaway 1987).

The contribution of archaeomagnetism to regional chronology building is well illustrated in archaeological research in the Hohokam area of Arizona. In the early 1980s, hundreds of AM samples were col-lected from Hohokam sites in southern Arizona. Eighmy and McGuire (1989) collected data on over 312 AM dates that could be assigned to the various Hohokam phases both in the Phoenix and Tucson areas. Dean (1991) also considered the large set of AM dates, along with radiocarbon dates, from the Phoenix and Tucson area in a wide-rang-ing reanalysis of the Hohokam phase sequence. At the time Eighmy, McGuire, and Dean were performing their reanalyses, between 10 and 50 AM dates were available for each phase. Eighmy, McGuire, and Dean calculated midpoint and terminal dates for each phase based on these samples. From these analyses, important cultural historical and processual hypotheses were proposed. For example, Eighmy and McGuire proposed that phases, defined primarily in terms of pottery types, were not temporally discrete as is often assumed but overlapped substantially in time (Figure 6.4).

Additionally, since the introduction of the technique, North Ameri-can archaeomagnetists have wrestled with the problems of specifying the best collecting techniques and identifying the best sampling materi-als. In terms of collecting techniques, collector training (Lange and Murphy 1990), sample size (Eighmy and Mitchell 1994:451), mold size (Smith 1990), and use of the sun compass (Hathaway and Krause 1990) have been studied. North American archaeomagnetists have also been interested in identifying soil conditions producing the best AM samples (Hathaway et al. 1990), the effects of firing histories (Hath-away 1990), and the effects of inundation in water (Wolfman 1978) on AM results.

One of the most influential contributions of North American archaeomagnetism has been that of Robert Sternberg on the problems of curve construction and statistical dating of samples (Sternberg 1982, 1989; Sternberg and McGuire 1990a, 1990b). Sternberg devel-oped a method for objectively building curves based on the principle of averaging the VGP locations of samples of a given age. This technique has been variously termed the moving window technique or the temporal

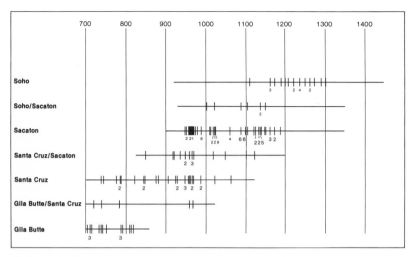

FIGURE 6.4 Temporal overlap of Phoenix area features assigned to various phases in the Hohokam sequence. Archaeologists were asked to assign a large sample of features to appropriate phases and phase transitions based on archaeological context information (primarily ceramic information). The features were then dated archaeomagnetically and arrayed by archaeomagnetic age within each phase and transition group. The results clearly show that features assigned to a given phase could temporally overlap with the features assigned to preceding and succeeding phases. (Eighmy and McGuire 1989)

averaging approach. Similar methods have been found useful in Europe, and Batt (1997) found it convenient to adopt Sternberg's moving window method directly for curve building in Great Britain. Because this method relies on well-dated (independent from AM dating) and well-documented VGPs, an important component to the health and vitality of archaeomagnetism has been continual efforts to maintain an accurate database on independently dated pole positions (Eighmy et al. 1987; Eighmy et al. 1990; Eighmy and Klein 1988, 1990; LaBelle and Eighmy 1995; Sternberg 1997). The technique has been important for North American archaeomagnetism because it has forced the field to consider objective and replicable methods for curve construction and to document more carefully the control samples used in master curve construction.

The alternative approach to that proposed by Sternberg has been promoted by DuBois (1989) and Wolfman (1990c). It relies more on spatial averaging (as opposed to temporal averaging) of an array of VGPs by simply drawing a freehand line through the scatter of VGPs with much less dependence on a knowledge of the age of the VGPs. Based on this method, DuBois (1989) and Wolfman (1990a) have proposed curves for the Southwestern and Midcontinental regions of the United States and for Mesoamerica (Wolfman 1990c). A part of the difference in the appearance of the DuBois curve and SWCV595 in Figure 6.1 is due to the difference in the methods used to construct the curves. As practiced by DuBois, the spatial averaging approach has two major drawbacks. One is that the data on which the spatially averaged Southwest curve (called by DuBois an archaeomagnetic apparent polar curve) has never been published fully, appearing only as scatter plots on polar projections (DuBois 1989). Wolfman (1990a, 1990b), on the other hand, has published the data used in drawing his Midcontinental and Mesoamerican curves. The other drawback is the fact that curves are drawn freehand and appear to have more detailed movements than the data justify. Having called attention to the problems with DuBois's curve construction, it must be added that the temporal averaging technique of Sternberg produces curves that are probably not faithful depictions of field changes either. Cox and Blinman (1996) point out that when the technique calculates mean curve locations from a sample of VGPs, that is distributed in the shape of a curve, the mean locations are artificially placed in the inside of the curved distribution (see also May and Butler 1986). Thus, a priority research problem within archaeomagnetism remains the task of discovering an accurate, as well as objective, technique for curve construction.

CURRENT EXPECTATIONS WITH RESPECT TO ARCHAEOMAGNETIC DATING

Archaeomagnetic master curves are available for the Southwestern, Plains, and Midcontinental regions of the United States. In North America, AM sampling is routinely performed only in the Southwest. Samples are often collected on the Plains and occasionally in the Midwest. They are never collected in California, the Northwest Coast, the Great Basin, Canada, or the Southeastern or Eastern United States. In areas where curves have been developed or tested, dating precision (more or less at the 95 percent significance level) is on the order of 75–200 years. Under optimal conditions, date ranges as small as 25 years can occur. Usually, a sample has more than one date option because the VGP plots near more than one curve segment. However, archaeologists are usually able to reject all but one of the date options based on archaeological context. It is difficult to judge the accuracy of any date because the target date is seldom known in advance. However, if we use the subjective judgment of archaeologists, it is possible to observe the frequency with which they consider AM dates to be accurate. According to this measure, it appears that AM dates are disregarded as being inexplicably outside the range of archaeological expectations about as often as are radiocarbon dates (Eighmy et al. 1993). On the other hand, tree-ring cutting, and even noncutting, dates are considered accurate at a much higher frequency.

Over the past 30 years, archaeomagnetism has made notable contributions to a better understanding of the past in two areas. The first is dating prehistoric events. While the problem of temporal control is often overlooked or minimized by archaeologists, it is fundamental to understanding social and ecological processes of the past. The emerging interest in evolutionary archaeology has a seldom stated but clearly dependent assumption that temporal control in archaeology is such that it can resolve temporal changes at a precise level. Temporal resolution in archaeology will have to be about one-tenth the total length of the processes studied in order for archaeology to make useful, empirically based, contributions to the study of evolutionary archaeology. AM dates are a vital contribution to this dating effort.

Second, archaeomagnetism has contributed significantly to documenting the history of the geomagnetic field. Recently, Lund has written:

[North American archaeomagnetic and lava flow data] should be considered the most accurate paleosecular variation record from North America in as much as these paleomagnetic data are thermoremnant magnetizations (TRMs) retained in archeological artifacts and lava flows during cooling from high temperatures, and the sampled materials can all be absolutely oriented with respect to geographical north. A TRM is universally viewed as a more accurate recorder of the geomagnetic field than is DRM/PDRM [detrital remnant magnetism/partial detrital remnant magnetism] , because it provides an instantaneous "snap-shot" of field variability (rather than a 50–200 year average) and usually has lower sample noise levels. (Lund 1996:8008)

These paleosecular variation records are significant in not only providing a history of change in the geomagnetic field but also providing the data for models of the geomagnetic field, its change, and genesis.

Nevertheless, it is safe to say that archaeomagnetism fails to meet the expectations of some archaeologists who have used the technique.

In the Southwest, archaeomagnetism cannot consistently produce dates that are more precise than tree-ring or ceramic dates. In areas where radiocarbon dating remains the primary dating tool, archaeologists are satisfied with the precision of AM dates because the AM and radiocarbon precisions are similar. In the U.S. Southwest, dendrochronology can usually tell archaeologists the construction dates for habitation structures within a 10-year period, and often less. Similarly, it is claimed that ceramic seriations can produce dates for ceramic assemblages that are as precise as those produced by AM and radiocarbon methods (e.g., Christenson 1994; Duff 1966; Love 1993). Under these circumstances, additional absolute dating methods like archaeomagnetism are viewed as unnecessary expenditures of time and money.

The decision not to use AM dating or radiocarbon dating when ceramic assemblages can be dated with great precision may be appropriate. If one knows, *a priori*, from looking at an assemblage of sherds, the duration of a site occupation to within a few decades, then archaeomagnetism and radiocarbon dating will not help establish the age of specific events during the site occupation with any greater precision. Nor will archaeomagnetism be much help with consistently sorting out the relative age of events that occurred over a short period of time ($\leq$ 100 years). VGPs and master curves can not be determined with enough precision for this sort of detail. However, if one is interested in testing hypotheses about site age or the validity of ceramic seriations or if one is uncertain about how ceramic assemblages are formed and uncertain as to what events ceramic assemblages reflect in the site formation process, then taking AM samples and any other absolute dating technique will be appropriate. Similarly, collecting a series of AM samples from a single component can be a useful exercise even if the component is of short duration. The utility of this strategy comes not from attempting to sort out the feature ages in a relative and highly precise temporal order but from combining the series of individual feature ages to produce a more precise estimate of the component age.

Limits to the Growth of Archaeomagnetism in North America

While it is clear that tremendous progress has been made in AM dating over the past thirty years, the technique is not integrated into archaeological infrastructure and research programs at an appropriate level. For example, compare the position that radiocarbon dating enjoys today with that of archaeomagnetism. In 1998, the Internet had sites for 17 ¹⁴C labs and five accelerator labs operating in North America. Granted, radiocarbon began in the early 1950s, nearly 15 years before AM dating began, but, obviously, the growth in ¹⁴C labs has been much healthier than the growth in the number of AM labs. Most important to this contrast between radiocarbon and AM dating is the fact that archaeologically oriented radiocarbon research is often carried out by archaeologists who are not radiocarbon specialists. Rarely are AM samples collected in North America outside the U.S. Southwest, and when they are collected in other areas, it is usually due to the direct involvement of one of the few AM specialists.

With respect to the number of laboratory facilities and the variety of research projects, the situation in archaeomagnetism is more similar to dendrochronology than it is to radiocarbon. As in archaeomagnetism, there are very few dendrochronology labs in North America, and the number of prehistoric samples collected outside the U.S. Southwest is very small, and archaeologically related tree-ring research is almost nonexistent outside the U.S. Southwest. However, this limit on the growth of tree-ring labs and research is due to the inherent limit to the number of places where tree-ring samples can be cross-dated. It needs to be pointed out that no such inherent limit exists with AM samples; in situ pieces of fired clay can be expected in all portions of North America.

Another way to think about the limited growth in North American archaeomagnetism is to compare it to European archaeomagnetism. There, we see much more vitality with active research and strong institutional support in six or seven different research centers in France, England, and Germany. Therefore, I believe that there is tremendous room for growth in AM dating in North America.

The Crisis in Archaeomagnetism

While the growth potential for North American archaeomagnetism is high, several obstacles stand in the way of realizing this potential. As a result, archaeomagnetism in North America is at an important crossroad. Further progress in the field will necessitate removal of these obstacles. Three of these obstacles can be mentioned, but they all seem to relate in one way or another to the general problem of training the next generation of archaeomagnetists. The first obstacle is the low number of AM specialists; the second is the institutional affiliation of these few specialists; and the third is the nature of archaeological/archaeometric training, in general, in North America.

Low Number of Archaeomagnetic Specialists.

In North America in 1994, two geophysicists, DuBois and Sternberg, and two archaeologists, Wolfman and I, were actively pursuing AM dating research. Since then, DuBois has retired and Wolfman has died, leaving only two AM specialists with institutional affiliation in North America. It is true that others have extensive experience in the laboratory as well as the field side of archaeomagnetism. DuBois not only trained Wolfman and me, he also trained Tom Windes in AM collection and worked with him on dating problems (Windes 1987). Wolfman trained Jeff Cox. Sternberg has trained Rich Lange, Barbara Murphy, and Bill Deaver. I have trained numerous students—most notably Kathy Baker, Kay Barnett, Sharilee Counce, Holly Hathaway, Pam Klein, George Krause, Stacey Lengyel, Jason LaBelle, and Gary Smith. With the possible exception of Jeff Cox and Stacey Lengyel, none of these people are likely to continue actively pursuing AM research as a primary career focus.

Institutional Affiliation of the North American
Archaeomagnetists.

Neither of the two people with a primary career focus on archaeomagnetism, Sternberg and I, are located at Ph.D.-granting institutions.

Nature of Archaeological Training in North America.

Unlike the practice in Europe and Canada, archaeological training in the United States is conducted in social science programs. I was trained as a four-field anthropologist, and I probably would not have stayed in archaeology if it had not had a strong social-science component. To this day, I find the problems of sociocultural change and variation much more interesting than problems of geomagnetism. Nevertheless, this four-field, social-science orientation of most of our graduate programs mitigates against the probability of attracting students with the right aptitudes and interests to pursue AM research (Rapp 1992; Kelley and Williamson 1996). This problem has been recognized for years, and Gumerman and Phillips put it this way: "Radical reorganization of archaeological training is necessary for the vigorous intellectual evolution of the discipline. Inappropriate for most contemporary archaeological training is the traditional four-field anthropology department that requires grounding in linguistics, physical and cultural anthropology as well as archaeology" (Gumerman and Phillips 1978:188).

Archaeomagnetic research depends heavily on physics, chemistry, and geophysics—skills that are very rare among archaeology graduate students. We need more archaeological/archaeometric training programs like those being developed at the Universities of Illinois, Arizona, Boston, Michigan, Washington, Minnesota, Toronto, Pennsylvania, and Wisconsin; and all archaeological programs need to have a strong hard science and quantitative component so that we begin the process of attracting the right type of students.

The problem of archaeometric training within anthropology programs may go deeper than the hard science limitations in many of these programs. In the first place, one often sees interests within the cultural components of these programs far from those of the traditional ethnographer, ethnologist, or ethnohistorian. Kelley and Williamson (1996:16) describe this phenomenon as vacating the core of anthropology. Too few of the modern cultural anthropology offerings are in the core areas (e.g., ethnography, cultural ecology, social organization, subsistence economy, etc.) that the archaeology student would find useful. In the second place, the influence of deconstructionist theory in many anthropology programs has resulted in anthropology curricula, faculty, and students that tend to view knowledge claims as relative and traditional, positivist scientific research as futile. As a result, these programs seem to have less and less to offer archaeologists and almost no flexibility within which archaeologists, interested in a hard-science specialization, can obtain the training necessary to further archaeological research of this type.

CHAPTER 7

Obsidian Hydration Dating, Past and Present

CHARLOTTE BECK
Department of Anthropology
Hamilton College

GEORGE T. JONES
Department of Anthropology
Hamilton College

When obsidian hydration dating (OHD) was first introduced by Irving Friedman and Robert Smith in 1960 (Friedman and Smith 1960) it seemed to offer great promise as a numerical-age ("absolute")[1] dating approach for two reasons. First, it was relatively inexpensive in comparison to other methods such as radiocarbon, but second, and more importantly, it could be used to date the artifacts themselves, rather than materials that often had to be related to artifacts through association. The early optimism faded, however, as questions arose concerning the appropriate equation to describe the hydration process as well as the effects of chemical composition of the obsidian, effective hydration temperature (EHT), and relative humidity on the hydration rate. Despite the complexities of the hydration process as we currently understand them, however, research continues. But as a result of the difficulties experienced with the method, OHD has not had major consequences for prehistory, per se. It has not, for example, been important in solving problems of world interest, such as the exact timing of extinctions toward the end of the Pleistocene or the earliest domestication of plants and animals, as has been the case for radiocarbon; nor has it provided precise local chronologies, as has been the case for dendrochronology. In regions where obsidian is plentiful, however, such as in the arid western United States, OHD has become a common component of many dating programs. Rather than the dating of specific events, OHD provides us with a means for examining trade networks, assessing stratigraphic mixing, and evaluating artifact types as chronological markers. But perhaps its most important use is as a means of analyzing the surface artifact record, not just dating it but assessing contemporaneity among artifacts and thus separating different depositional events and/or periods.

THE OBSIDIAN HYDRATION DATING METHOD

The OHD method is based on the fact that a freshly broken surface of obsidian gradually absorbs moisture from its surroundings (Friedman and Smith 1960; Michels 1973; Michels and Tsong 1980). The progress of this absorption is marked by a diffusion front that separates the hydrated glass (the hydration rind) from unaltered glass. The rind can be seen in thin section under a microscope when illuminated by polarizing light. Measurement of the depth of the hydration rind, combined with knowledge of the rate at which the rind expands, provides a means of estimating the age of the artifact.

Although OHD was first presented as a dating method in 1960 (Friedman and Smith 1960), its history actually begins in 1955 with the publication of "Water and Other Volatiles in Volcanic Glasses," by C. S. Ross and R. L. Smith. Ross and Smith (1955) were the first to recognize that perlite, which often contains nodules of obsidian, is in fact hydrated obsidian; perlite contains about 3.5% water while unhydrated obsidian contains only 0.3% water, and the index of refraction, which has a consistent relationship with water content, differs markedly between the two. Ross and Smith (1955) found that as an obsidian surface takes on water, the hydrated portion increases in density, which causes a mechanical strain. The difference in the index of refraction together with the birefringence (refraction of light in two slightly different directions to form two rays) resulting from the mechanical strain are visible under a microscope.

Friedman and Smith (1958) took this research a step further by demonstrating that the deuterium (heavy hydrogen) concentration in perlite is similar to that in the surface water of the surrounding environment. This suggested that obsidian hydrated under normal atmospheric conditions on the earth's surface, as had been suspected earlier by Ross and Smith (1955). When they introduced the OHD method in 1960, Friedman and Smith (1960) presented test results confirming that hydration occurs under normal atmospheric conditions; these results also suggested that hydration occurs at a fixed rate, as a function of the square root of time. In a companion paper to that of Friedman and Smith, Evans and Meggers (1960) presented an archaeological application and evaluation of the newly proposed method. They cautioned, however, that "numerous pitfalls lie in the path of an uncritical user at the present stage of the research" (Evans and Meggers 1960:523). Their statement proved prescient.

In their original presentation, Friedman and Smith (1960) described the factors they believed influence the rate of hydration, which they suggested were primarily temperature and gross chemical composition; relative humidity, they believed, was not an important factor. The OHD method seemed to be very promising in areas where obsidian was plentiful, and researchers began to use it right away. Two dissertations that focused on the method were completed shortly after its introduction, the first by Donovan Clark in 1961 (Clark 1961) and the second by Clark's student Joseph Michels in 1965 (Michels 1965). Michels (1965) was enthusiastic about the potential of OHD in archaeology. Though he recognized that problems would continue for OHD as a numerical-age approach until all of the factors influencing the hydration process were better understood, he saw great possibilities for it as a relative approach. It was inexpensive to use when compared to radiocarbon dating: Michels calculated that for the cost of one ^{14}C date, 80 or more obsidian dates could be obtained (Michels 1967:212). As a relative approach, Michels (1967) suggested OHD could be used in a number of ways, such as tracing the history of an artifact style at a site, solving the problem of artifact reuse (e.g., Clark 1961, 1964; Green 1964), delineating trade complexes (Green 1964), examining the intensity of site occupations through time, and examining the contemporaneity of artifacts within a surface assemblage. In an innovative paper in *American Antiquity*, Michels (1969) used OHD to test stratigraphic mixing at the Mammoth Junction site in California. Even though researchers at the time were unaware that obsidians of even slightly different chemical compositions can hydrate at different rates, Michels's results did show that the range of hydration measurements differed (but overlapped) by stratum in the predicted manner.

Unfortunately Michels's enthusiasm was not contagious, probably because his ideas were somewhat ahead of their time. No one, for instance, was very interested in testing stratigraphy because formation processes had not yet become an issue; no one was particularly interested in testing for contemporaneity among surface artifacts because there was still a strong belief that the surface record lacked chronological integrity. Instead, efforts concentrated on the development of numerical-age estimation, the calculation of hydration rates, and the appropriate equation to use in the derivation of those rates, and subsequently, the factors that influenced the rate. In fact, while Meighan et al. (1968a) applauded Michels's enthusiasm over OHD, they pointed out that most efforts had been spent discussing the method and that only five empirical studies had been published to date, with an additional small number having been presented in papers read at meetings.

The trends in issues regarding the OHD method appear to be decadal: the 1960s were dominated by discussions of the correct rate equation; the 1970s by discussions of the effects of chemical composition on the hydration rate; the 1980s by induced experiments, debates concerning experimentally versus empirically derived hydration rates, and discussions of how to control for EHT; and the 1990s by the effects of relative humidity on the hydration rate. We discuss each of these issues separately.

The Hydration Rate Equation

The debate over the correct hydration rate equation began shortly after the presentation of the OHD method. Irving Friedman and Robert L. Smith (1960) suggested that the hydration of obsidian could be described as a diffusion process, and thus the rate at a given temperature could be defined by the diffusion equation:

$$x^2 = kt \text{ (which can also be written } x = kt^{1/2}) \tag{1}$$

where,

x = depth of penetration of water in microns
k = constant for a given temperature
t = time in years

D. L. Clark (1961, 1964), in a correlation between artifacts and ^{14}C dates from California, derived a hydration rate defined by the equation:

$$x = kt^{3/4} \tag{2}$$

Clark stated, however, that "Whether the rate follows $t^{1/2}$ of $t^{3/4}$ remains to be established as more data are provided" (Clark 1964:177).

An experiment by W. Haller (1963) suggested that the diffusion coefficient is a function of water concentration, and the two are directly related. In response, Friedman et al. (1966) conducted experiments in which they induced hydration of samples that were heated to 100°C in a water pressure environment for up to four years. They defined the diffusion rate constant, k, by the Arrhenius equation:

$$k = Ae^{-E/RT} \tag{3}$$

where,

k = diffusion constant at temperature T
A = a constant (depending on physical or chemical properties of the glass)

E = activation energy of the hydration process (calories per mole)

R = universal gas constant (calories per degree per mole)

T = absolute temperature (degrees Kelvin)

Friedman et al. (1966:324) agreed with Haller (1963) that "the diffusion rate constant, k, is not only a function of temperature but is also strongly dependent on the water content of the glass," but stated that "the diffusion rate that we are discussing is the lowest diffusion constant along a concentration gradient; it is the one that controls the overall penetration rate of water into the glass." Their experiments supported the use of Friedman and Smith's original diffusion equation to define the hydration process.

In 1968 the Friedman and Smith (1960) equation was challenged once again, this time by Meighan et al. (1968a), who published a rate for the coast of western Mexico based on a simple linear function:

$$x = kt \qquad\qquad\qquad (4)$$

Friedman and Evans (1968:814) defended their original diffusion function, stating that "Meighan et al. [1968a] do not present any evidence that makes necessary the use of a linear hydration rate." Friedman and Evans (1968) suggested that the linearity of the Meighan et al. (1968a) rate was due to their dealing with a short time span; had they examined an older archaeological record, they would have found the rate fit a curvilinear model.

The debate over the appropriate rate equation continued into the 1970s (e.g., Doremus 1975; Ericson 1975; Ericson, MacKenzie, and Berger 1976; Findlow et al. 1975; Friedman et al. 1970; Johnson 1969; Katsui and Kondo 1965, 1976; Kimberlin 1976; Lee et al. 1974; Meighan 1970, 1976, 1983; Meighan and Haynes 1970; Meighan et al. 1968b) and was never really brought to a close (e.g., Anovitz et al. 1999). Empirical rates continue to be based on varied equations (e.g., Basgall 1983; Bettinger 1989; Hall 1983, 1984; Hall and Jackson 1989; R. Jackson 1984b) while experimental rates (see below) generally follow the Friedman and Smith equation (e.g., Michels et al. 1983; Stevenson, Carpenter, and Scheetz 1989; Stevenson and Scheetz 1989; Stevenson et al. 1993, 1996, 1998; but see Anovitz et al. 1999; McGrail et al. 1988). The reasons for this difference deserve some discussion.

It is difficult to evaluate the empirical rates calculated during the 1960s because of the ignorance at the time of the effects of chemical composition on hydration rates. Kimberlin (1976), for example, reexamined the artifacts from the Morret site upon which Meighan et al. (1968a) based their linear rate and found that five distinct chemical groups are represented in that assemblage; with our current understanding of the sensitivity of the hydration rate to chemical composition, the Meighan et al. (1968a) rate is rendered meaningless. But even when controlling for source and environmental variables (see below), rates continue to be calculated that deviate from the Friedman and Smith model; why is this the case?

One possible explanation relates to the assumptions made by archaeologists about site formation processes. First, the obsidian artifacts used to formulate a rate are assumed to be contemporaneous with the dated material (i.e., charcoal, tree-rings, projectile point types) against which the hydration rate is calibrated, but this assumption is not always valid (Jackson 1984b; Jones and Beck 1992; Ridings 1991). Second, researchers rarely take into account the error factors attached to radiocarbon dates; these error factors are compounded when used to construct a hydration rate (Friedman and Trembour 1978). Third, differences in EHT can occur even for artifacts within the same stratum (Friedman and Long 1976; Ridings 1991; see below), and thus hydration readings will differ. Finally, data on formation processes suggest that a simple model of site formation—that deposition is followed shortly by burial, ensuring constant thermal and humidity histories at each successive depth—rarely obtains in nature (Hall and Jackson 1989; Hughes 1992; Tremaine 1991). More realistically, artifacts often have quite complex depositional histories, which might include burial, exposure, and reburial over time and which would greatly affect the hydration rate (Beck and Jones 1994). It is quite possible that, theoretically, the hydration rate is defined by the diffusion equation presented by Friedman and Smith (1960) but that in any archaeological situation, these factors might cause an empirically derived rate of hydration to behave slightly differently. Anovitz et al. (1999) have recently argued, however, that *neither* the Friedman and Smith (1960) equation *nor* the Arrhenius equation (Friedman et al. 1966; see equation 3 above) appropriately describes the diffusion process because the diffusion of water in obsidian is concentration dependent, an argument made in 1963 by Haller and modeled in 1975 by Doremus. Anovitz et al. (1999) argue that, in general, the diffusion coefficient will increase with water content, causing the hydration rate to continually, but not necessarily uniformly, increase during the diffusion process. As a result, the hydration rim will grow faster than

predicted by the Friedman and Smith (1960) equation, and the estimated age will be too old. And so, the debate goes on.

Chemical Composition

In their 1960 presentation of the method, Friedman and
Smith recognized that variation in chemical composition of the obsidian could affect the hydration rate. They recognized that different colors or different degrees of banding or mottling in obsidians are the
result of differences in chemical composition or of the physical properties of cooling. They stated that "obsidian of different compositions
may have different rates of hydration and a different temperature
coefficient of the rate of hydration" (Friedman and Smith 1960:485)
and suggested that only continued testing of obsidians from all over
the world could solve this problem. Because little was known, however, concerning the extent to which this variable could affect the
hydration rate, Friedman and Smith's (1960) comparisons were of
broad groups, such as "rhyolitic" versus "trachytic" obsidians. Such
broad comparisons led other researchers to assume that there was little chemical variation among rhyolitic obsidians and that it was temperature that caused the greatest differences in hydration rates
(Michels and Tsong 1980).

One of the first attempts to investigate whether chemical composition influenced hydration rates was made by LeRoy Johnson (1969)
in his discussion of hydration rate calculation for the Klamath Basin
in California. Johnson's hydration results showed large standard
deviations for each stratigraphic level, which he stated could be due
either to chemical composition or to stratigraphic mixing. Johnson
believed that the major chemical difference was in silica content,
which he tested using the refractive index. His results showed that
there was no substantial difference in this index among the artifacts
tested. He thus concluded that the large standard deviations were
due to stratigraphic mixing.

Researchers were nevertheless beginning to suspect that even small
differences in chemical composition might be important. Friedman et
al. (1970:65–66) stated:

> Little is known about the specific chemical differences that exist
> between obsidians obtained from different outcrops or quarries in one
> small area. Even less is known about the influence of such minor chemi-
> cal differences, if they exist, on the rates of hydration of such obsidians.
> In the course of our research, we have found small anomalies in sets of

data, that may be related to minor chemical differences among the artifacts. (Friedman et al. 1970:65–66)

Friedman et al. (1970) presented an example from the Yayahyala site in the state of Hidalgo, Mexico, where two colors of obsidian were present, gray and green. The gray artifacts had hydration readings of less than three microns while the green artifacts had readings of greater than three microns. These differences, they suggested, could be the result of differences in chemical composition.

Michels (1971) found a similar pattern. He conducted an OHD study of 2,036 artifacts from 20 different sites in the Valley of Mexico and also found that green and gray obsidian were present and that the green obsidian hydrated over 2.5 times as fast as the gray obsidian (see also Michels 1973; Michels and Bebrich 1971).

By the mid-1970s the effects of differences in hydration rates for obsidians from different source areas were being recognized. Findlow et al. (1975:345) published "the first 'source-specific' hydration rate available to date Southwestern obsidian artifacts." In the following year, several papers in R. E. Taylor's (1976) *Advances in Obsidian Glass Studies* presented studies that demonstrated the differences in hydration rates for obsidians from different sources (e.g., Ericson and Berger 1976; Kimberlin 1976; Reeves and Ward 1976; Stross et al. 1976). But it was Friedman and Long (1976) who discovered which particular elements affected the hydration rate. They presented the results of a long-term experiment in which they induced hydration at elevated temperatures under controlled laboratory conditions on obsidian collected from 12 different locations. They found a relationship between both silica dioxide (SiO_2) and the refractive index of the nonhydrated glass and the hydration rate. They also found, however, that a combination of components was more closely related to the rate than SiO_2 alone, and thus presented what they termed the "chemical index":

$$SiO_2 - 45(CaO + MgO) - 20(H_2O^+) \qquad (5)$$

By using this index and the EHT, they said, the hydration rate for any obsidian could be calculated.

Following the discovery that the hydration rate is source dependent, the literature became dominated by source characterization studies (e.g., Asaro et al. 1978; Ericson and Kimberlin 1977; Nelson et al. 1977; Newman and Nielson 1985; Smith et al. 1977; Stross et al. 1978). It was found that, although it was the combination of major and minor elements that actually affected the hydration rate, it was the trace elements that actually best distinguished one obsidian from another. Source characterization studies of obsidian, however, had been going on for at least 10 years prior to the recognition of their importance for OHD. In the early 1960s, Renfrew and others began the investigation of obsidian source identification using trace elements for the purpose of delineating trade routes in the Near East (e.g., Cann and Renfrew 1964; Renfrew et al. 1965, 1966). The method they used was spectrographic analysis, which had been used previously for the analysis of metal artifacts (e.g., Briton and Richards 1963). These studies were shortly followed by studies by Jack and Heizer (1968) of Mesoamerican obsidians and Jack and Carmichael (1969) for California and Oregon obsidians, both using x-ray fluorescence (XRF) spectrometry; by Gordus et al. (1968) and Griffin et al. (1969) for obsidians present in Hopewell sites, using neutron activation; and by Stross et al. (1968) for obsidians in various parts of the Americas using both approaches, all for the study of prehistoric trade. It was not until the mid-1970s that source characterization studies were seen as important for OHD. The earlier source studies for OHD were dominated by those using neutron activation (e.g., Ericson 1977a, 1977b, 1981; Ericson and Berger 1976; Ericson and Kimberlin 1977; Ericson, Hagan, and Chesterman 1976; Kimberlin 1976) but with technological improvements in the XRF approach (Hampel 1984; Hughes 1984, 1986), this method has become equally popular.

By 1980 obsidian source analysis was becoming more common but by no means a routine part of all OHD studies (e.g., Meighan 1981; Ridings 1991, 1996). Discussion in the early 1980s focused on fine-tuning and standardizing these analyses (e.g., Hampel 1984; Hughes 1984; Nelson 1984). "Short-cut" methods (Meighan 1984) and visual approaches (Bettinger et al. 1984) were also investigated in light of the high cost of full-scale chemical analysis (at least $15 per sample in 1984 [Bettinger et al. 1984], $25 to $35 per sample today); OHD was no longer an inexpensive approach.

The early 1980s also saw more detailed chemical studies of volcanic fields that contained several different outcrops of obsidian. R. E. Hughes (1982) demonstrated that flows in the Medicine Lake Highlands previously believed to represent the same geologic source (e.g., Jack 1976; Jack and Carmichael 1969) actually differed chemically. Hughes (1988) later examined the Coso volcanic field, finding similar heterogeneity (see also Ericson 1989; Hall 1983; Hughes 1989). These and other studies (e.g., Hughes 1994; Hughes and Smith 1993) revealed the possible complexity of volcanic fields and ash-flow tuffs, and stressed the importance of extensive study of each obsidian "source" to demonstrate chemical homogeneity.

Temperature

Temperature has long been known to have a strong impact on the hydration rate. Friedman and Smith (1960) demonstrated that artifacts of the same age from arctic environments hydrated much more slowly than did artifacts of the same age from tropical environments. They suggested that "detailed studies of soil temperatures are needed to understand the influence of the temperature variation upon the rate because the mean annual temperature rates in some regions give only an approximate indication of the actual temperatures to which obsidian artifacts were subjected while buried in different kinds of soils at different depths" (Friedman and Smith 1960:483–484). A few years later Friedman et al. (1966:326) stated that "the effective hydration temperature [EHT] is not the average temperature but rather an estimated temperature at which hydration proceeds at the indicated rate if the temperature is maintained constantly." Further, "in nature, the effective hydration temperature [EHT] depends not only on the maximum temperature, but also on the length of time that the high temperatures are maintained" (Friedman et al. 1966:326). But it was believed that the effects of temperature could be controlled by limiting studies to areas within which the environment was fairly "uniform."

The temperature coefficient of the rate of hydration, although probably the largest variable, does seem to be the easiest of the variables to assess and correct. As Friedman et al. (1970:65) noted: "We need but to construct hydration curves for different climatic zones. . . . More closely defined zones will ultimately allow closer control of this variable. Indeed we should soon know the temperature dependence of the 'constant' k in the hydration rate equations, and this will allow us to calculate a hydration rate curve for any given site."

Within a few years, however, Friedman and his colleagues began to recognize that simply limiting a study to a particular climatic zone was not sufficient, for the effects of temperature on the hydration rate were too complex. In 1976, Friedman and Long derived hydration rates for obsidians from a number of different locations based on induced hydration experiments, stating that "in principle, if we can measure the temperature to which an obsidian sample has been exposed and know its chemical composition we can calculate its average rate of hydration" (Friedman and Long 1976:348).

The measurement of that temperature, however, did not prove to be easily accomplished. Friedman and Long (1976:34) recognized that obsidian on the ground surface or buried to a depth of approximately 10 cm would experience wide diurnal fluctuations in temperature. They argued that, because the hydration rate varies as a power function and not linearly, an average or mean temperature could not be used to calculate a rate. Instead, the equation for the constant, k, must be solved repeatedly using temperatures for small time intervals and then an average computed for the individual values of k. Because temperatures fluctuate much less as depth increases, they argued, deeply buried obsidian would not be so affected, and a single temperature could be used for the calculation of an average rate. Thus, Friedman and Long (1976) were the first to point out that the depth at which artifacts were buried could also affect the rate at which they hydrated (although this point was hinted at by Friedman and Smith in 1960). They also noted that "the depths of burial to yield these conditions vary with soil diffusivity, albedo, snow cover, climate, and so forth" (Friedman and Long 1976:34). In other words, temperatures at a particular depth vary with location and climatic conditions, and thus the EHT is specific to each location and depth.

In an attempt to estimate EHT Friedman and Long (1976) measured soil temperatures at the surface and at different depths at three locations, in Montana, Oregon, and Mexico (see also Friedman 1976). Temperatures were read every two hours at the surface and every five days for subsurface locations. These temperatures were then used to calculate values for the rate constant, k, and thus, average hydration rate.

By the late 1970s, investigations turned to looking for the best approach for measuring EHT. A thermal cell that could be buried in the ground was devised by Ambrose (1976; see also Ambrose 1984) to measure temperature at various depths over a period of time. The Ambrose cell is based on the diffusion of water vapor through the walls of the cell, a temperature-dependent process. Ambrose's (1976) experiments with the new thermal cell confirmed Friedman and Long's (1976) studies that showed an increase in temperature by 1°C will increase the hydration rate by 10%. Friedman and his colleagues used another type of thermal cell that depends on the hydrolysis of sucrose into an inverted sugar (a mixture of glucose and fructose), the rate of which is temperature and pH-dependent (Friedman and Long 1976;

Friedman and Norton 1981; Norton and Friedman 1981; Olmstead et al. 1981). Trembour and Friedman (1984:82) compared these two approaches, preferring the Ambrose cell "because of its comparative simplicity, compactness, ruggedness and economy." In 1986, Trembour et al. described a modified Ambrose cell, designed to measure relative humidity, decrease cell size, and increase cell capacity and use-life (Trembour et al. 1986:186; see also Trembour et al. 1988); this device became known as the "Friedman cell" (see Ridings 1996).

The experiments by Friedman and his colleagues measuring air, surface, and soil temperatures in an attempt to estimate EHT also investigated the utility of induced hydration of obsidian under laboratory conditions and elevated temperature and pressure in order to gain a better understanding of the hydration process. The first induced experiments were reported in 1966 by Friedman et al. In their experiment, samples of freshly flaked obsidian from the Jemez Mountains of New Mexico were suspended in a furnace heated to 100°C; water was slowly dropped into the furnace to maintain a steam atmosphere (Friedman et al. 1966:323). Over a period of four years specimens were periodically removed from the furnace and a thin section cut for hydration measurement. Using the results of these experiments, Friedman et al. (1966) established the relationship between the diffusion rate constant and absolute temperature using the Arrhenius equation (equation 3 above). They also demonstrated that the hydration rate conformed to the original diffusion equation specified by Friedman and Smith (1960). Friedman and Long (1976) reported on expanded experiments that investigated a wider range of temperatures, ranging between 95°C and 245°C. The results of these experiments were used to investigate not only the relation between EHT and the hydration rate but also between the rate and chemical composition. Friedman and Long (1976) also used these results to create experimental hydration rates for the obsidians studied.

The utility of the experimental approach to derive hydration rates for use in OHD was obvious. Following Friedman's lead, others began to conduct induced experiments (e.g., Ericson 1978; Michels 1981, 1982, 1983; Michels et al. 1983; Tsong et al. 1981). Michels et al. (1983) described the method in detail, emphasizing its potential for the derivation of hydration rates for use in OHD. They discussed the complexity of the effects of EHT and the difficulties of reconstructing this variable. As an alternative they recommended the use of an equation derived by Lee (1969):

$$T_a = -1.2316 + 1.065T_e - 0.1607R_t \qquad (6)$$

where,

T_a = mean annual temperature
R_t = annual temperature
T_e = environmental effective mean temperature

A recent study by R. Ridings (1996), however, suggested that the use of Lee's equation can lead to drastically erroneous results (see also Jones et al. 1997; Stevenson, Carpenter, and Scheetz 1989).

Convinced of the utility of induced hydration for the calculation of hydration rates, Michels began performing this procedure under contract in his Pennsylvania laboratory (MOLAB). He produced the first MOLAB Technical Report in 1981 (Michels 1981), which presented a rate for Batza Tena obsidian in Alaska. Over the next eight years Michels produced 86 technical reports, in which he presented initial or revised rates for 62 obsidian sources all over the world, including the United States, Guatemala, Mexico, Honduras, Ecuador, Sardinia, Greece, Kenya, and Ethiopia (see Skinner and Tremaine 1993 for a list of these reports). Subsequently, however, some of these rates were called into question on empirical grounds. For example, Michels (1982) derived a rate for Casa Diablo obsidian in California that placed occupations of that region as early as 16,000–19,000 B.P. while the projectile points on which the hydration measurements were taken indicated a time depth no greater than 5000–6000 B.P. (Hall 1983; R. Jackson 1984a). Concerning this rate Robert Jackson noted:

> It is somewhat surprising that Michels accepts his experimentally derived rate, considering the spurious results it produces when applied to his own data from the Mammoth Junction site. This example suggests that there may be serious problems with at least some rates derived from induced experiments, and until the method can provide archaeologically meaningful results it should be regarded as no more accurate than other methods and should be rigorously tested against archaeological data. (R. Jackson 1984a:176)

Adding fuel to the fire, subsequent experiments demonstrated that the conditions of an induced experiment can substantially affect the results. For example, Bates et al. (1988) conducted induced experiments in both hydrothermal solution (as Michels used) and a saturated vapor environment (as Friedman et al. 1966 and Friedman and Long 1976 used)[2]; they found that these different conditions produced different reaction rates (see also Abrajano et al. 1986). This was an important discovery because artifacts are generally found in deposits saturated with water vapor (Stevenson, Bates, Abrajano, and Scheetz 1989:4). Further, Michels's experiments were conducted at temperatures of 150°C to 250°C for durations of up to six days in a pressure reactor. Temperatures greater than 200°C were found by other researchers to be problematic, especially in concert with a hydrothermal environment. Experiments by Stevenson, Bates, Abrajano, and Scheetz (1989; see also Stevenson, Carpenter, and Scheetz 1989) and Tremaine and Frederickson (1988; see also Tremaine 1989) showed that for hydration rims developed at temperatures of 200°C and higher in a hydrothermal environment the diffusion fronts appear to lose definition, inhibiting the ability to measure the hydration rim (Tremaine 1989:30). Further, Bates et al. (1988) found that under those same experimental conditions, there can be dissolution (i.e., removal of the hydration rim), which led them to suggest that the actual depth of hydration induced was underestimated. Because of these results, experiments are currently performed in vapor environments and at temperatures not exceeding 180°C (e.g., Mazer et al. 1991).

The confusion arising from the results of induced hydration studies has led a number of researchers to argue that until proper experimental conditions are established, empirically derived rates are more accurate (e.g., Gilreath and Hildebrandt 1997; Hall and Jackson 1989). Using stratigraphically sealed obsidian samples, rates are created by calibrating hydration rind measurements with ^{14}C dates, dendrochronological dates, or time-sensitive projectile points (e.g., Bettinger 1989; R. Jackson 1984b). This approach, however, depends on the assumption that there is a direct temporal association between dated material and obsidian, which experimentalists argue is more problematic than errors resulting from the laboratory approach. Zeier (1989), in a comparison of empirically and experimentally derived rates for the Medicine Lake source in Oregon, found the experimentally derived rates to be more accurate. Basgall and McGuire (1988), on the other hand, found an empirically derived rate to work best for the Coso source in southern California. We should point out, however, that over 15 empirically and experimentally derived rates have been calculated for the Coso source (e.g., Basgall and True 1985; Cleland 1990; Drews and Elston 1983; Ericson 1977a; Friedman and Obradovich 1981; Koerper et al. 1986; McGuire et al. 1982; Meighan 1978, 1981; Michels 1983; Stevenson and Scheetz 1989), but no single rate has had much general success when applied to measurements from the larger region (Basgall

1993:50). This problem may be due in part to differences in chemical composition within the source area documented by Hughes (1988). Basgall (1990), however, in a comparison of rates suggested that much, if not most, of the variability in these rates is due to EHT, which he demonstrated could vary considerably from locality to locality. Stevenson et al. (1993) believe the variation may be due in large part to the intrinsic water content of the obsidian, which they demonstrated also varies considerably, even within a single flow of the Coso field. Intrinsic water content was shown by Mazer et al. (1992; see also Stevenson et al. 1998) to be the primary factor controlling the hydration rate.

It may be that the empirical and experimental approaches will never result in comparable results for complications arise from the application of a rate derived in a *closed system*, that is, in a laboratory where time, temperature, pressure, etc., can be controlled, to artifacts in an *open system*, where there are numerous cultural and natural transformation processes operating (Hughes 1992).

Relative Humidity

It has been only fairly recently that relative humidity has been shown to affect the hydration rate. In their original presentation, Friedman and Smith saw no indication that relative humidity was a factor in the hydration process: "If our analysis of the hydration process of obsidian is correct, the concentration gradient across the diffusion front is constant and independent of the relative humidity in either the soil or air environment surrounding the specimen" (Friedman and Smith 1960:482). Their reasoning was that the hydrated layer becomes "saturated" at 3.5% water; in any natural environment there is enough water for the outer surface to become saturated and thus higher humidities would have no impact.

This reasoning was accepted until the mid-1980s. Leach and Hamel (1984:399), for instance, stated that "the humidity of the environment in which a piece of obsidian comes to rest does influence hydration too," but citing Trembour (personal communication 1983) they went on to say that "for most archaeological sites it can be ignored because relative humidity reaches 100% at 10–15 cm depth" (Leach and Hamel 1984:399). Friedman and his colleagues suspected that humidity was indeed a factor when they modified the Ambrose cell to measure relative humidity (Trembour et al. 1986). But empirical demonstration came in 1991 from Mazer et al., who induced hydration in obsidians from Coso (California), Mule Creek (New Mexico), and Orito Quarry

(Easter Island) at 95%, 90%, and 60% relative humidity, using EHTs of 150°C and 175°C. The rate of hydration for each obsidian was constant at 60% and 90% relative humidity for each temperature, but between 90% and 100% the rate changed significantly (between 10% and 30%), depending upon the composition of the glass. Mazer et al. (1991:510) concluded that obsidian hydration is a "relatively simple process of water diffusion that is controlled by the environmental variables temperature and humidity." They suggested that the combined effects of these two variables can cause extreme variations in the hydration rate.

In a subsequent experiment where specimens were tested at ambient temperatures of 40°C and 70°C, Friedman et al. (1994) found that the rate of hydration increased from 27% to 100% relative humidity, in contrast to the results of Mazer et al. (1991; see also Ebert et al. 1991). They noted, however, that in discussions with Mazer they concluded that the difference in results was due to the different temperatures used in the two experiments.

An additional pattern observed by Friedman et al. (1994) is that surface and subsurface samples did not appear to have hydrated at substantially different rates, as should be the case given the difference in EHT between these two situations. Based on the rates and temperatures presented by Friedman and Long (1976), for example, a rate should increase on the order of 70% with an increase in temperature of 10°C. Friedman et al. (1994:188) suggested that "this apparent lack of a temperature effect on the hydration rate may be due to the compensating effect of the lower relative humidity experienced by surface samples, which tended to counter the effect of solar heating." This relationship would be most pronounced in a desert environment, such as that of the Great Basin, in which surface relative humidities are often less than 10% (Beck and Jones 1994) and would explain other studies where the difference between surface and subsurface hydration readings did not differ as much as expected (e.g., Hall and Jackson 1989; Origer and Wickstrom 1982).

Measurement of the Hydration Rind

In 1960, Friedman and Smith described the technique by which the hydration rim thickness was measured. A thin section was cut at right angles to the edge using a 0.015-inch thick continuous-rim diamond cut-off saw blade. The sawed-out section was ground down until it was between 1/16- and 1/32-inch thick, cemented to a glass

microscope slide, and then ground further to a thickness of between
0.002 and 0.003 inch. Friedman and Smith suggested that "with luck,
the skill acquired through practice, three to six thin sections can be
made per hour and 70% to 90% of the slides will be satisfactory"
(Friedman and Smith 1960:479). Once the slide was completed, the
hydration rind was measured under a microscope. Measurements were
made with a 12.5x filar micrometer ocular; a 45x objective was used
for rims greater than 2.0 microns while a 100x oil immersion apochro-
matic objective was used for thinner rims (Friedman and Smith
1960:479–480). Friedman and Smith stated that the birefringence due
to physical strain in the hydrated layer would be brightened using
cross-polarized light, but "the measurement must be made in plain
light" (Friedman and Smith 1960:480).

In 1973, Michels recommended the use of an image-splitting eyepiece because it depends "only on the operator's ability to shear apart
and then overlap two identical images. It has been shown that this
technique is capable of measuring with a precision of at least an order
of magnitude greater than the resolution of the optical system being
used, because it does not depend on being able to resolve the measured
objects, but rather simply on being able to match intensity variations"
(Michels 1973:205). Michels reported a measurement error of ±0.1
micron using this eyepiece. Scheetz and Stevenson (1988:111), however, suggested that under the best circumstances the maximum resolution that can be achieved is 0.21 microns.

In 1984, Jackson conducted a test in order to evaluate the consistency of hydration readings between laboratories. He gathered two
sets of slides, one from Napa Valley and one from Owens Valley, both
in California; both sets of slides were examined by the University of
California, Davis Obsidian Hydration Laboratory, and the Obsidian
Hydration Laboratory at Sonoma State University. A good correlation
was found between the labs with regard to the Napa Valley specimens
but not for the Owens Valley specimens. In the latter case, the techni-
cian at the Sonoma State lab stated that the slides were "poorly pre-
pared' or they exhibited "ragged edges" (R. Jackson 1984a:108–109).
Jackson suggested that "this particular example illustrates that such
affective variables do intervene in the measurement process and that,
in some cases, these can be attributed to differences in sample preparation" (R. Jackson 1984a:109). He concluded that some type of monitoring system should be put into place, that intra- and interlaboratory
comparisons should be made continuously, and that multiple hydration

cuts on the same artifact by the same and different technicians should be made and measured (see also R. Jackson 1990). And, because individual hydration readings may occasionally be in error, hydration results for single specimens should not be relied upon.

The traditional optical approach continues to be the predominant method used to measure hydration rims (e.g., Friedman et al. 1997; Stevenson et al. 1996), although other techniques have been investigated, such as resonant nuclear reaction (e.g., Laursen and Lanford 1978; Leach and Naylor 1981; Lee et al. 1974) and sputter-induced optical emission (Leach and Hamel 1984; Tsong et al. 1978). As Ambrose (1993) points out, however, these techniques have not been widely applied since their early report. Recently Ambrose (1993) proposed the use of computer imaging technology to overcome the problems inherent in optical measurement of the hydration rim. He argued that the constraint on precision arises from the optical resolution of the microscopes that are used and "the need for the operators to make judgments in alignment of the measuring device with the outer and inner boundaries of the hydration-induced optical effect" (Ambrose 1993:79–80). According to Ambrose, "the basic difference with imaging technology for measurement is that the visual judgment is avoided, the minimum unit of differentiation being the pixel, with light intensity being the means for displaying the image either as a gray scale value, or some defined spectral scale; by recording the microscope optical image as a computer based digitized image the minimum distance that can be represented is one pixel" (Ambrose 1993:81).

Ambrose's tests demonstrated that the error factor involved in this approach, although not as small as expected (0.11 micron), was smaller than that achieved when using the standard optical approach. Thus, computer imaging appears to have promise in the measurement of hydration rinds and reducing measurement error (see Stevenson et al. 1996).

Anovitz et al. (1999) have proposed the use of secondary ion mass spectrometry (SIMS) as an alternative to the optical approach. They argue that the optically measured hydration depth varies with the water profile as measured by SIMS. Their experiments suggest that the boundary between hydrated and unhydrated glass is gradational rather than sharp and that the sharp diffusion front observed optically is in part a function of the optical properties of visible light, rendering the results of the optical approach, at best, uncertain. They believe the hydration profile as measured by SIMS to be a more reliable as well as a more accurate representation of the water diffusion process with respect to obsidian.

CURRENT STATUS

The current status of OHD may actually be more problematic than it was in 1960 when the method was first presented, largely because we know so much more about the hydration process. Researchers continue to attempt to solve the problems that have been present from the beginning. The debate, for example, concerning the appropriate equation to define the hydration rate goes on (e.g., Anovitz et al. 1999; Stevenson et al. 1993, 1996, 1998). The debate over the derivation of hydration rates continues (e.g., Gilreath and Hildebrandt 1997; Stevenson et al. 1993, 1996, 1998). In an attempt to avoid the problems that appear to be inherent to the high-temperature induced experiments, Stevenson et al. (1993; see also Stevenson et al. 1996, 1998) suggested an alternative approach, based on intrinsic water content of the obsidian. Recent work by Mazer et al. (1992; see also Anovitz et al. 1999; Stevenson et al. 1998) has shown a strong relationship between the structural water content of obsidian and the hydration rate, and using an estimate of the hydroxyl (OH) concentration of a particular glass, the hydration rate for that glass can be estimated (Stevenson et al. 1996). This approach, however, is in its infancy, and as such, some researchers are reluctant at this point to use it (e.g., Gilreath and Hildebrandt 1997). Effort continues to be invested in both laboratory and empirical investigation of the method and of the factors that influence the hydration rate. Recent studies, for example, have shown that EHTs can differ by depth (Jones et al. 1997; Ridings 1991, 1996) or factors such as vegetation cover, exposure, and variation in soil properties (Jones et al. 1997; see also Jones et al. 1995) at the microregional level. As a result Jones et al. (1997:514) have suggested that it is important to develop measures of EHT variation for each site to be dated.

In addition, Ridings (1996) has shown that Lee's temperature equation, Ambrose's thermal cells, and the Friedman thermal cells give similar results for sites near the equator, but moving toward the poles the results grow less comparable. She concluded that for sites located some distance from the equator, such as those in North America, "depth-specific rates of hydration based on EHTs from thermal cells are not likely to be representative of artifact hydration histories in localities where the amplitude of the annual surface temperature wave is large"

(Ridings 1996:145–146). We should point out, however, that source characterization analysis was not done for the artifacts used in this study, and until it is known that the variations observed are not in part due to differences in chemical composition, these conclusions must remain tentative.

Effort also continues to be invested in the empirical development of more precise hydration rates for particular sources (e.g., Hull 1996), and use of the method, both as a relative approach and for the calculation of numerical-age dates, is greater than ever (e.g., Gilreath and Hildebrandt 1997; Shackley 1996; see also references in Skinner and Tremaine 1993). But the tyranny of the radiocarbon method has diminished the impact of OHD; when you have radiocarbon dates, why use a less precise method like OHD? The obvious answer to this question, of course, is that radiocarbon dates are often not numerous and OHD provides an alternative or an approach to be used in conjunction with radiocarbon dating, and thus OHD continues to play a large part in both research and contract projects in regions where obsidian is present.

OHD AND THE PREHISTORY OF THE AMERICAN DESERT WEST

As suggested at the beginning of this paper, the impact of OHD on North American prehistory has not been in providing precise dates or solving long-debated substantive problems. Indeed, no chronometric tool rivals radiocarbon in this regard, save dendrochronology in the American Southwest where a particular, well-preserved record enables this method. But because OHD is applied directly to the artifact, it has been used in unique ways not possible with most other dating approaches. The potential of the method as originally proclaimed by Michels (1967) remains the same: for substantive issues like the delineation of trade networks, where dates apply directly to the medium of exchange, and to issues relating to site formation histories, such as evaluating the problem of artifact reuse, examining the intensity of site occupations through time, and evaluating stratigraphic mixing. In the American Desert West OHD is most frequently used in the examination of raw material conveyance, the evaluation of particular artifact types as chronological markers, the examination of the history of source use, and the dating and evaluation of contemporaneity among surface artifacts. We believe that the last, its application to the surface artifact record, may be its greatest impact and its most promising future. To illustrate the potential of OHD we discuss several applications in detail.

Issues of Material Conveyance

An issue of considerable current interest concerns temporal and spatial patterns of lithic material conveyance. OHD is especially valuable because obsidian is one medium of conveyance. The specific archaeological issues are numerous—the history of regional exchange systems, the diagnosis of local and regional settlement patterns, the evaluation of territorial ranges, and mobility. Obsidian exchange in California has been well documented by a number of researchers (Bouey and Basgall 1984; Ericson 1977a, 1977b, 1981, 1982; Ericson and Meighan 1984; Ericson et al. 1989; Hall 1984; T. Jackson 1984, 1986, 1988, 1989; T. Jackson and Ericson 1994; Koerper et al. 1986; Singer and Ericson 1977) using a combination of chemical characterization and obsidian hydration. An allied topic, the history of source exploitation, has been examined for several source areas in California and Oregon, including Coso–Sugarloaf (Elston and Zeier 1984; Gilreath and Hildebrandt 1997), Bodie Hills (T. Jackson 1984; Singer and Ericson 1977), Casa Diablo (Hall and Basgall 1994; T. Jackson 1984), and the Medicine Lake Highland (Hughes 1982).

Regarding studies of prehistoric exchange, however, Basgall states that "It is the case, of course, that obsidian distribution reflects directly only geographic displacement of material from its place of origin, yet many archaeologists persist in viewing regional source profiles as relatively straightforward signatures of trade, territoriality, and other behaviors that operate within a strong sociocultural matrix" (1989:111). Basgall goes on to say that although obsidian distribution in some instances may reflect exchange or other complexities of social interaction, "among many hunter-gatherer populations lithic procurement is a fundamental component of subsistence settlement organization and occurs primarily or wholly within that context" (Basgall 1989:111).

Using a combination of OHD and source characterization analysis Basgall demonstrated that early in the central-eastern California occupation sequence obsidian source diversity is greater than later in the sequence and that this pattern is due to "relatively more mobile, extensive subsistence-settlement systems that brought groups in proximity to a wider range of lithic resources during their annual foraging cycle" (Basgall 1989:123). Later source use, he says, appears to focus on a more limited set of sources, likely due to increased territoriality, which limited access to sources, and the development of exchange networks.

In our own work in eastern Nevada (e.g., Beck and Jones 1990, 1992, 1994; Jones and Beck 1990) we have pursued a similar problem to Basgall's, using OHD and source characterization to delineate terminal Pleistocene/early Holocene mobility patterns. We have documented conveyance of obsidian in a north-south pattern covering 400 km. The most predominant obsidian sources represented in the earliest assemblages lie to the north and south of our research area, about 200 km in each direction. Among other indications, the high frequency of obsidians from such great distances suggests mobility within a large areal range. During the early Holocene, there is a shift in source use, incorporating sources to the east, which eventually come to dominate the assemblage. Although the reasons for the shift in source representation over time are uncertain, our ability to recognize this shift in the configuration of geographic ranges is made possible by the development of age control using OHD for the artifacts that serve as proxies for movement patterns. These changes in source use correspond to changes in resource distribution in this area during the terminal Pleistocene and early Holocene periods (Beck and Jones 1997).

Testing Time-Sensitive Artifact Types

Typological cross-dating is the most commonly used approach for dating the surface record (or the subsurface record where no other dating approach is available). Most commonly used in this approach are ceramic types, but for preceramic periods or in areas such as the Great Basin where ceramics were never widely used, other artifact categories, such as projectile points, have been used for the construction of types (see Beck 1998, 1999).

An issue that has both substantive and theoretical import in Great Basin archaeology concerns whether projectile points of different types are, in fact, valid as chronological indicators. Most archaeologists, not just those working in the Great Basin, have operated as if this were fact (e.g., Christenson 1986; Shott 1993; Thomas 1981) and that the main issue simply is refining the dating for each point type by amassing more radiocarbon dates and looking more closely at local patterns to assess chronological variation across space. But in a set of provocative papers now a decade old (Flenniken and Raymond 1986; Flenniken and Wilke 1989), Jeffrey Flenniken, Anan Raymond, and Phil Wilke called into question the validity of projectile point types as chronological indicators. Their argument is that dart points often exhibit breakage and resharpening on both the blade and stem, which can drastically change the form of the point and thus the type to which it is assigned. What archaeologists find, according to this argument, are

expended, "used-up" points that likely started out their use-lives looking quite different. Thus, they concluded, projectile point types cannot
serve as valid time-markers.

Since projectile points are a critical dating tool, these arguments
warranted careful study. The issue has been tackled from several directions (e.g., Beck 1995, 1998; Bettinger et al. 1991; Thomas 1986b), yet
it seems more than clear that this is one substantive problem in which
OHD can be profitably applied. David Rhode (1994a) presented results
of the analysis of projectile points from Yucca Mountain in southern
Nevada. One of the goals of this research was to test the utility of
Great Basin projectile point types for dating using OHD. These results
showed that for the Yucca Mountain points, at least, the types had distinct, although overlapping, distributions of hydration readings in the
expected relative order. Studies by R. Jackson (1984b), Hall and Jackson (1989) and Gilreath and Hildebrandt (1997) for southern California, and the authors (Beck and Jones 1994; Jones and Beck 1990) for
eastern Nevada have shown similar results. In short, what had been
taken as fact on the basis of stratigraphic evidence (that Great Basin
projectile point types follow a regular sequential pattern) has been
confirmed by OHD.

OHD *and the Surface Artifact Record*

To generalize, we can state that every substantive archaeological problem requires chronological assessment, whether the issue is
to monitor and explain change or to be able to isolate materials of the
same age in order to accurately describe an ecological or social configuration. In the arid western United States, where much of the archaeological record lies on the surface, such control is often difficult. In
fact, one of the most common surface expressions, the nondiagnostic
lithic scatter, is so labeled precisely because of its resistance to chronologic inference. Often containing few or no temporally sensitive artifacts like projectile points or ceramics, lithic scatters are routinely
dismissed in both research and contract settings because of their
apparent ubiquity on the one hand and for the analytic difficulties
they pose on the other. It is in this context that OHD has such great
potential, by bringing some measure of chronologic control to a wide
array of temporally "faceless" artifact assemblages and thus expanding the sample of archaeological phenomena that can be used to
answer any particular question.

Quite early in OHD studies, researchers (e.g., Friedman and Long

1976; Trembour and Friedman 1984) warned that temperature extremes like those experienced by artifacts on the surface could seriously distort the chronological signal in hydration rinds. Not only was it reasonable to expect rind widths of those artifacts to be much wider than those of buried specimens of the same age (Layton 1973) but also to possibly have developed "abnormally" because of temperature extremes (see related discussion above of induced hydration). When put to the empirical test, however, these concerns appear somewhat misplaced. In a comparison of buried and surface projectile points from the Santa Rosa Plain in California, for example, Origer and Wickstrom (1982) concluded that while the range of hydration measurements for surface specimens was slightly larger than that for buried specimens, there were no statistical differences between them. In a study of projectile points of Casa Diablo glass in California, Hall and Jackson found "relatively minimal divergence between hydration values obtained on surface and subsurface specimens" (Hall and Jackson 1989:44). Theoretically there should have been large differences between the surface and subsurface readings, but the lack of difference, as discussed earlier, is likely due to the countering effects of low humidity (cf. Friedman et al. 1994). Whatever the case, the application of OHD to surface assemblages appears no more problematic than its application to subsurface assemblages, where the depositional history cannot be known (Beck and Jones 1994).

One of the most extensive OHD programs has been developed in connection with site inventory and evaluation in projects at Fort Irwin in southern California. Work by Mark Basgall, Matt Hall, Claude Warren, and many others (e.g., Basgall 1993, 1995; Basgall and Hall 1993; Basgall and McGuire 1988; Basgall et al. 1988; Gilreath et al. 1988; Hall 1993; Warren 1990) has developed a large inventory of surface sites, spanning the late Pleistocene to the historic period. But a significant proportion of surface sites contain few or no associated diagnostic projectile points, a characteristic not uncommon in any part of the Desert West. Most of the obsidian represented in the Fort Irwin assemblages is from the Coso volcanic field (Basgall 1993). For chronologic study, OHD results were calibrated using both radiocarbon dates and diagnostic projectile point types. For the latter, hydration values were compiled for all projectile points made from Coso obsidian, and then, ranges of hydration values were established for each point type. For assemblages with no diagnostics, hydration ranges for nondiagnostic obsidian flakes in each assemblage were identified with the hydration ranges established for the projectile point types, thus placing these assemblages in time.

Basgall (1995) presented the hydration results from hundreds of artifacts from the northern Mojave Desert. OHD was used to evaluate the relative ages of assemblages containing either large stemmed points or Pinto points (see Beck and Jones 1997 for a discussion of these point forms). While the former have greater time depth, the period of overlap, if any, with Pinto was uncertain. Basgall showed a bimodal distribution in hydration readings for these two point forms, the means of which were significantly different. He concluded, based on the few radiocarbon dates from Fort Irwin sites in combination with a rate he developed for the Coso source, that, although there may be some short temporal overlap, stemmed points are representative of early-Holocene occupations while Pinto points are representative of mid-Holocene occupations.

Because OHD is applied to individual artifacts, this approach can be taken a step further than traditional typological cross-dating in that contemporaneity (or lack thereof) can be demonstrated between the remainder of the obsidian assemblage and the projectile points, something that is rarely considered when simply relying on projectile point types. One of the fundamental interpretive questions of archaeology concerns component formation. That is, whether an assemblage is the result of short-term activities or multiple depositional events over a longer period of time. The projectile points present in an assemblage may indicate relatively short-term use when in fact debitage or other tool categories may have been deposited over a longer term. Because it dates individual artifacts, OHD can be used to assess contemporaneity among artifacts within assemblages as well as the duration and continuity of deposition.

Archaeologists working on the Paleoarchaic (11,500–7500 B.P.) (see Beck and Jones 1997) record of the Great Basin have had decidedly little success in developing chronologic sequences of surface sites using typological cross-dating. Although component mixture often plays a role, the main obstacle to chronological control lies in the low frequency of projectile points in assemblages and the long conservation of forms—most types span 3,000 to 4,000 years (Beck and Jones 1997). Faced with this problem, we have supplemented our typologically based dating program with OHD. We have obtained over 650 rind measurements on artifacts from 13 assemblages. Combining the lack of radiocarbon-calibrated hydration rates and our concern more generally about the comparability of surface and buried samples as to temperature and humidity histories, we have used OHD as a relative tool, attempting to compare assemblages as to contemporaneity, occupation span, component mixture, to develop a chronological sequence.

Chemical analysis of 666 obsidian specimens indicated the presence of 34 different geochemical obsidian types (Beck and Jones 1994; Jones and Beck 1990). Most of these, however, are represented in very small numbers; only six are represented by 20 or more specimens, and these have been the focus of our dating studies. When hydration readings were arranged within sources, several assemblages exhibited much longer ranges, suggesting that these assemblages are representative of longer occupation spans, a conclusion supported by the wider range of projectile point types represented.

In addition to an assessment of contemporaneity between projectile points and the remaining obsidian in each assemblage, the 13 assemblages were ordered serially based on mean hydration values within the six most prevalent geochemical obsidian types to create a relative chronological order. Although there is a good deal of overlap in the distribution of hydration values from assemblage to assemblage, mean hydration values in general increase in each obsidian type as one moves downward in the order. With the chronological ordering of OHD results, a pronounced shift in source use was evident, from a high reliance on Browns Bench obsidian over 200 km to the north to the inclusion of and finally dominance of sources from western Utah (Beck and Jones 1992, 1994). In the absence of the relative order based on OHD, we would have been left to wonder if the variation in source representation across assemblages was simply an expression of the variability expected over this entire period or if it held a temporal component. That it is a temporal pattern leads to investigations of parallel time series. Therefore, the order based on OHD yielded not only a relative chronology for the 13 assemblages, but indicated the contemporaneity (or lack thereof) of particular obsidian source use.

SUMMARY AND CONCLUSION

OHD has been with us now for nearly 40 years, and from the foregoing discussion it may appear that the method is no better a dating tool than it was when it was first introduced in 1960. This is not the case, however. We have gained considerable knowledge over those years, both concerning the complexity of the hydration process and how to control uncertainties. The measurement of chemical composition, for instance, while virtually nonexistent in the early 1970s, has today become commonplace in obsidian studies. Attempts to establish EHT and relative humidity of the hydrating environment, although not yet commonplace, have become more prevalent. And though we still do not completely understand the hydration process (e.g., Anovitz et al. 1999), the method has seen increasing use over the years, especially as a relative-age approach.

Given the limitations identified, significant interpretive use of OHD data may actually be in areas other than determining the age of a deposit. We have discussed several such areas, including studies of material conveyance (e.g., mobility, exchange), contemporaneity among artifacts in a surface assemblage, and evaluation of artifact reuse and stratigraphic mixing. By far the most numerous studies have to do with material conveyance, especially in the Desert West where prehistoric (as well as historic) peoples were, for the most part, hunter-gatherers who may have traveled hundreds of kilometers in a single year. Issues of mobility and exchange are crucial in the understanding of prehistoric land use strategies, and since obsidian was commonly a medium of conveyance (either obtained directly from the source or through exchange), OHD plays an important role because measurements are taken directly on the artifacts.

Although studies of artifact contemporaneity and reuse are considerably fewer, they are becoming more prevalent as more serious attention is given to the importance of the surface artifact record. The importance of dating the surface record cannot be overstated. In studies of hunter-gatherers, especially as we move back farther in time, lithic artifacts comprise an increasing majority of the archaeological record, and at least in the Desert West, probably 75%–80%, if not more, of this record occurs on the surface. If we are unable to evaluate this record chronologically, we can never hope to make sense of prehistoric hunter-gatherer land use strategies, especially those of the late Pleistocene and early Holocene. OHD is one of the few methods that can be applied to this record (Beck 1994), and its advantage is that it can be applied directly to the artifact. Importantly as well, in all of the types of studies mentioned above, numerical-age dates are not required. Although it would be nice to have "absolute" dates, all that is necessary are within-source hydration rim measurements that can be compared relative to one another, which of course diminishes the problems faced in the establishment of a hydration rate.

In discussing its utility, we might consider the accuracy and precision (as defined in chapter 1) of OHD in the various contexts in which it has been used. Both are enhanced by limiting the amount of error introduced to the estimate. Without going too deeply into this matter, we can see several sources of error that reduce confidence in any estimate. Errors can be introduced through measurement of the hydration rind or determinations of chemical composition, but the greatest errors are likely due to the difficulties in measuring EHT and relative humidity as well as in reconstructing the depositional histories of the artifacts dated. On the other hand, as Jim Feathers (1997a) points out in a recent discussion of luminescence dating, precision at least is *increased* when the target event can be dated directly. If the target event is the death of the wood found as charcoal in a hearth then radiocarbon or tree-ring dating can be used to directly date that event. If, however, the target event is the age of the lithic assemblage adjacent to the hearth, then these methods do not date the target event, and the relevance of those dates must be argued through association. It is precisely because OHD dates the artifact directly that it remains an important dating method and that it has great potential for the future.

CHAPTER 8

Luminescence Dating and Why It Deserves Wider Application

JAMES K. FEATHERS
Department of Anthropology
University of Washington

Luminescence dating was introduced to American archaeologists more than 30 years ago and was touted as a technique that could directly date events of archaeological interest (Ralph and Han 1966). Despite that promise enhanced by 30 years of research and development, and acceptance by other parts of the world (e.g., Bowman 1991), the technique still lacks wide popularity in the United States. In a book addressing how dating methods have affected the understanding of American prehistory, luminescence does not have much to show. This paper explores why luminescence has not gained a footing in American archaeology and attempts to demonstrate why it could and should.

The method is based on the accumulation of radiation effects in crystalline materials, such as ceramics and sediments. The natural radioactivity present in these materials and their surroundings causes ionization of atoms, which leads to subsequent trapping of charged particles at defects in the crystal lattice. Exposure to sufficient heat or light releases the charge from these traps and results in a luminescence signal whose intensity is proportional to the time elapsed since the previous detrapping event or when the material was last exposed to sufficient heat or light. Luminescence can date ceramics or heat-treated lithics to the time of their last heating, usually the manufacturing event, or sediments to the time of their last exposure to light, or burial. Measurement involves determining the amount of radiation necessary to produce the natural luminescence signal (called the equivalent dose) and the natural dose rate. Dividing the equivalent dose by the dose rate results in an age.

The low standing of luminescence dating in American archaeology can be attributed to two sets of reasons, which can be categorized as those stemming from the supply side and those coming from the demand side. The supply side accounts for the failings of luminescence itself, in particular how it has been practiced in the United States. The demand side addresses the perceptions of dating by American archaeologists and how that has limited the role of luminescence.

Supply Side

The phenomenon of luminescence has been known for centuries, although the basic physics was not formalized until the late 1940s (Garlick and Gibson 1948; Randall and Wilkins 1945). The first suggestion that it could be used for dating archaeological or geological materials was made by a group of chemists led by Farrington Daniels at the University of Wisconsin in the early 1950s (Daniels et al. 1953). Daniels was interested in practical applications for luminescence, particularly as a means to detect radiation exposure, or dosimetry. This followed from the observation that luminescence intensity was proportional to absorbed radiation. Further, if the radiation dose rate was known, the luminescence intensity could be related to age. Daniels was most excited about the potential for dating the crystallization of geologic materials but also mentioned the possibility of dating the last heating episode of ancient pottery.

That ancient pottery did possess a luminescence signal that was responsive to radiation dose was demonstrated by researchers in Germany (Grögler et al. 1960) and at the University of California at Los Angeles (Kennedy and Knopff 1960). Both groups also suggested a method for determining age. Several laboratories then set out to perfect the dating method. Most notable were the Applied Science Center for Archaeology (ASCA, later MASCA) at the University Museum, University of Pennsylvania; the Research Laboratory for Archaeology at Oxford University; Nara University in Japan; and the Danish Atomic Energy Commission, Research Establishment Risø in Roskilde, Denmark. All the early work was in thermoluminescence (TL), or luminescence stimulated by heat. Luminescence stimulated by light, or optically stimulated luminescence (OSL), was not developed as a dating method until the 1980s.

Americans were thus involved from the beginning in the initial research in luminescence dating, but the subsequent history of the four labs (Winter 1971) is a telling account of success and failure in developmental research. I focus on the Pennsylvania group, which was not successful, and the Oxford group, which under the leadership of Martin Aitken (1985, 1992, 1994), laid the groundwork for luminescence dating as it is practiced today. The Japanese laboratory took a similar approach as the Pennsylvania group (Ichikawa 1965) and did not become a major influence, although the laboratory continued to function into the 1980s (e.g., Kojo 1991). Little luminescence dating research has been undertaken in Japan, although the Japanese later became leaders in the related dating technique of electron spin resonance (e.g., Ikeya 1978). The Danish lab, under the guidance of Vagn Mejdahl, followed the Oxford lead (Mejdahl 1969) and is now one of the prominent laboratories in the world, having made several important contributions in method and instrumentation through the years (e.g., Bøtter-Jensen 1988; Bøtter-Jensen et al. 1993; Bøtter-Jensen et al. 1994; Mejdahl 1983, 1988; Mejdahl and Bøtter-Jensen 1994).

Developing a viable dating technique did not prove simple at either institution, however. Several obstacles, most of which were only dimly realized at the outset, had to be overcome.

The work at Pennsylvania began in the early 1960s under Elizabeth K. Ralph, one of ASCA's founders, and research chemist Mark C. Han (MASCA Newsletter 1965). From the beginning, they recognized the value of luminescence for dating pottery directly and thereby avoiding the association problems of radiocarbon (Taylor 1987). But the dating procedure (Ralph and Han 1966, 1968, 1969, 1971) they worked out could not capitalize on this advantage.

Ralph and Han began by assuming that the luminescence signal was primarily a function of, or at least proportional to, radiation from heavy, energetic alpha particles. They therefore thought it necessary only to measure the alpha dose rate, which could be done relatively easily by scintillation screens, as had been demonstrated in biology (Turner et al. 1958). Contributions from betas (particularly from ^{40}K) and gammas (from sources external to the sherds) were believed insignificant or at least relatively invariable from sherd to sherd.

Ralph and Han attempted to measure the natural luminescence by grinding the entire sherd sample to less than 75 μm and depositing thin coatings on aluminum foil. These were then heated to measure TL. They quickly realized that the luminescence varied greatly among sherds of the same radioactivity and even from different portions of the same sherd. This they correctly interpreted as the result of variation in sensitivity to radiation and corrected for it by giving artificial radiation and glowing out each portion a second time. This calibration resulted in what they termed "specific thermoluminescence":

Sp. TL = (N-TL)/α(A-TL)

where,

N-TL =   the natural thermoluminescence

A-TL =   the second glow thermoluminescence stimulated by artificial irradiation

α =   the alpha dose rate

They were reluctant to attempt any absolute, or ratio-scale, age determinations because of uncertainties in radioactivity measurements, particularly the varying efficiencies in producing luminescence from alpha, beta, and gamma radiation. They therefore opted for relative, interval-scale dating. They hoped to convert these to calendrical ages through construction of a calibration curve where specific TL of known-age samples was plotted against the true age (Figure 8.1). Some of the "true" ages came from historical records, but many were from associated radiocarbon dates. The correlations, while suggestive of TL's potential as a dating tool, were far from perfect and fully empirical, based on a limited dataset. Using the curve to derive calendar dates for sherds of unknown age could not be reliable, particularly because of their assumptions about radioactivity. Moreover, because radiocarbon associations formed the basis of the curves, the advantage of luminescence was obviated.

In fact, the Pennsylvania laboratory never did produce viable dates for materials of unknown ages. Some published dates (e.g., Bronson and Han 1972) were strongly disputed on archaeological grounds (Loofs 1974) as well as from luminescence considerations (Aitken et al. 1983; Carriveau and Harbottle 1983) and were later withdrawn by MASCA. A list of all TL dates considered valid by S. J. Fleming (1979) did not include any from the Pennsylvania lab. Fleming, a pioneer in luminescence dating at Oxford, was brought to MASCA in 1978 with a promise to regularly publish TL dates (Fleming 1978), but nothing more was heard from the Pennsylvania lab.

In hindsight, the Pennsylvania approach had three major shortcomings. First, the assumption that the alpha count rate was a sufficient measure of radioactivity ignored the large and varied contributions of beta radiation from ^{40}K and of gamma radiation from the environment. Plus, alpha radiation has proved to be much less effective at inducing luminescence than betas or gammas, making it an unlikely representative of the total radiation. While they began to realize the different

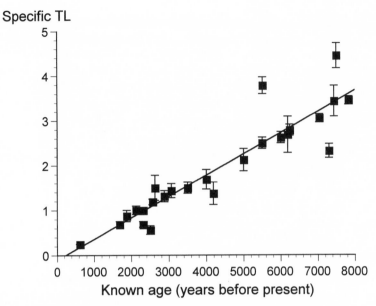

FIGURE 8.1 Relationship of specific luminescence to known ages using data derived from the University of Pennsylvania laboratory. The graph is a composite of two figures appearing in Ralph and Han (1969).

effectiveness of alphas (Han 1975; Ralph and Han 1971), the group never got a handle on radiation determinations necessary to derive accurate ages.

Second, by using a ground portion of the entire sherd, they ignored accumulating evidence of heterogeneity in sherds both in luminescence susceptibility and radioactivity. Accurate dating could not be done until these severe dosimetry problems were resolved.

Third, by calibrating the natural luminescence by a second-glow artificial irradiation, they did not realize the potential errors from heat-caused sensitivity changes (Han 1975 began to struggle with the issue) or nonlinearity in dose response.

American geologists became interested in luminescence dating following Daniels's suggestion and published a number of studies in the late 1950s and 1960s. The interest was in dating the formation of rocks or deciphering their thermal history. For the time ranges involved, the alpha radiation was expected to create defect traps as well as populate existing traps with excited electrons (e.g., Levy 1968). Dating then had the very difficult problem of not only determining the rate of trap filling but also the rate of trap creation. While some empirical methods were offered (e.g., Zeller 1968), the practical difficulties prevented a continuation of this line of research. Most geologic work at this time centered more on making luminescence characterization studies of particular minerals and pointing out many obstacles, such as complicated kinetics, in relating glow curve characteristics to time (e.g., Bonfiglioli 1968; see McKeever 1985). While some success in geologic dating has since been reported for meteorites (Sears 1988) and some kinds of calcites like stalagmites and flow stones (Debenham and Aitken 1984; Franklin et al. 1988), the main thrust of geologic applications of luminescence came later with the dating of sediments to their last exposure to light, an application with importance in archaeology as well (Roberts 1997). This was originally suggested by Russians (Morozov 1968), first made practical by a Canadian (Wintle and Huntley 1979, 1980), and further developed by Europeans and Australians. Americans played a limited role.

The Oxford group began by considering the problem of trap creation versus trap filling and concluded that a dating method based on trap creation was not practical (Tite and Wayne 1962). Tite (1966) later showed that trap creation was insignificant for time spans represented by pottery. They also demonstrated that alpha effectiveness in producing luminescence was much less than that of betas and gammas and that this effectiveness was likely to vary from sherd to sherd (Aitken et al. 1967). Failure to consider alpha effectiveness was probably the major reason early attempts at absolute ages were grossly inaccurate (Aitken et al. 1968). The lesser role of alphas makes gammas more important, and therefore consideration of the external radiation environment is necessary. They also showed early on that spurious chemoluminescence had to be controlled by heating samples in inert atmospheres and that preparation and measurements should take place in subdued light because of optical bleaching (Aitken et al. 1963).

A key observation was that neither the luminescence nor the radioactivity, particularly from short-ranged alphas, was distributed evenly within pottery (Fremlin and Srirath 1964). Using a ground portion of the entire sherd is apt to give misleading results, particularly when calibrating against artificial dose, which would affect the entire sample. Two solutions to this problem were developed at Oxford. Both depend on extracting from the sherds materials with similar dosimetric environments. The first solution was to use coarse grains of minerals with relatively small internal sources of radiation (Fleming 1966). If the grains are large enough, the alpha contribution is negligible and the luminescence can be evaluated only in terms of betas and gammas. The second approach was to only use grains fine enough that no attenuation of the alphas would occur (Zimmerman 1967) and to evaluate luminescence in terms of alphas, betas, and to a lesser extent gammas.

Finally, the Oxford group demonstrated that the growth of luminescence in pottery was not always linear; it is often supralinear at low doses and therefore requires mathematical correction (Tite 1966). Moreover, heating a sample changed the susceptibility to luminescence so that equivalent dose could not be accurately derived by regenerating the luminescence. Evaluating the luminescence by adding artificial dose to natural samples (additive dose) and the supralinearity by a regeneration was the proposed solution (Fleming 1970; Zimmerman 1971).

By the early 1970s, most of the obstacles toward achieving absolute dates on pottery had been overcome by the Oxford group (see review by Seeley 1975). While continued refinements have been made, the basic procedures for pottery have remained unchanged. If dating pottery is not now routine, it is only because luminescence dating depends heavily on localized factors that in any one situation can frustrate dating efforts. Kojo (1991) provides an American example where Southwest sherds of known age produced precise and accurate TL dates in two situations but not in a third. The author (who used a Japanese laboratory for the work) proposed that an underestimation in the latter may be due to radon emanation, but other possibilities, such as anomalous fading, were not considered.

There were some American attempts to follow the Oxford lead. Most prominent was at Washington University in St. Louis, where physicist Robert Walker engaged David and Joan Zimmerman, both students of Aitken's at Oxford, to establish a Center for Archeometry. Dating work on archaeological materials as well as meteorites (Walker's interest) was undertaken (e.g., Kornmeier and Sutton 1985; Sutton 1985), but the laboratory suffered a major setback with D. Zimmerman's untimely death in 1978 and was eventually closed. Another effort to use luminescence to date heat-treated chert artifacts was begun in the late 1970s at the University of Florida. After some initial work (Maurer and Purdy 1986; Purdy 1985), the project ceased due to lack of continued funding. In 1982, Beta Analytic, a commercial radiocarbon laboratory, opened a TL branch (called Alpha Analytic), but the effort proved uneconomical and was shut down in 1987. More recently, dating work at the University of Maryland (laboratory since closed), Ohio State University, Western Washington University (laboratory now moved to the

Desert Research Institute in Reno), and the University of Washington (Feathers 1997a) has begun to establish luminescence as a viable dating alternative in the United States.

Nevertheless, the legacy of the early American failures lives on. The National Science Foundation was reluctant for many years to put much money into luminescence dating. A brief survey of introductory textbooks to archaeology or ceramics shows that most cite only the early MASCA work (e.g., Fagan 1975, 1988; Hester et al. 1975; Sharer and Ashmore 1979), dismiss the reliability of the technique (Ashmore and Sharer 1996; Joukowsky 1980; Sinopoli 1991), give it only brief mention (Thomas 1989), or fail to mention it at all (Rathje and Schiffer 1982; see Rice 1987 for an exception). The luminescence section in the various editions of Fagan's *In the Beginning* (from 1975 to 1988), remained unchanged despite substantial development in technique and method. This contrasts with European treatment where Sheridan Bowman (1991), for example, puts luminescence on an equal footing with radiocarbon as the two most important dating techniques for archaeology.

DEMAND SIDE

While reliable luminescence work has been slow to emerge in the United States, lack of access cannot fully explain the low interest in luminescence by American archaeologists. Canada has no less than four laboratories, and Europeans have from time to time made forays into American archaeology (e.g., Huxtable et al. 1972; Stokes 1992). The low interest stems from the perception of its usefulness, or lack thereof, to American archaeology.

A common perception of luminescence (in Europe as well as America) is as a technique to be used only where radiocarbon dating is not possible. Bowman (1991) lists four situations where luminescence is useful: (1) beyond the range of radiocarbon, (2) where no organic materials are preserved, (3) where association of the organics to the event of interest is poor, and (4) during periods where the radiocarbon calibration curve is so flat that luminescence can provide better accuracy. Indeed, the most celebrated achievements of luminescence are the dating of the origins of anatomically modern humans (Mercier et al. 1995) and the initial settlement of Australia (Roberts et al. 1994), both of which are beyond the reach of radiocarbon.

Luminescence dating is thus seen as the poor cousin of radiocarbon dating, a technique with inherently better precision. Such comparison, I think, shortchanges luminescence for at least two reasons. One is confusion between precision and accuracy (Dunnell and Readhead 1988). Radiocarbon may have better precision, but a more important comparison may be in accuracy. The other reason is more to the point. Luminescence can be very useful for addressing certain chronological research issues. In these situations, it might be more appropriate to favor luminescence and turn to radiocarbon (or some other dating technique) only where luminescence is not viable.

Precision vs. Accuracy

Radiocarbon has good precision because only a few variables, generally just count rate or carbon isotopic abundance, require measurement. Luminescence requires the measurement of a multitude of variables, each with its own error term, which when propagated lower precision. However, when it comes to arriving at the correct answer (accuracy), radiocarbon has some disadvantages. One, because of temporal variation in the cosmic flux, radiocarbon dates must be calibrated to achieve calendrical dates. In periods where the calibration curve is relatively flat, radiocarbon can come up with multiple possibilities, covering a range that obviates the precision advantage. Luminescence directly produces calendrical dates that require no further calibration. The basic luminescence equation (equivalent dose divided by dose rate) is written in terms of time before present, and no systematic error common to all samples biases the result.

A more important disadvantage of radiocarbon dating is the problem of association. The event dated by radiocarbon is the isolation from the carbon cycle by the death of living cells. Except in the case where the organic material is the object of interest (development of corn agriculture, e.g., Crawford et al. 1997), radiocarbon dates must be historically linked to other events of archaeological interest, such as artifact manufacture. This is done by association. This is not required by luminescence, which in many cases dates artifact manufacturing events directly. Historical association is an accuracy problem that has long been recognized, but seldom are error terms assigned to the bridging arguments that must be made to make the association (Dean 1978), probably because they are almost impossible to quantify. Only qualitative arguments, based on locational proximity and integrity of context, are usually given. A fair comparison of the two methods in any situation must include all systematic errors (including association), as well as random error.

An example of problems in association-based dating has been in determining the antiquity of mound building in the Southeast. The demonstration of pre–Poverty Point mounds has been controversial (Russo 1994) because diagnostic artifacts or radiocarbon dates that can be unequivocally associated with the construction of the mounds are rare (Gibson 1994). But if the mound construction material or a buried surface has been adequately exposed to sunlight, luminescence dating of the sediments can potentially address a construction episode directly. In a pilot project to test the feasibility of dating mounds by luminescence, the University of Washington laboratory recently completed analysis of three sediment samples collected from buried surfaces at Watson Brake mounds and Poverty Point in northeastern Louisiana (Feathers 1997b). By comparing results from TL and OSL, we were able to demonstrate that the sediments were in fact poorly exposed in antiquity, but further analysis of the OSL showed that one of the samples from Watson Brake was sufficiently exposed for an OSL date. The other two samples provided only maximum dates (Table 8.1). But this analysis, not the best that luminescence can offer, nevertheless unambiguously demonstrated the antiquity of Watson Brake and also showed that Poverty Point was occupied much later than is often assumed.

TABLE 8.1. Luminescence Dates for Mound Sites in Southeastern Louisiana

Site	Luminescence Date
Watson Brake Ridge	4003 ± 444 B.P.
Watson Brake Mound B	5538 ± 936 B.P.*
Poverty Point Ridge	2142 ± 424 B.P.*

* = Maximum date.

Measuring Change

Association-based dating is also not very useful for measuring rates of change, the tempo at which one set of artifacts rises in frequency at the expense of another set. The rate of change is important for understanding the mechanism of change. A good example is the rise in frequency of shell-tempered pottery in the Eastern woodlands. Shell-tempered pottery replaced earlier pottery tempered with other materials during the Late Prehistoric over much of this region. How quickly did shell replace the other tempers? This question can be directly addressed by luminescence. One simply dates a large number of sherds producing a possible age range for each one. One then takes any length of time, counts how many dates for each kind of pottery intersects that time, and compares them to an earlier or later equal span of time. The rate of change can then be quantified with an error term.

The task is much more difficult with association-based dating, unless one-to-one association of dates to sherds is possible, and this is probably never the case. The best that can be accomplished is to associate groups of sherds with a date, at an often debilitating cost in resolution. For example, shell-tempered pottery appeared in high frequencies by the eleventh century in northern Alabama. But it first appeared at least a century earlier in assemblages that also contained a large number of grog-tempered sherds. Archaeologists have dated by association three periods of time: period A when only grog-tempered pottery was made, period B when both grog- and shell-tempered pottery were made, and period C when mostly shell-tempered pottery was made. Because all of the pottery from period B is associated with the radiocarbon dates for that period, archaeologists do not know if the grog- and shell-tempered pottery was made at the same time or if all the grog-tempered pottery dates to the early part of period B and all the shell-tempered pottery dates to the late part of period B. Current debate around the rise of social complexity in the mid-South revolves in part around the rate of ceramic change (Blitz 1993; Jenkins 1981; Mistovich 1988; Steponaitis 1983; Welch 1994). If all the shell-tempered pottery appeared at once, the argument for an external source for complexity (as in a migration) is strengthened. If the pottery change was gradual, internal sources might seem more reasonable. Only direct dating of the pottery can resolve the issue.

More serious methodological problems arise with association-based dating if one assumes, as is often the case, that the association between a kind of pottery and a radiocarbon date in one place holds for the same kind of pottery found in other places. Shell-tempered pottery has been so often associated with the Late Prehistoric that its appearance in older contexts is often assumed to mean some postdepositional intrusion or mixing (Allsbrook 1995; Webb and DeJarnette 1942). The argument is circular and prevents understanding how a particular artifact like shell-tempered pottery came into prominence, short of assuming some large-scale transformational change: no shell-tempered pottery before the Late Prehistoric, suddenly shell-tempered pottery everywhere (Plog 1973). The alternative, that shell-tempered pottery first appeared in low frequencies and then rose in prominence, is precluded by the assumption, even though it is plainly possible.

Another example where association-based dating may be obscuring the process of change is the early pottery sequence of southeastern Mesoamerica. This is a region that has long had chronological problems due to stratigraphic complexities, lack of sites exhibiting the full sequence, and poor preservation of organics. The region also has archaeological importance because of the early appearance of social complexity. An assumption governing traditional approaches to the chronology is that the stylistic sequence of ceramics is panregional, the development passing through the same series of "horizons" at every location. The available radiocarbon record has been interpreted in a way that reinforces the horizon concept (Blake et al. 1995). Because of difficulties with association, not all radiocarbon dates are believed accurate reflections of the ceramic ages. Using a statistical approach, all significant outlying dates from the mean of all ^{14}C determinations associated with a particular kind of ceramic are eliminated. By assuming any outliers are due to inaccurate associations, however, this approach precludes another possible interpretation: that more than one ceramic tradition is available in the area and the sequence may vary from place to place in both content and timing according to purely local developments defined by variable selective pressures or degree of interaction with other groups (Neff and Arroyo 1996). Again, directly dating the ceramics can resolve the competing interpretations—something currently being undertaken by the University of Washington laboratory. Although only a handful of ceramic dates are available at present, a comparison of these dates with the sequence of Blake et al. (1995) (Table 8.2) suggests the pottery is not going to fall into neat chronological steps. The various subdivisions of the widespread Ocós tradition have considerable overlap. The Cuadros tradition (of which Navarijo is a precursor in the Guatemala region; Neff and Arroyo 1996) also extends earlier and later than the conventional dates (even though the earliest date from Salvador Aquino seems rather anomalous).

In each of the above examples, association-based dating, because it cannot resolve the chronology of change, is unable to provide data that can distinguish between competing interpretations of how the change took place. This contrasts with the direct dating possible with luminescence, which should be the method of choice for these kinds of questions.

TABLE 8.2. Luminescence Versus Radiocarbon Dating, Southeastern
Mesoamerica Prevailing Radiocarbon Model (Blake et al. 1995)

Pottery	Radiocarbon Dates (years B.C.)
Ocós Tradition	
Barra	1850–1650
Locona	1650–1500
Ocós	1500–1350
Cherla (Navarijo)	1350–1200
Cuadros Tradition	
Cuadros	1200–1100
Jocotal	1000–950

	Luminescence Dates	
Sherd	Type	TL Date (years B.C.)
Salvador Aquino 3	Cuadros	3498 ± 975*
Leonidas 7	Barra	1872 ± 359
Quiñonez 3	Ocós	1856 ± 433*
Sinaloa 4	Navarijo	1606 ± 291*
Leonidas 5	Locona	1263 ± 469
San Carlos 3	Ocós	1252 ± 285
Leonidas 3	Locona	1149 ± 383
Leonidas 2	Locona	1146 ± 271
Sinaloa 2	Cuadros	784 ± 232

* = These dates must be accepted with caution due to problems in the luminescence
analysis.

Landscape Archaeology

Beginning at least with the settlement studies of Willey (1953)
and certainly accelerated by the demands of CRM, archaeologists have
increasingly become interested in changes through time of entire
human landscapes (Rossignol and Wandsnider 1992). This kind of
study in many cases relies on artifacts collected from the surface,
where association-based dating is particularly deficient. Establishing
historical relatedness is rather problematic where long periods of accumulation can make the record more or less continuous across space or
result in "palimpsests" of successive occupations (Beck 1994:3–13).
(The same problems exist, of course, for buried materials that, while
presently capped, were once on the surface themselves.) Here the establishment of historical associations requires dating rather than the dating
being dependent on associations (Dunnell 1992).

The University of Washington laboratory has been involved in the past several years with dating surface ceramics from the Desert West. Table 8.3 shows some dates derived from seven brownware ceramics from the southern Great Basin (Feathers and Rhode 1997). Brownwares have been associated with Numic speakers, and their distribution has been used to infer a Numic expansion into the Great Basin during the Late Prehistoric, but temporal controls have been poor. The dates achieve a level of resolution that has not been possible with traditional dating, which has lumped all the brownwares into a 600–800 year time span. While many more dates are needed to chart the Numic expansion, these initial dates suggest the bulk of brownwares, at least in the southern region (see also Rhode 1994b) date after A.D. 1400.

TABLE 8.3. Luminescence Dates of Brownware Ceramics from the Great Basin (Feathers and Rhode 1997)

Age (A.D.)
1762 ± 21
1540 ± 49
1450 ± 79
1840 ± 26
1638 ± 85
1787 ± 41
1476 ± 55

Even in regions that are better known, mapping changes in settlement patterns will require dating of small sites containing nondiagnostic artifacts. Much of what is known about Mississippian settlement comes from work at large centers. In many areas these centers are surrounded by dozens of small, unremarkable sherd scatters, whose relationship to the large centers is often unknown. The University of Washington laboratory is beginning a project to date several small sites in the Southeast. One date (A.D. 1140 ± 88) already obtained from upland regions of eastern Mississippi is much earlier than would be expected from conventional understanding of settlement dynamics, which place the small upland sites in the Late Prehistoric and protohistoric (Peacock 1995, Peacock and Rafferty 1995).

CONCLUSIONS

The underutilization of luminescence dating in American archaeology can be traced both to an inadequate product delivered by early American practitioners of luminescence (as well as ignorance of the developments in Europe) and to a perception of luminescence as simply a second-choice dating method turned to when other dating methods cannot be applied. This perception must change, however, as American archaeologists begin to address questions other than simple cultural history, such as technological change, localized variations in development, and landscape evolution. The methodological deficiencies of association-based dating in addressing these questions become apparent when luminescence dates are compared to those obtained conventionally.

At the same time, the technique of luminescence dating has become more and more refined, as the theoretical basis for the method is becoming better understood (McKeever and Chen 1997). Research in sediment dating, in particular, has seen many recent advances (Prescott and Robertson 1997; Roberts 1997). Precision better than 10% is often achieved for both sediments and ceramics (e.g., Mejdahl and Bøtter-Jensen 1994). Intercomparison among laboratories is just beginning with promising results (e.g., Michab et al. 1998; Rees-Jones et al. 1997). Costs are coming down. A TL date on pottery costs less than an AMS date.

A wider application of luminescence dating has the potential of changing and refining a great deal of what we understand about prehistory.

PART IV

Historical Records and Narrative

Dendrochronology and Historical Records: Concordance and Conflict in Navajo Archaeology

RONALD H. TOWNER
Laboratory of Tree-Ring Research
University of Arizona

Tree-ring and historical records are the most precise dating techniques available for studying the recent past. Whether or not an individual historic reference or tree-ring date accurately places a specific event in time, however, is a question archaeologists must seriously consider. Historical records have provided the only independent means of verifying tree-ring dates; dendrochronology, on the other hand, has often confirmed historical reconstructions and provided a check on historical references.

Historical records and tree-ring dates are both precise and, presumably, accurate. Historical records are often precise to the year, month, day, or even hour. Tree-ring dates are precise to the year, and in some cases, to the tree-growing season (Dean and Warren 1983). The accuracy of tree-ring dates is confirmed by their agreement with hundreds, if not thousands, of like specimens that cross-date with the master tree-ring chronology for a given area. Likewise, the accuracy of historical documents is confirmed by their agreement with other documents reporting the same event or phenomena. Prior to their acceptance by archaeologists and historians, however, both dendrochronological dates and historical records must be assessed in terms of their accuracy and reliability.

Because of their precision, dendrochronology and historical records have been intertwined since dendrochronology's beginnings early in the twentieth century. Unlike the use of tree-rings to calibrate radiocarbon or ceramic time scales, dendrochronology and historical records have in this country maintained their status as independent dating techniques. In the early 1900s, when Andrew Ellicott Douglass was developing the methods of dendrochronology, he was living in the Flagstaff area—an area that was being actively logged. By examining the stumps and cross sections of ponderosa pine trees, Douglass identified the "Flagstaff signature" ring series that contained small rings at specific years in the late 1880s, 1890s, and early 1900s (Webb 1983). The first significant test of Douglass's fledgling method occurred in 1904 when he deduced, by cross-dating tree-ring series, that a particular tree in the area had been cut 10 years previously. Douglass confirmed his deduction in discussions with the farmer who admitted that he had, in fact, cut the tree in 1894 (Webb 1983:104). Thus a historical record, in this case an oral history, was used to confirm the tree felling date offered by Douglass. This short exchange demonstrated the veracity of his technique and suggested that, with no small uniformitarianist assumption, his method could be used to apply year-by-year tree-ring chronologies to events prior to the historic period. Douglass went on to develop tree-ring chronologies for a number of areas using purely dendrochronological methods. His first test of cross-dating outside the Flagstaff area occurred when he examined specimens from the Prescott, Arizona, area and discerned the same pattern of wide and narrow rings in the late 1800s and early 1900s. This ring-series "signature" demonstrated that dendrochronology could have wide geographic applicability. Although Douglass later used archaeological data to select specific sites for dendrochronological sampling (Nash 1997a), the tree-ring dates he derived were independent of those data—a point reiterated by Dean (1969a). For the purposes of this volume, however, it is important to remember that the first test of the accuracy of tree-ring cross-dating had been provided by an oral history.

In contrast to the independent development of tree-ring dating in North American archaeology, the initial archaeological tree-ring chronologies developed by Bruno Huber for oak specimens in Europe relied on abundant historical documents, primarily building construction dates, to firmly anchor the series in time (Baillie 1982, 1995; Huber and Giertz 1969; Liese 1978). Because churches and other buildings were constructed during the historic period, and often had their construction dates noted on corner stones, they provided key "anchor points" connecting living trees with archaeological chronologies (Baillie 1995). Additional specimens were used to fill the "gaps" and create long tree-ring chronologies. When the European chronologies were extended into the prehistoric period using bog wood and other sample types, however, only dendrochronological methods were used. With the establishment of long oak chronologies in Europe (Baillie 1982, 1995), it became possible to check historical records against tree-ring dates, and vice-versa. In this regard, European archaeologists interested in the period of overlap between tree-ring dates and historical records have had much more experience evaluating the relationship between the two dating techniques, for the historical record in North America begins much later in time.

The European case is relevant to this discussion in several ways. In the years since the development of the long chronologies, European dendrochronologists have been called upon to date numerous historical events that were thought to have occurred at known times. The construction dates of various Viking ships (Bonde 1994), the harvesting dates of the wood used in historical paintings (Eckstein et al. 1986; Fletcher 1986), and the volcanic eruption of Santorini (Baillie 1982, 1995), to name just a few significant events, have all been subject to dendrochronological analysis. In each of these cases, the dendrochronologically derived dates have proven to be more accurate than historically or archaeologically derived dates. Although there have been controversies and initial disagreements, such as those surrounding the precise date of the eruption of Santorini (Baillie 1982, 1995), European historians have come to rely on tree-ring dating much more than have their American counterparts studying the historical period. In their analyses, tree-ring dates are always given precedence over historical records when discord is discovered between the two datasets. As Niels Bonde and Arne Christensen (1993) write: "Within recent decades dendrochronology has established itself as one of the most important scientific dating methods in northwest European archaeology.... The result is often so precise that every recognized theory which conflicts with it is immediately discredited." This has not been the case in North American archaeology or history.

This paper examines the use of historical documents and dendrochronology in one of the few areas of contemporary American research where these techniques overlap: the study of the Navajo past. Research concerning the Navajo occupation of the northern Southwest can utilize thousands of tree-ring dates from Navajo sites, as well as numerous historical documents, and provides an excellent opportunity to assess the relative importance and efficacy of each technique for interpreting the recent past.

EVALUATING HISTORICAL RECORDS

Through the use of rigorous methods and analyses that are beyond the scope of this paper, historians have been able to assess the authenticity and reliability of historical records across a wide geographic area and in a number of different contexts. They have concluded that specific documents must meet certain criteria before being accepted as "authentic and reliable" sources (Gottschalk 1955). These criteria include but are not limited to the following: (1) the nature of the document, (2) the language of the document, (3) the proximity of the document's author to the subject of the document, (4) the temporal relationship between the writing of the document and the subject being discussed, (5) the cultural and political relationship of the author to the subject, and (6) the number of independent accounts that verify or discredit the account provided by the subject.

The nature of the document refers to whether a document offers primary, secondary, or tertiary accounts. Primary accounts are preferable because they have not been subject to change, or error, via transmission. The childhood game of "telephone," as well as adult gossip and hearsay, should alert researchers to the interpretive dangers associated with secondary documents. Wood (1990:83) indicates that "secondary documents…are to be used with caution." This is not, however, to say that secondary documents are without merit. They often summarize important information and provide valuable data and references. It must be remembered, however, that secondary documents offer interpretations of primary documents and are therefore one step removed from the event of interest.

The language of a document is important for several reasons. If the document being used is a translation of an original, questions may arise as to the accuracy of the translation. One need only look at the different versions of the Bible, and the schisms they have caused, to realize the dangers of translations. More relevant for Southwestern archaeologists, Chardon (1980) shows how the measure "league" had seven different distances associated with it, depending on the translation used. Not everyone can, or should, read sixteenth-century Castilian Spanish, but it should be obvious that if different translations of a text are available, all should be consulted.

The proximity of a document's author to the topic presented directly influences the nature of a document. One must ask: Was the author an "eyewitness" to the subject? If not, one must determine how he or she acquired the information presented. "The testimony of one

who was on the scene...is generally more credible than that of someone who was not there; the testimony of a nonwitness is hearsay evidence...and must be regarded with suspicion" (Wood 1990:88).

The temporal relationship of a document to the subject being discussed is important because memories often fail and perceptions and
ideologies tend to change. Was the document written during or
immediately after a particular event, or was it written long after the
fact? In this case, diaries kept by participants may be the most useful
type of document for describing a specific event. For example, Lewis
and Clark's journals (Clark 1964) provide abundant, and relatively
accurate, information on the flora, fauna, and geography of the
northern Rocky Mountains and lower Columbia River drainage. In
contrast, "memoirs" written decades later are often far less informative. To use a recent example, Richard Nixon's memoirs (Nixon
1978) differ markedly from contemporary newspaper accounts of the
same events.

The cultural and political relationship of the writer to the recorded
event can be critical for assessing the reliability of an account. Because
many of the early documents pertaining to the peoples of the Southwest were written by Spaniards, one needs to know if the author actually knew and understood what he or she was witnessing. Was the
author relying on an interpreter? If so, how fluent was the interpreter
in Spanish and the many and varied Native American languages with
which he or she was dealing? Is there a political agenda hidden in the
account (Shafer 1980)? That is, was the author trying to promote or
downplay his or her role in an event? Was he or she trying to gain
additional funding or support for a cause? Is the document part of
"official testimony" that may have been impacted by the possible ramifications of that testimony, as was the case with the Spanish Inquisi-
tion? An interesting example of possible cultural misunderstanding is
provided by Edmund Ladd's (1998) contention that the Zuni were
conducting ceremonies when Coronado arrived. Ladd suggests that the
Zuni asked the Conquistador and his Entrada to wait until the end of
the ceremonial cycle to enter the pueblo, but Coronado interpreted
their request as an act of defiance and started a battle that had immediate and long-term consequences.

Truly independent corroboration can substantially strengthen the
reliability of a document. Wood (1990:90) indicates that "a single statement, even by an unimpeachable source, can never be accepted without
reservation," as is the case with single tree-ring dates (Ahlstrom 1985).

Wood also notes, however, that seemingly independent historic observations may have originated from a single source, and that, therefore, duplication does not imply corroboration.

EVALUATING TREE-RING DATA

Like historical documents, tree-ring dates must be evaluated individually within their contexts. Unlike historical documents, we know the individual dates are accurate if they are properly cross-dated. We know they are accurate because the tree-ring sequences cross-date with hundreds or thousands of other trees that responded in the same way to broad climatic patterns across a broad area. If a sample does not cross-date with the master chronology, it is simply not given a date.

The interpretation of tree-ring dates, however, must be performed using specific methods. Dendrochronologists such as Haury (1935), Bannister (1962), Dean (1978), Ahlstrom (1985), and Nash (1997b) have developed specific criteria for evaluating tree-ring dates; these include (1) the types of dates, (2) the date range, (3) the range of cutting dates, (4) the presence of date clusters, (5) the identification of construction events, (6) the possible behavioral explanations for "anomalous" dates, and (7) the presence of other lines of evidence that support (or do not support) the dates.

Tree-ring dates give precise years of cambial growth on specific samples. Thus, as Dean (1978) pointed out two decades ago, the dated event on a tree-ring sample is a biological, not cultural, phenomenon. It is completely independent of archaeological or cultural events. It is necessary for archaeologists and dendrochronologists to relate the biological event of ring growth to the cultural event of interest.

Noncutting tree-ring dates indicate the growth year of the last ring on a sample, not the year the tree died. Thus, single noncutting dates can provide only a terminal date before which tree death could not have occurred. In contrast, cutting dates denote the year of tree death. Assuming the tree was cut by humans, cutting dates generally date both a biological (tree death) and a behavioral (tree felling) event. A single cutting date, however, may not date the target event of interest (Dean 1978). The tree-ring date itself is an accurate and precise measure of the year (and possibly season) of tree death, but if the event of interest is the use of dead wood, for example, the date may be irrelevant.

Date clustering is perhaps dendrochronology's greatest strength (Ahlstrom 1985; Haury 1935). A cluster of cutting dates, defined as

three or more cutting dates in the same tree-growing year, helps identify anomalous dates and various past human behaviors. Ahlstrom
(1985) suggests that a strong terminal cluster in a date distribution,
defined as a group of cutting dates at the end of a distribution, is a
good indicator of building construction. Anomalous dates, for example a cutting date that occurs several years earlier than a terminal cluster, may indicate behaviors such as beam reuse. Similarly, a tree-ring
date that postdates construction typically indicates repair of a structure. Date clustering is important and can be accomplished only by the
collection and dating of an adequate number of samples.

It is clear that both dendrochronologists and historians have developed methods for evaluating their respective datasets. It is imperative,
however, that archaeologists investigating the Protohistoric and Early
Historic periods (Wilcox and Masse 1981) learn to employ these methods in their analyses. The discussion that follows suggests that few
researchers interested in the Navajo occupation of the Southwest have
used either discipline to the fullest extent possible.

TREE-RING DATING, HISTORY, AND NAVAJO ARCHAEOLOGY

Navajo archaeology offers one of the best frameworks in
American archaeology for evaluating the relationship between tree-
ring dates and historical records. The examples offered below discuss
the use of dendrochronological and historical data to assess the
Navajo entry into, occupation of, and abandonment of their traditional homeland of Dinétah in northwestern New Mexico. Other
examples of overlap between historical documents and tree-ring dates
generally relate to one particular site, such as Walpi (Ahlstrom et al.
1991) or Acoma (Robinson 1990). The Navajo case, however, includes
more than 1,000 sites spread over much of northwestern New Mexico
and northeastern Arizona. There are literally hundreds of tree-ring
dates from these sites and an abundance of historical documents and
oral histories relating to the Navajo occupation of and mobility within
the northern Southwest. With one notable exception, however, both
archaeologists and historians have generally used historical records
uncritically and ignored much of the archaeological and dendrochronological data.

Concordance in Navajo Archaeology: The Black Mesa Project
The best example of concordance between tree-ring data and

written or oral histories is contained in the archaeological research record of Black Mesa, in northeastern Arizona. As part of the Black Mesa Archaeological Project (BMAP), more than a thousand Navajo archaeological sites were examined and ethnographic interviews were conducted with the "owners" of those sites whenever possible (Rocek 1995; Russell 1983). All dendrochronologically sampled sites had been abandoned and were uninhabited but still belonged to the original owners or their descendants. Intensive dendrochronological sampling of a variety of structure types yielded a plethora of both cutting and noncutting dates relevant to the Navajo occupation of the area (Dean and Russell 1978; Rocek 1995).

Dean and Russell (1978) compared the oral histories recorded for the sites with the dendrochronological data in order to examine a number of variables relating to wood use behavior, including construction dates, construction seasonality, frequency of repair and remodeling, the use of stockpiled and dead wood in construction, species preferences, and a number of other variables for a variety of structures. These datasets were gathered independently and only later compared.

In general, the ethnographic data agreed with the dendrochronological data for most variables, including year and season of tree procurement, structure construction and repair dates, and site occupation duration. Historical events, such as the influenza epidemic of 1918–1919 and the stock reduction program of the 1930s, are clearly documented in the dendrochronological and historical records, and were confirmed by oral histories.

The influenza epidemic of 1918–1919 resulted in the death of millions of people world wide, and inhabitants of Black Mesa were not excluded from its wrath. Hogans in which a death occurred ("Chindi hogans") were abandoned and never reoccupied. Tree-ring cutting dates show a significant gap in tree harvesting activities at the same time, and demonstrate a lack of repairs on Chindi hogans (Dean and Russell 1978). The forced stock reduction program of the 1930s left its own archaeological and dendrochronological signatures. Because sheep were a primary target of stock reduction, their numbers declined dramatically (Bailey and Bailey 1986). Rocek (1995:108–111) demonstrated that the size of dated sheep corrals declined coincidentally.

The only area of consistent discordance between oral histories and dendrochronology of the BMAP occurred over species identification. Some informants stated specific preferences for using a particular species in a specific structure type (usually hogans), but the true species distribution was found to reflect local environmental conditions regardless of the stated preferences (Dean and Russell 1978).

The BMAP study is important because it is one of the few examples of ethnohistoric and dendrochronological information being used to address the same set of research issues, and certainly the best. Importantly, the dendrochronological and ethnographic data tend to affirm each other, although each database was derived independently.

Discordance in Navajo Archaeology and Dendrochronology

Many aspects of Navajo archaeology, particularly for periods prior to A.D. 1800, have been explored using historical, ethnohistorical, and dendrochronological data (Brugge 1983, 1986; Hester 1962). Tree-ring dates and ethnohistorical data tend to be utilized in these analyses only if they agree with Euro-American documents. Although the historical documents for the pre-1800 era are sparser than for later periods, the archaeological and ethnohistorical data are routinely ignored in favor of the limited Spanish accounts. The three examples of conflict between historical and dendrochronological data presented below were chosen because each relates to a critical period in Navajo cultural development and ethnogenesis. Thus, the bias toward Euro-American documents has had important consequences for our understanding of the Navajo occupation of the northern Southwest.

The Athabaskan Entry into the Southwest. The first example concerns the initial immigration of Athabaskans into the Southwest. The most accepted model of this process is the Late Entry–High Plains model (Wilcox 1981) and suggests that the Athabaskan ancestors of the Navajo, identified as the "Querecho," entered the Southwest via the High Plains of Colorado and New Mexico just prior to Coronado's Entrada of 1540, possibly as early as 1525, but certainly later than A.D. 1500 (Gunnerson 1987; Gunnerson and Gunnerson 1988). Wilcox's model presents an elegant theoretical argument for the use of Puebloan "hinterlands" by the Athabaskans (Wilcox 1981:324), but its empirical underpinnings are based on questionable ethnohistorical data. Historic accounts suggest that while Coronado camped at Pecos Pueblo (Cucuye) in 1540–1541, one of the Pecoseños told him that "the Querechos" had only been "visiting" Pecos for 16 years prior to Coronado's Entrada. In other words, if the Querechos were Athabaskans, they had been in the vicinity of Pecos only since about A.D. 1525 (Gunnerson and Gunnerson 1988). The historical reference for this model is thus a questionable second-hand reference that describes a process, not an event, and that was translated through at least two languages.

The archaeological and dendrochronological support for the Late Entry–High Plains model is virtually nonexistent. As of this writing, there are no known, well-dated, pre-1540 Athabaskan sites on the High Plains. James Gunnerson (1969, 1987) describes Apachean sites in northeastern New Mexico, but none can be demonstrated to have been occupied earlier than the late 1600s. Wilcox (1981:234) suggested more than 15 years ago that "once some of these sites [pre-1540 Athabaskan sites] are identified—or are shown not to exist—it will be possible to better evaluate this model and alternatives to it." In the nearly two decades since Wilcox proposed his model and after much additional field work, the earliest Athabaskan sites on the High Plains are still the Apache sites described by Gunnerson (1969).

Significantly, there are no historical documents relating to the traditional Navajo homeland in northwestern New Mexico where the earliest dated Navajo sites are located. This lack of written documentation does not mean, of course, that the Navajo were not present in Dinétah at the time; it is simply a function of Spanish interest elsewhere. On the other hand, there are tree-ring dated Navajo habitation sites—not generalized Athabaskan camps—in northwestern New Mexico that date to the 1500s (Hancock 1997; Sesler and Hovezak 1996) and radiocarbon-dated sites that date to the early 1400s and late 1300s (Hogan 1989; Reed and Horn 1990). These data suggest that the earliest sites occupied by Athabaskan-speaking peoples in the Southwest are not on the High Plains at all but occur in the upper San Juan drainage. Nevertheless, many archaeologists and historians still accept the Late Entry–High Plains model as *the* explanation of Athabaskan entry into the Southwest (cf. Hendricks and Wilson 1996; Schaafsma 1996).

In fairness to Wilcox, all of the early tree-ring-dated Navajo sites were investigated after his 1981 publication appeared (Wilcox 1981), and at that time, the only archaeological evidence of a pre-1680 Navajo occupation of the Dinétah was Hall's (1951) tree-ring dates from a single hogan. Nevertheless, Navajo oral traditions are clear and unambiguous regarding the location of their homeland as Dinétah. Largely uncritical acceptance of meager historical data led Wilcox to develop the Late Entry–High Plains model.

The Refugee Influx. The second example of discordance between historical and dendrochronological data concerns the supposedly massive immigration of Puebloans into the Navajo country following the

Pueblo Revolt of A.D. 1680 and the subsequent Spanish Reconquest of the area between 1692 and 1696 (Hester 1962; Schaafsma 1996). The supposed immigrant populations, known as Puebloan refugees, are postulated to have "had a dramatic impact on all aspects of Navajo life" (Hester 1962). Indeed, Garrick Bailey and Roberta Bailey (1986) suggest that Navajo culture itself—as distinct from that of other Athabaskans—developed as a direct result of the refugee influx at the end of the seventeenth century.

The primary historical evidence for the Puebloan refugee influx consists of a comment by an unidentified man from Jemez, New Mexico, to Adolph Bandelier that "some Jemez moved to the Navajo to escape the Spanish and stayed about 10 years" (Bandelier 1890–1892). Additional support for the "refugee influx" comes from the Rabal Document (Hill 1940), which contains testimony of soldiers, recorded in 1744, who had participated in campaigns against the Navajo in the early 1700s. Their statements, recorded after a delay of more than 25 years, were given during investigations into supposed violations by the Spanish administrations. The testimony is therefore likely to be biased by selective recollection, attempts to avoid self-incrimination, and a host of other factors that have not been considered.

Archaeologists have also failed to consider another important aspect of the historical record. The entradas that brought Spanish soldiers into the Navajo country served two purposes: They sought to punish the Navajos for raiding various pueblos and sought to rescue Puebloans from their Navajo captors. The Spaniards did in fact return numerous Puebloans to the Rio Grande Valley, but they were captives, not refugees. Hogan's (1991) reanalysis of the historical data has shown that the majority of Puebloans who fled the Rio Grande Valley after 1680 went to other pueblos, such as Hopi and Zuni, and not to the Navajo country after all.

Kidder (1920) used Bandelier's informant data and Morris's archaeological evidence (Carlson 1965) to posit ethnic coresidence of Pueblo and Navajo populations in the pueblitos of Dinétah. Historians such as Jack Forbes (1960) and Frank McNitt (1972) cited Kidder's work to confirm the immigration of Puebloan refugees into the Navajo country. Patrick Hogan's (1991) recent research, however, shows that historians cited Kidder for the massive immigration and that later archaeologists closed the circle by citing the historians. Thus, until quite recently, what has been lacking is an independent assessment of the historical and archaeological evidence pertaining to the hypothesized immigration.

Reexamination of the archaeological and dendrochronological evidence for a massive immigration suggests that the hypothesis has been severely overstated as a factor in Navajo cultural development.

Two types of archaeological evidence have been used to support the Puebloan immigration model: Gobernador Polychrome ceramics and pueblito masonry structures. Gobernador Polychrome, a high-fired, tricolor ware, has been described as "Navaho made but Pueblo inspired" (Keur 1944), and has been cited as strong evidence of a refugee influx (Hester 1962). Recently, however, Michael Marshall (1991, 1995) demonstrated that Gobernador Polychrome rarely constitutes more than 10% of the ceramics on any pueblito site and that Puebloan trade wares rarely constitute as much as 8% of the ceramics. If Gobernador Polychrome was made by Puebloan refugees, they apparently produced very little of it. In addition, Reed and Reed (1996) and Sesler and Hovezak (1996) demonstrated that Gobernador Polychrome was manufactured prior to the Pueblo Revolt of 1680 and possibly as early as 1630. These new data do not invalidate the idea that Gobernador Polychrome was "inspired" by Puebloans, but they do eliminate post-Revolt refugees as the source of that inspiration.

The masonry pueblitos of Dinétah were hypothesized to be refugee constructions because they were made of stone, which is not a traditional Navajo building material, and dated to the historic period on the basis of evidence for metal tools and historic period ceramics (Kidder 1920). With one notable exception, pueblito masonry is "columnar-style construction" (Powers and Johnson 1987) and is more similar to Apache masonry (Donaldson and Welch 1995) than to traditional Puebloan or Anasazi styles. Nevertheless, Hogan (1991) argued that Navajo masons used local archaeological ruins as "templates" for their construction efforts.

Extensive dendrochronological analysis of nearly 1,000 tree-ring samples from more than 60 pueblitos demonstrates conclusively that all but two of the supposed refugee sites were built almost 20 years *after* the supposed refugee influx and that the vast majority of the "refugee pueblitos" were built more than 30 years after the purported mass migration (Towner 1996, 1997). There are no other sites in the Navajo country that were occupied during the interval when refugees could have been entering the area. Despite the historical and archaeological evidence, however, the "Refugee Hypothesis" is still widely accepted (Plog 1997).

Tapacito Ruin (LA 2298). The third example of discordance between tree-ring data and the historical record involves the one notable exception mentioned above. Tapacito Ruin (LA 2298) is a four-room, core-veneer masonry structure located on a bench above Largo Canyon. It is characterized by a number of attributes that make it unlike other pueblitos in the area. It is situated on a bench, not a large boulder or mesa rim. It is constructed with a massive core-veneer masonry style, it has a quartered-square ground plan, and lacks a ground-level entrance. The ceramic assemblage is anomalous when compared to other sites in the area. Finally, the dendrochronological data do not jibe with other sites in the area. Tapacito ruin is well dated: 12 cutting dates cluster at 1694, and 11 noncutting dates form a sequence prior to that year. The tree-ring date distribution thus approaches that of an "ideal" site constructed with only freshly cut timbers that have since suffered minimal erosion (Ahlstrom 1985). Analysis of terminal ring development indicates that Tapacito was constructed in the late summer or early fall of 1694 (Towner and Dean 1992). Based on the tree-ring dates, its unique architecture, and its ceramic assemblage, it has been interpreted as "the only true refugee site in the Dinétah" (Towner and Dean 1992). Interestingly, the construction is only slightly later than Don Diego de Vargas's attack on Jemez Pueblo, which historic accounts suggest occurred in late July 1694 (Espinosa 1988). Navajo traditions indicate that Tapacito is the ancestral home of the Coyote Pass Clan, a clan that has strong connections to the Jemez.

Recently, an archaeologist and a historian used original journal entries to trace the route of Roque de Madrid's military campaign against the Navajo in 1705 (Hendricks and Wilson 1996). Hendricks and Wilson (1996) suggest that the last battle of Madrid's campaign occurred at the confluence of Tapacito Creek and Cañon Largo. The Spaniards remained on the valley bottom but sent some of their Indian auxiliaries back up Tapacito Creek to attack the Navajos from behind. Madrid made no mention of any masonry structure near the battle site, but Hendricks and Wilson believe that Madrid's Indian auxiliaries "could hardly have missed seeing such a structure and undoubtedly would have told the Spaniards about it" (Hendricks and Wilson 1996:86). On that basis, they suggest that "the pueblito at LA 2298 had not been constructed in 1705, and whenever it was built, the wood in it was salvaged and used from another dwelling. The intact roof over one room also argues that the structure is more recent in age" (Hendricks and Wilson 1996:86).

Tapacito Ruin is one of the most securely dated structures in the

Dinétah. At least 12 trees were cut in the summer or early fall of A.D. 1694 and were used in the structure. Masonry beam sockets and other architectural details of the ruin show that the timbers were cut specifically to fit that structure. In addition, no tree-ring dates later than 1694 have been recovered despite complete sampling of every beam on the site. Although a few other pueblitos in the area contain timbers that yielded cutting dates, no other site in the Dinétah contains as strong a terminal cluster as Tapacito Ruin. Finally, there are no 1694 cutting dates at any other site in the Dinétah. If, as Hendricks and Wilson (1996) propose, Tapacito Ruin was built after 1705 with beams salvaged from other sites, the construction crew fortuitously managed to collect a dozen specimens that were all cut 11 years earlier. That a structure was built with a dozen 11-year-old beams and not a single freshly cut timber is not outside the realm of statistical probability, but it challenges the credulity of the corpus of data, method, and theory developed by dendrochronologists over the past seven decades and ignores what is currently known about Navajo wood use behavior (Dean and Russell 1978). In all probability, Tapacito Ruin was built in 1694 with timbers cut expressly for that purpose, and it seems likely that it was constructed by founders of the Coyote Pass Clan.

There are several ways to explain both the battle as described and the pueblito as present when the battle occurred. First, Tapacito Ruin is not precisely at the confluence of Tapacito Creek and Cañon Largo but instead lies approximately three-fourths of a mile north of the confluence; it is also more than "about 20 meters back from the [bluff] edge" (Hendricks and Wilson 1996:85). It is not visible from the valley bottom and lies at least 100 meters from the edge of the bench. In addition, though the area around the site is usually described as a bench, it is better characterized as a structural bench covered with undulating eolian hills. Tapacito, a single-story masonry structure, is not visible until one passes within a radius of about 40 meters, even when it is approached from behind. It can therefore easily be missed. Finally, if the pueblito was not a Navajo structure, but a Puebloan (Jemez?) family dwelling (Towner and Dean 1992), political or kinship ties may have prevented some of the Indian auxiliaries from informing the Spaniards about Tapacito even if they had seen it. Secure tree-ring dates at one of the best dated structures in the Southwest have been dismissed because the site was not mentioned in the historical documents by people who may never have seen it and who may have had reasons for not discussing it, even if asked.

Climate and the Navajo Abandonment of Dinétah. Climate, in the form of a particularly severe drought in 1748, has been suggested as a cause for the abandonment of the Navajo homeland in the mid-1700s. The historical evidence in this case comes from a secondary reference (Reeve 1959:20) that "the Navajo, suffering from drought, were amenable to the missionaries' suggestion that they move south to the Cebolletta region." Lest one infer that this "cause-and-effect" environmental determinism is a relic of preprocessual archaeology, it has recently been repeated and expanded: "A drought that began in the 1730s" forced the Navajo to abandon their homeland by 1748 (Marshall 1995: 203). The historical reference cited for such a drought is a secondary source (Reeve 1958). The primary reference is a comment by priests who wanted to establish a mission among the Navajo at Cebolletta approximately 60 miles to the south (Hill 1940). The primary document must be viewed with some suspicion because the priests had an agenda and may have depicted the Navajo as willing participants in mass religious conversions. Simply put, the priests needed to convince their secular and religious superiors that their expenditure of funds and energy would yield important benefits, namely the conversion of many Navajos to Christianity.

A dendroclimatic reconstruction of precipitation in the Gobernador area indicates that 1748 was a serious drought year; indeed it is the driest year in the entire 1,348-year chronology (Towner 1997). Two of the preceding three years, however, 1745 and 1746, were above-average years in terms of precipitation and the succeeding year, 1749, was the wettest in almost 30 years. The "drought" of 1748 was thus a single-year event. Other dry years, including 1707, 1715, 1729, and 1735, have not been given such emphasis by those who see climate as a cause of abandonment. These dry years are not mentioned in historical texts, either.

In addition to the paleoclimatic data, the archaeological data indicate that several Navajo pueblitos were constructed after the supposed drought and that the area was not abandoned. At least seven construction episodes, and possibly more, at as many as eight sites occurred in the years following 1748 (Towner 1997). Indeed, Pueblito construction expanded into new areas, such as north of the San Juan River, during this period. The latest tree-ring-dated sites in the area indicate the Dinétah was still in use in 1762 (Fetterman 1996). It is apparent from these data that climate was not one of the "pushes" behind the Navajo exodus from their homeland. The "drought" of 1748 was a one-year event, sandwiched between very wet years, and therefore did not cause the abandonment of the Navajo homeland. Current evidence suggests that the abandonment occurred in the mid-1750s as a result of Ute raiding and the increasing importance of sheep in the Navajo economy.

CONCLUSIONS

The archaeological and ethnohistorical data are in general agreement that Navajo culture developed in the Upper San Juan area prior to 1500; Navajos absorbed Puebloans into their culture via a number of mechanisms, but there was no massive influx of refugees; Tapacito Ruin was built in the fall of 1694 and was either missed or went unreported by Roque de Madrid's forces; and the Navajo population of the Dinétah abandoned the area in the mid-1750s and moved south and west to join extant Navajo populations. It is apparent that dendrochronology has, as yet, apparently, had little impact on the interpretation of Navajo history. Many of the major questions in Navajo archaeology have been "resolved" with uncritical acceptance of historical records in lieu of sound analyses of archaeological and dendrochronological data as well as Navajo oral traditions.

Why has there been such a strong reliance on historical documents to the near exclusion of other lines of evidence? Archaeologists are rarely, if ever, trained as historians. They do not routinely examine primary documents and typically rely on secondary sources (cf. Forbes 1960, McNitt 1972). If they use primary sources, archaeologists rarely evaluate them with any degree of analytical rigor. Unless there is some glaring discrepancy between the historical records and the archaeological data, the unevaluated historical references are usually given primacy.

A second problem is that few archaeologists are trained in the interpretation of dendrochronological data. It is not unusual for archaeologists working in the Navajo area to collect minuscule numbers of samples from a site, when in fact, all potentially datable timbers should be sampled. Archaeologists often do not recognize the differing interpretive potential for cutting and noncutting dates, and do not recognize the importance of date clusters. Anomalous dates are often simply ignored. Tree-ring dating can contribute significantly to illuminating the archaeological record of the Navajo occupation of the Southwest, but only if dates are interpreted properly.

Finally, few, if any, historians are trained in archaeological inference

and not surprisingly tend to rely on written records rather than archaeological evidence. It is now clear that the historical analyses pertaining
to the Navajo were conducted decades ago and need reevaluation,
especially because new documents have been discovered (e.g., Hendricks and Wilson 1996). Historians generally accept tree-ring dates
uncritically, ignore them outright, or simply give them secondary
weight. However, tree-ring dates are independent chronological markers and therefore must, if available, be included in any rigorous analysis. If we follow the lead of European historians and archaeologists,
tree-ring dates will soon be given primacy over historical accounts
(Bonde and Christensen 1993). In so doing, archaeologists would follow Sidney Stallings's analytical footsteps. When, in 1932, his good
friend and fellow dendrochronologist John McGregor inquired about
a drought reported in historic documents to have hit the northern Rio
Grande valley in the 1680s, Stallings replied:

> There is no good evidence of an extreme drought....A few specimens
> show a slightly smaller set of rings during this time, but it is not an unusu-
> ally small set....The slightly dry spell during this decade appears to have
> been scattered locally, and even in such spots was not on the whole
> extreme. All this is contradictory to the testimony of the Indians follow-
> ing the Reconquest, but one must bear in mind that this decade was one
> of social instability around the [Rio Grande] Pueblo population, which
> would surely affect to some degree their pursuit of agriculture. Further,
> such testimony was exactly what the Spaniards wanted to hear, and
> whether completely true or not, it would have been the politic thing to
> say. (Stallings to McGregor, November 20, 1932)

Researchers interested in the Protohistoric and Early Historic periods must consider remedies to the current situation. Archaeologists
should receive more training in the limitations of dendrochronological
and historical data. In recent years various contract archaeologists
(Brown 1998; Dykeman and Wharton 1994; Sesler and Hovezak
1998) have demonstrated increasing sophistication in addressing the
problems of chronometric analysis of Protohistoric period remains,
and such examples should be brought to the attention of interested students and academics alike. Current Native American Graves Protection and Repatriation Act (NAGPRA) regulations make it imperative that
we be accurate and precise in our dating of sites in order to help sub-
stantiate claims of cultural affiliations. Projects on which tree-ring and
historical data can be independently evaluated, like the BMAP, should

be promoted. Finally, we must reaffirm our belief in the scientific method as a means for interpreting past human behavior and events. This does not mean that nonquantitative data should be ignored but that they should be evaluated with a higher degree of rigor. Such an approach will become even more important as we develop increasingly sophisticated methods for evaluating Native American oral traditions and ethnohistorical data (Vansina 1985).

Acknowledgments. My thanks go first to Steve Nash for his efforts in making the SAA symposium and this volume successful; without Steve's efforts neither would have been possible. Gary Funkhouser's wizardry with climatic reconstruction has been very important to Navajo archaeology in the past few years, even if few people realize it. Conversations with Jeff Dean and Scott Russell over the years have been very helpful. Richard V. N. Ahlstrom's comments improved this document substantially. Finally, my thanks to David R. Wilcox and David M. Brugge—both scholars and gentlemen—whose ideas have stimulated those interested in Navajo archaeology for decades. Any errors of fact, interpretation, or logic, are, of course, my own.

CHAPTER 10

Narrating Archaeology

A HISTORIOGRAPHY AND NOTES TOWARD A
SOCIOLOGY OF ARCHAEOLOGICAL KNOWLEDGE

JENNIFER L. CROISSANT
Program on Culture, Science, Technology, and Society
University of Arizona

IN THE BEGINNING

Histories are shaped by questions internal to disciplines, limited by available records, and constituted by scholarly conduct and discourses. These constitutive factors of production apply to both the knowledge produced by archaeologists and the histories about archaeology produced by archaeologists and others. This historiography of archaeology is an analysis of prior historical accounts of archaeology and forms the beginnings of an analytic review of the discipline's view of itself. The goal is to set the stage for retelling disciplinary histories and moving from an account of the historical particulars to the processes of development of archaeological thought.

Historiographic projects, as Trigger (1989) notes, are relevant in a number of dimensions. They provide a means of uncovering the biases of prior stories about the field, for inducing reflexivity about the goals and directions of a discipline, and for revealing neglected problems worth investigation (see Graham et al. 1983; Laudan 1993). The historiography of archaeology and archaeological dating also provides resources for the sociological investigation of archaeological knowledge, and accords insights into the power of narrative in developing and sustaining professional and intellectual communities.

In this chapter, I discuss the role of narrative in archaeological theory and the roles that dating techniques have played in the emergence of particular narrative forms in and about archaeology. First, I review some theoretical antecedents to the outlook presented here. I examine theories of narrative from history and briefly introduce some key concepts in the sociology of knowledge that will be useful for the analysis of the materials presented here. In the second section, I outline four broad categories of narratives in archaeology: micronarratives of research reports; macronarratives of history and culture that are the work of archaeology; narratives of the field itself; and the histories of archaeology as written by various inter- and intradisciplinary commentators for various purposes. From this latter category, the stories of the emergence and distribution of new dating techniques becomes evidence for a case study in the sociology of knowledge. Thus, in the third section of the chapter, I review historical accounts concerned with the origins of new ideas and techniques, the organization of knowledge and discipline formation, the role of instrumentation and evidence in theory, and the distribution of innovations. For archaeologists, this analysis can help to provide a ground for the reevaluation of dating techniques perhaps forgotten or neglected, and to critically consider the limits of others. The conclusion of the chapter outlines the framework for sociologically grounded histories of disciplines and studies of narrative in archaeology. I suggest some of the ways the history of archaeology and archaeological dating techniques are particularly illustrative as case studies of major theoretical issues in the sociology of knowledge.

The Storytellers

In this chapter I will transgress some territorial and epistemological boundaries. This is an "etic" project, not an "emic" one. As an interloper in the field of archaeology, I wish to let you know that my intentions are not hostile; I am just sincerely curious about the archaeological tribe and its intellectual landscape. I come to this topic from the controversial specialty of science and technology studies, from a theoretical orientation in general sociological theory and the sociology of knowledge (Zuckerman 1988), and from a territory infused with feminist concerns.

Several storytellers provide the primary resources for discussing the roles of narrative in archaeological thought. They come from fields that are close cousins to archaeology in terms of their concerns with historicity, evidence, and culture but nonetheless remain disparate in their solutions to these questions. From the history of technology, the history of science, and the history and philosophy of history more generally, we have much to gain in developing a critical appreciation of the power of narrative in archaeological thought.

The profession of history, broadly defined, has had a long and troubled discourse over the roles of theory and narrative in historical scholarship.[1] Until recently, the role of theory in the history of technology has been relatively unproblematic. In a debate in the journal *Technology and Culture*, R. A. Buchanan (1991), John Law (1991), and Philip Scranton (1991) argue over the role that theory plays in the development of historical accounts. Buchanan (1991) argues for a strong dichotomy between narrative and theory, and further argues that historians should stick to the business of pure description. Law (1991), arguing for the relevance of theory in developing historical counts and espousing a methodology of historical sociology where the past is used for sociological theory building, nonetheless reifies the distinction between narrative and theory as separate but equal enterprises. Scranton (1991:388), taking not the middle ground but moving to a met-analysis of the discourse, noted the dichotomy and mentions, though only in passing, the emergence of analyses, such as Hayden White's (1987), of the theoretical substance of narrative.

Hayden White argues against the narrative/theory, or description/explanation, dichotomy. Because "a narrative account is always a figurative account, an allegory" (White 1987:48), "scientistic" discourse is prejudiced against narrative, finding it atheoretical. However, he notes: "Narrative is not merely a neutral discursive form that may or may not be used to represent real events in their aspect as developmental processes but rather entails ontological and epistemic choices with distinct ideological and even specifically political implications" (White, 1987:ix). Similarly, Beverly Burris (1993) notes that "Narrative knowledge...does not give priority to the questions of its own legitimation and...it certifies itself in the pragmatics of its own transmission without having recourse to argumentation and proof." While narrative discourse accepts science as one of many varieties of narrative cultures, science does not reciprocate with similar tolerance" (Burris 1993:48, citing Lyotard 1984:25–27). This opposition of science and narrative has appeared in historical accounts of archaeology. For example, Daniel is ambiguous as to whether archaeology *is* a science, noting that "science contributes to archaeology" and dating techniques are "scientific aids to [archaeological] research" (Daniel 1975:353). Archaeologists have, at various points in time while telling the stories of their discipline, tried to distance themselves from the narrative work of the discipline in favor of analysis, as if the two were unequivocally distinct.

As historians, historians of archaeology operate within three basic kinds of historical representation: the annals, the chronology, and the narrative history (White 1987:4). The annals, the catalogs of aggregate data, manifest no formal narrative properties of a beginning, middle, or end, little prioritization of information, and no identifiable voice of a narrator or author. This form, however, does invoke its own ontological and causal choices. The chronicle, the list of dates without a theme or moral, without a synthetic ending or conclusion, similarly only implies causality, but ontology and causality are nonetheless latent in the selection of items ordered. The historical narrative, however, conjoins chronology and causality in that the standard notion of causality that requires that a claim that y is caused by x must first establish that x preceded y in time. Narrative history manipulates this assumption in its presentation of the establishment of a sequence of activities and events, that, while also having thematic unity, cohere in a causal unity.

White (1987:94) describes four forms of narrative. There is the investigative narrative, which provides an account or even a mimesis of the research process; the conventional narration of events; the didactic narrative providing a moral lesson, and the discursive narrative that relates past events within contemporary concerns. Often more than one genre is employed within a given account, though one is likely dominant as establishing chronology and causality. Within each genre, four themes are available: pragmatic narratives that focus on the intents of actors; conditional narratives that relate events to material causes; psychological narratives that focus on the will of actors; and ethical narratives that focus on moral life as shaped by material, ideal, and practical considerations. While an exposition of these in detail is beyond the scope of this paper, these establish a pattern of variation that can be related to the micro- and macrosociological states of the discipline under study. So, for example, Daniel's (1967) review of major authors in archaeological thought might be characterized as an idealist event-based chronology, focusing on the psychological and pragmatic concerns of individual actors. In contrast, Martin Hall's (1990) account of South African archaeology is largely a review of ideological components driven by the political and economic relations of various periods of scholarship in a discursive relation to the present state of the field.

As the debate between Buchanan (1991), Law (1991), and Scranton (1991) shows, particularistic or ideographic approaches to history are largely still opposed to nomothetic or generalizing projects. This distinction, however, rests on the assumption that narratives are atheoretical, when, in and of themselves, they are entirely theoretical, although the dimensions of theory are only implicit in the narrative constructions. Because causality is implied by chronology, although not articulated as theory nor framed in analytic or hypothetico-deductive terms, the distinction is rather a matter of degree (of theoretical specification) than kind (atheoretical versus theoretical or descriptive versus problem-centered research). One will note, of course, that much of the controversy over the role of theory in historical narrative, and in the history of technology in particular, echoes the transformations of the discipline of archaeology in the 1960s and 1970s, often portrayed as a shift from historical to processualist work. As I note later, the history of archaeology as produced by archaeologists is still largely represented by a particularistic, historical mode, rather than a "processual" mode or theory-driven history. The irony of this is explored in the final sections of the chapter.

ARCHAEOLOGICAL NARRATIVES: EMBEDDED, SEDIMENTED, STRATIFIED

In looking at varieties of archeological texts, I have found three major kinds of narratives present in archeological writing. In the first instance, we have the basic narrative of historical chronology that is now the raison d'être of the field—the macronarratives of both popular culture and professional discourse. How old is it? What is the origin of the human species? Who arrived where first? Where did they come from? How did they interact with their neighbors? The environment? At a second level, we can read the narratives constituting disciplinary histories: Who arrived at the major first discoveries of the field? Where has archaeology come from? How do archaeologists think? This will be the focus of this section, although the third level is also important. The third genre of archaeological narration is present in the micronarratives written into reports and publications, which describe the research process, methodologies, and the modes of evidentiary reasoning, induction, and inference constituting knowledge claims in the field. Where have these facts come from? How and to whom were they first visible? What were the procedures? What were the measures? By what processes were facts defined, discovered, authenticated, and analyzed?

I want to focus on the second level, the disciplinary histories, though I will also briefly remark on the narrative structure of archeological texts and make some suggestions for understanding the micro- and macronarratives that frame archeological thought as mediated by the middle-range of discipline structure. To this end, I have examined review essays, book-length treatments of the history of archaeology, anthologies presenting diverse perspectives on the origins of the field, dissertation literature reviews, textbooks, presentations, published articles, and the other chapters in this book, to provide some initial "evidence" for the analysis that follows. I will focus on publicly available histories of archaeology written for archaeologists (or more specifically, archaeology students at the graduate level), and comment on the relevance of other specific texts as necessary.

Other scholars have conceived similar projects on the role of narratives in archaeological thought and practice. I found Alice Kehoe's (1992) short essay and Margaret Conkey and Sarah Williams's analysis (1992) particularly inspiring, and Diane Gifford-Gonzalez's (1993) analysis of visual representations of "paleolithic life" similarly informative (see also Stephanie Moser 1996). Katina Lillios has noted the contradictory state of critiques of narratives of social collapse as formulated in theory and scholarship in relationship to their absence from teaching materials (Lillios 1996). She noted the influence of Misia Landau's (1984) analysis of the convergence of evolutionary narratives with heroic myths and other folk tales. In another study, Bettina Arnold (1996) described the (ab)use of archaeology in constructing national identity based on heroic folk narratives of Nazi Germany transformed into archaeology as theory. And Christopher Fung (1996) described how the conventional narratives and periodization of Mesoamerica have created conceptual difficulties in interpreting the Maya civilization. Other precedents for this work include that of Lester Embree (1992), who has written phenomenological accounts of archaeology and collected an important volume on metarchaeology, and Guy Gibbon (1989) who provided an account of the emergence of "New Archaeology." However, note that these scholars are not archaeologists per se, a point to which I will return later.

In terms of the micronarratives of scientific publications and scholarly journals, I will be very brief here, giving only a few examples of some kinds of textual analyses of archaeology's documents. Joan Gero (1996) focused on the role of narratives in constructing accounts of the field and the strengths and limitations of greater reflexivity about conducting and representing fieldwork.[2] Jean-Claude Gardin (1980) took note of the structure and content of archaeological writings in terms of the distinction between compilatory versus explanatory publications, as part of a critique of logical positivism in archaeology.

While a more detailed look at the narratives of evidence, proof, and reasoning in archaeological texts would be fascinating,[3] let me turn now to the accounts that more directly take on the stories archaeologists have constructed about themselves. There are a number of reasons for writing histories of a discipline, and these vary over time and with the social position of the authors. What accounts for the systematic variations in the discipline's accounts of itself? As sociologist Nicholas Mullins noted, "the belief system of a scientific group includes its view of its own history and the sets of beliefs, theories, etc. which its members share" (Mullins 1972:70). Similarly, Embree noted that "all groups tell stories about their past, and one ignores legend at one's peril" (Embree 1989:68).

What I am working on then is a study of narratives about archaeology, including the origin stories for the discipline, heroic figures, tropes, and chronologies. What I am interested in determining, as a researcher in science studies, is "How do they know?" One must ask, in any given field of knowledge, what constitutes evidence (Galison, 1987)? Who is a reliable interlocutor (McCook 1996; Shapin 1996)? How does the field manage its legitimacy? What frames the cultural coherence of the field (Fleck 1979)? What are the norms of scientific conduct (Merton 1973)? What model of science is archaeology being compared to, either profitably or in its perceived inadequacy? How has knowledge been institutionalized? The current study uses narrative analysis to critically read the history of archaeology as a means for sociological explanation for the structure and content of its knowledge. The focus of this book on dating techniques becomes evidence for my analysis.

As Mullins noted above, an examination of a scientific group's view of its own history helps to illustrate the emergence of discipline-specific objects of study, criteria, and norms of conduct. These, when placed in the context of both genealogical, network, social roles, and institutional analysis of fields of inquiry can lead to a fully sociological conception of knowledge (Ben-David 1960; Ben-David and Collins 1966; Collins 1989; Mullins 1972). As Steven Shapin (1982:196) describes it, this approach is able to account for the ways in which "people produce knowledge against the background of their culture's inherited knowledge, their collectively situated purposes, and the information they receive from natural reality."

Hayden White (1987) argued that narrative choices reflect political as well as basic epistemic choices. We need not think of these political choices as being exclusively matters of the state and ideology but also operating in the more mesopolitical realm of disciplinary structure. Randall Collins (1989) discusses the structure of intellectual competition in relation to expanding or contracting resources. The number, strength, and density of intellectual lineages and schools greatly affects the framing of research questions in a discipline. One of the key problems in intellectual arenas is the need to maximize distinctiveness or originality, yet not go too far afield from extant paradigmatic approaches and exemplars. For example, Trigger (1978) rhetorically works to minimize the novelty of the then-new processualist and behavioralist archaeologies by making the most of the precedents set by Clyde Kluckhohn (1939) and Walter Taylor (1948) in the 1940s as practicing a generalizing or nomothetic archaeology. Processualists' early accounts of archaeology's development maximized the revolutionary tenor of their work, yet more recent accounts tend to operate in a more assimilationist vein. The narratological causality at work is one of a fulfillment of past promise (and certainly not just the effects of some prior causes) (White 1987:149), reflecting the solidification of the intellectual lineages.

Looking more specifically at narrations of the role that dating techniques play in the history of archaeology, it is often unclear whether the techniques are causal in a deterministic sense, merely facilitative of intellectual change, or in fact epiphenomenal in relation to the intellectual interests driving the field. For archaeologists, like historians, chronology and causality, the essences of narrative, are the tools for representation where the object of study is time itself. As Nash (1997a) has noted, while this seems obvious to contemporary observers, this has not always been so. Chronology had to be established as the central and organizing frame for archaeology, for example through dendrochronology and other techniques for establishing relative and absolute dates. David Browman and Douglass Givens (1996) argue, for example, that Wissler (1917) worked hard to articulate the role of chronology, eschewing collections and antiquarianism (what White [1987] might recognize as the *annals* of history) prevalent in early twentieth-century American archaeology. Wissler's attempts to "really tell the story" (Wissler 1917:100) with the technique of stratigraphy were framed in competition with evolutionary narratives and typologies that tended to minimize material changes perceived in the Americas.

One apparent tension in reading much of the general history of archaeology, also manifest in the history of the invention of dating techniques, is the problem of the individualizing, and often hagiographic, biographical modes.[4] This mode of scholarship emphasizes individual inventors and downplays the role of networks of competitors and correspondents in developing solutions to intellectual questions. For example, A. E. Douglass, in Webb's (1983) account, has two distinctive careers, one in astronomy and one in dendrochronology, despite the calendric of overlap Douglass's foremost interests. This not only provides a fractured narrative, it undermines Webb's own goal of providing a coherent and positive picture of Douglass's episteme. The "Gladwin" controversy is represented as brief and conclusively solved, rather than the 17-year oscillating and often quite personal argument between two personae (Nash 1997a, 1999), while the problem of the objectivity of the dendrochronological methods is downplayed. The needs for patronage and the effects of prewar philanthropy and amateurs on the intellectual milieu are similarly unexplored in any detail (e.g., Nash 1999).

Thus the history of archaeology itself has a long tradition, showing in part a trajectory similar to more general historical studies of science, technology, and medicine (see Rosenberg 1983; Shapin 1982; Staudenmaier 1985), especially since the first practitioners in the history of archaeology are very frequently the "senior statesmen" of the field, often reminiscing on their long tenures in the discipline (e.g., Judd 1968). Various forms of biography also emerge, and eventually specialists in the history of the discipline, often outsiders not trained in the field directly, emerge. While this chapter must remain inconclusive, it is apparent that there have been several waves of history-making about archaeology (beyond literature reviews that serve very specific functions), most recently a wave that emerged in the late 1970s with Bruce Trigger's (1978) work, and another that appeared in the 1990s with Michael Shanks and Christopher Tilley's (1992) work and ones such as that by Peter Robertshaw (1990). We also see the emergence of external specialists (Embree 1992; Fagette 1996).

In an analogous example, John M. Staudenmaier (1985) can be viewed as a historian of the history of technology. His book-length review of the origins of the field, focused on the Society for the History of Technology, outlines the dimensions of research, themes, and points of dissent in the scholarly community of historians of technology. This text not only serves as reference and primer for students of the history of technology but also points to pathways as yet untrammeled. As Trigger (1989) or Daniel (1975) do for archaeology, Staudenmaier (1985) represents an important moment in the discipline of the history of technology: the emergence of scholars specializing largely in the production of metanarratives of the field's emergence, current state, and potential directions.

Glyn Daniel serves as a similar figure, along with scholars such as Bruce Trigger or Gordon Willey and Jeremy Sabloff, in archaeology. Daniel's (1968) chronological dictionary of foundational texts is a classic example of the "men and ideas" approach to the study of scientific knowledge. He echoes the stock periodization of antiquarianism, professionalization, and mature sciences that is featured in nearly all accounts of the history of archaeology, although often subdivided or labeled differently (cf. Willey and Sabloff 1980). This model mirrors the Kuhnian formulation of disciplinary trajectories, although still within an accumulationist model of knowledge acquisition. Daniel's (1968) accounts, as chronicles with their list of dates, events, and people, only imply causality, but ontology and causality are nonetheless latent in the selection of scholars and events.

Willey and Sabloff (1980:1) characterize archaeology as a discipline "whose goals are *to narrate* the sequent story of that [human cultural and social] past and *to explain* the events that composed it" (emphasis in the original). This formulation relies on the narrative/explanation dichotomy. Their narrative of the history of archaeology is, however, in a particularistic mode, relying on a latent paradigmatic model of discipline formation and change. Browman and Givens (1996) similarly make the argument that the emergence of stratigraphy after 1910 in North American archaeology is a paradigm shift; they, too, misrepresent the idea of paradigms. The notion of a paradigm shift is a vague, unsociological term for a cognitive revolution that is best understood as an organizational transformation. Nowhere in the case of stratigraphy do we have the idea of anomaly as stimulus to theoretical change, as present in Kuhn's formulation. What we do have is a group of archaeologists looking for a way of regularizing archaeological practice, to avoid the ex post facto reconstructions of stratigraphic information. Browman and Givens's (1996) account of the emergence of stratigraphy in North American archaeology is valuable in that it documents the network of practitioners and variations in stratigraphic methodology among Kidder, Nelson, and Gamio and Boas. Yet it is largely a search for historical continuity with present practice, anachronistically dismissing prior practices rather than contextualizing them. We have, again, a history of archaeology that neglects the discipline's own precepts for the study of the past.

There is one additional tension, manifest throughout histories of the field. This is the dilemma of professionalization. It is never presented as a dilemma in the "emic" versions of the history of archaeology.

Archaeologists have had to work hard to establish professional criteria, to separate their practices from "pot hunting," to distance the field
from antiquarianism, to protect themselves from the incursions of
mere dabblers and amateurs and yet to enroll their support as a paying
public, and to carefully manage the credibility of contract and state
archaeology in relation to the discipline in academic institutions.[5] Yet
the professionalization of archaeology, as presented by "insiders," is
an intellectual triumph, rather than an organizational one. Paul
Fagette's (1996) argument about the influence of the New Deal in the
professionalization and intellectual stabilization of archaeology can
only have been written by someone who considers himself a historian,
not an archaeologist. Only rarely do the Works Progress Administration or Civilian Works Administration digs appear in internally generated accounts of the discipline and then only as the source of revenue
for scattered digs in the Southeastern United States or as brief stopover
points for archaeologists during their professional development. However, Fagette (1996) discusses the routinization of field methods, the
establishment of academic archaeological credentials as necessary for
government employment, and the very dense networks of practitioners
that emerged in the 1930s as central to the intellectual development of
American archaeology.[6]

The accomplishment of a legal oligopoly on practice, professionalization, and institution building are no mean feats, are far-from-settled
issues, are worthy of sociological study, and illustrate a number of
interesting points. Scientists regularly engage in "boundary work" to
separate credible from incredible witnesses (Gieryn and Figert 1990;
Shapin 1996) and to protect their "turf" from being overridden by
outsiders from other disciplines (see Ben-David and Collins 1966), or
in the case of archaeology, amateurs. "Etic," or external, accounts of
the history of archaeology (e.g., Fagette 1996) have the discipline tied
much more closely to the fortunes of anthropology than do accounts
presented by archaeological practitioners,[7] while the relationship with
anthropology is sometimes manipulated to provide a space for intellectual innovation. And at various points in time, archaeologists in North
America have worked to either align or distance themselves with scholarship in Europe.

The strategic nature of the representation of the history of the
discipline definitely requires further scrutiny. In the following section, I examine the chapters in this volume to determine what we can
learn from examinations of the specific trajectories of archaeological

instrumentation in developing a set of general propositions for understanding the development and propagation of new techniques.

INSTRUMENTATION, METHODOLOGY, AND THEORY

As Shapin (1982) noted, the history of science has been transformed from its beginnings in scientific biography through various
forms of internalist histories of ideas, histories of instrumentation, as
well as by later social and "externalist," or contextual, histories of
ideas and practice. Similarly, people studying archaeologists have done
much biography, history of ideas (cf. Trigger 1989), histories of instrumentation and technique (Nash 1997a, 1999; chapters presented in
this book), and have started to produce social and institutional
accounts (cf. Fagette 1996).

As an analogue, consider the development of medical visualization
devices. Even simple devices, such as the stethoscope, were at first presented unequivocally by medical historians as progress, couched in a
narrative of increasing ability to penetrate the body and see its "true"
features. More recent scholarship (Blume 1992; Reiser 1978; Stafford
1991), however, argues that we do not see into the real body any more
clearly but that new properties of the body are becoming available for
inspection, at the same time that other features of the body are made
more unintelligible. Further, the human body, they argue, is *manufactured* through these interactions, in which some of the "real" features
are foregrounded at the expense of others in reference to the dominant
conceptual frameworks of the time (Hirschauer 1991). As we
approach the millennium, most but not all of the histories of archaeological methods and techniques are of a kind with the "old" histories
of medicine, which are straightforward accounts of medical inventions
and their adoption. What might happen if we were to look more critically at the ways archaeological dating assists in the manufacture of
archaeological interpretation?

Towner's chapter examines the methodological value of historical
documentary accounts in light of independent tree-ring dates. He
notes, as does Nash, that Douglass first calibrated tree-ring dates
based on historical information, and notes that tree-ring dates are
given priority over textual accounts. While a valuable account from an
"emic" perspective, Towner's review of a particular set of problems in
the conflicts between dendrochronological and historical records does
little for establishing a sociological analysis of which evidentiary
source will take priority under what conditions, except to surmise that

archaeologists are not as rigorous in their interrogations of written texts as they should be.[8] Yet, to argue that tree-ring dates are unbiased in itself reflects a disciplinary commitment, insufficiently attentive to the various instabilities in tree-ring dating.

Stein distinguishes between stratigraphic excavation methodologies (digging and data recording techniques, really), and stratigraphic dating that works with geological evidence for providing a chronological framework. All archaeologists practice some form of stratigraphic excavation, and have since at least the 1920s. For "prehistorians" and those working without access to the written historical record, geological stratigraphic dating is an invaluable technique for establishing relative dates. The asymmetry, where prehistorians do not influence stratigraphy as recorded in the International Stratigraphic Guide, yet rely on it, is interesting. If a conflict over dates is generated, which community's chronology will take precedence? Consider Stein's example of the problem of the transition from the Middle to Upper Paleolithic in Europe. She argues that stratigraphy will help to solve the problem of defining the unit and date of change, yet it is not at all clear at this time which possible "markers" (skeletal morphology, deoxyribonucleic acid [DNA], isotopic dating, or tools) will take precedence. Similarly, it is not clear what geological stratigraphy will contribute to urban archaeologists, given the very different spatial and temporal scales in which they operate.

Stein correctly proposes that the different uses of the ideas and practices of stratigraphy are based on the historical trajectories of the subspecialties that engage them. This much is true, and she provides a particularistic account of the processes. The purpose of the chapter is clearly one of rapprochement and unification, rather than of analysis. We are left, too, with the question of whether stratigraphic techniques from geosciences impelled the interest in chronology in archaeology (which Trigger [1989] argues), or whether, as Willey and Sabloff (1980) argue, stratigraphy was adopted because the need for fixing chronological relationships had already been established.

Blinman, noting the "glorious circularity" of ceramic dating, presents a chronology of the solidification of ceramic dating and its limitations as a technique. Chronological calibration must often be established by other means, in part because of the complexity of both spatial as well as temporal variations in the production of ceramics. In this narration, it is again unclear whether or when ceramic dating is pursued because the basic goal is to establish chronology—dating for its own sake—or because questions about regional chronology, population, or other intellectual agendas require the establishment of a stable chronological background. Where are the debates? How has the community reorganized its paradigms in response to ceramic dating? How are students trained in this method? How stable are ceramic chronologies? Are they still subject to research in their own right, thus destabilizing their use as a transparent tool for dating sites? This problem, in which the technique itself is still subject to research and validation, is also present in Eighmy's chapter on archaeomagnetism and Feathers's on luminescence, and suggests that premature release of dates derived using a technique before it is fully stabilized and calibrated may increase resistance to the technology (see Nash 1997a, 1999 for examples in dendrochronology), even after technical problems are solved and calibration is achieved.

In Nash's account, Douglass clearly controlled and managed the release of dendrochronological dates so that the technique was well established, reliable, and reproducible, before entering into difficult arenas and posing challenges to established chronologies and frameworks. It is clearly a case where a research group knew the data that it needed, and went out and got them. Douglass and the select group of archaeologists with whom he worked were quite strategic in selecting sites that could validate their methods, and as the technique solidified, selecting sites that could be used to demonstrate its efficacy. There is nothing particularly wrong with this; it is in fact an important lesson, as I note below, for purveyors of new dating techniques.

Taylor provides the most comprehensive account of the development of radiocarbon dating, in terms of understanding the principles, access to the primary sources, and processes involved in the establishment of ^{14}C dating as valid and reliable. It is important to note that again, a technique had moved from being a research object to being a research tool after a conscious effort at stabilization and calibration, and with the recognition that modification of existing field practices would be important, though difficult, to implement. Radiocarbon dating's implication in establishing closure for large chronological questions is important. Here is an example where the technique was immediately important and literally pulled into the intellectual arena to solve problems of chronology.

Beck and Jones, in their account of OHD, are faced with a dating technique that, because the underlying physicochemical processes are exceedingly complex, has proved difficult to conclusively establish.

While OHD can provide, like luminescence dating, a direct rather than associational date for artifacts, it has entered the analytical playing field after many basic chronological questions have been answered and the discipline has turned to more esoteric ones.

Eighmy's practitioner's account of archaeomagnetism similarly tells us a great deal about barriers to adoption. As noted by Feathers, premature release of results of a new technology before the technique has been fully calibrated can lead to increased resistance to it, despite later improvements. Relative precision matters, as does complexity of measurement sampling. Perhaps we should consider this a didactic chronology of the history of archaeomagnetism, in that the morals of the story to be inferred include the challenge for stabilizing a chronometric resource, the problem of cost and complexity in evaluating effectiveness and enrolling users, and the problem of relative outsiders bringing new techniques to a field.

Feathers's account of luminescence is similarly partisan, and yet is important in thinking through the general processes of technique adoption. This is clearly a case where there is great difficulty in calibrating and stabilizing the technique. First calibrated in relation to radiocarbon dates, this immediately suggests that the transition from calibrated to calibrating technique is still not yet complete. It is also a complicated technique: at points in its history it required subdued lighting, inert atmospheres, special sampling regimes, the use of many variables, and a complex negotiation of dosimetric assumptions. It also enters a field established by radiocarbon dating and other techniques, namely associational techniques, which are already well established. This is a case to follow, to see if it is sufficiently stabilized to challenge extant chronologies, as the author suggests, or whether it will remain a secondary or corroborating source, or face extinction in the archaeological study of the Americas.

Looking across these accounts of archaeological dating techniques, we can consider the heuristic that has emerged from studies of other fields of science that "revolutionary" inventions are generally made by "outsiders" or those on the periphery rather than in the intellectual core of an area of study. In the case of archaeology, this is evidenced by the observations that new techniques in dating or materials characterization have almost uniformly been imported into the field by various "outsiders." While the case of stratigraphy does not quite apply because its emergence as a technique well before the boundaries around archaeology had been drawn, dendrochronology, radiocarbon dating, luminescence, and AM studies as described in this text clearly fit this model.

Those bringing new techniques from other areas are not burdened with prior expectations regarding the outcomes of dating tests or the theoretical disruptions that might occur from unanticipated dates, allowing them one measure of objectivity. However, they are still committed to establishing the reliability of their techniques. Their outsider status will likely provide a source of resistance and a lack of credibility to the established practitioners in a field. The converse, however, might also be true, as is the case with tree-ring dating (Nash 1997a), in that when a problem is brewing and an external technique can emerge to solve it, it is adopted, and rather quickly, by the "side" to which it is favorable. Thus the enthusiasm for radiocarbon dating and the energy with which collaborators sent Libby their samples for analysis increased.

I am particularly interested in the moment at which a metric makes the transition from something that must be calibrated to something that can calibrate. When does a technique become a relatively transparent research tool, rather than a research object in itself? For example, in 1934, Emil Haury communicated with Paul Martin of the Field Museum of Natural History, to see if the data collected from a tree-ring analysis made sense in the context of masonry and ceramic assemblages at Lowry Ruin. Martin relied on the dendrochronological data only as supplemental to his analysis of the site in the subsequent year's publications (Nash 1997a). By 1940, however, archaeological tree-ring data had sufficient stability to disrupt prior chronologies and theories within Southwestern sites. Similarly, early in its spread from the laboratory, Libby verified carbon dates by referencing known Egyptian dates, secured by the historical and archaeological record. Later, however, carbon became in-and-of-itself a source for validation. What, exactly, happened? Some techniques never clear that hurdle. Clearly this is a matter of stabilization. Routinization of sample collection, technique, instrumentation, and interpretation must be achieved so that group consensus of what constitutes reliable evidence can emerge. And it is not merely an accumulation of reliable dates, by volume or sheer mass of data, but a more subtle reprioritization of data and changes in practice that must occur. If a technique is providing data that are incompatible with extant frameworks, what are the conditions that foster revising the frameworks and thus accepting the technique or conversely that lead to the neglect of the apparently aberrant data? This has to do with the assumed veracity of the techniques, and there is a sociological threshold in action.

Finally, one problem that seems to be prevalent across all new dating techniques is a matter of accessibility. At a first-order level, this means as scientific techniques enter the field from other specialties, the potential users in archaeology must find them simple enough to understand (hence Eighmy's lament that there are not enough of the "right" kind of students in archaeology to make sense of archaeomagnetism). However, there is also the problem of the complexity, cost, and usability of the technique, especially in relation to extant techniques and needs for precision. Dendrochronology, by all accounts, is something that not just anyone can do. The laboratories are specialized, the techniques somewhat esoteric, though the general principles are deceptively straightforward. This made some, such as Harold Gladwin, suspicious of the technique, as the very practice thereof challenged his view of the scientific norms of universalism (cf. Merton 1973). If a technique is too fickle, its reproducibility and validity come into question. DuBois's research in geochronological magnetism led him to the archaeological record as a means for applying and calibrating his technique. It appeared, however, in the midst of a variety of techniques, many already calibrated, and most easier to use.

We can then start to think of various push and pull factors in the development and propagation of dating techniques. The pull factors include the need for establishing chronology and the importance of dating to specific research questions after chronology is established. Certain techniques (radiocarbon, dendrochronology) were pulled very effectively from the laboratory into the field after very careful calibration by their practitioners. Other techniques, however, such as luminescence, archaeomagnetism, and OHD, must be pushed, and they are pushed into an intellectual space already populated by apparently reliable techniques and stable chronologies against which they must be measured. Hence, the success or failure of dating techniques is clearly a phenomenon dependent on the social and intellectual conditions of the field and the strategic actions of its practitioners in that milieu. It is certainly not, as most narratives have it, a matter of unequivocal intellectual progress or ignorance on the part of resisters.

CONCLUSION

Without more coherent theories of discipline formation, and theories of the role of instrumentation in inquiry, histories of archaeology are likely to continue to recapitulate the narratives of unilineal evolution. Lillios (1996) notes that despite having been sanitized from racist colonial tropes to politically correct systems theories explaining the increasing complexity of civilizations, the unilineal narrative still serves as the organizing narrative structure of the field. Looking broadly at the history of science, then, there have been significant shifts in the field from the internalist biographical accounts or the history of ideas, which tended toward hagiography and Whiggism, to social and contextualist histories. This is not to say, however, that there has been unequivocal "development." The various forms of narrative, periodization, and relations to critique coexist. But the complexity of the historical accounts has shifted as the history of science has been professionalized from its origins as an activity of semiretired scientists (e.g., Judd 1968). Similarly, we can expect the development of historiographic complexity and the coexistence of multiple related forms of history in the history of archaeology as specialists in the history and philosophy of archaeology are trained. This is evidenced, for example, in Jonathan Reyman's (1992) or Peter Robertshaw's (1990) collections of methodologically diverse histories of archaeology, and we can expect more such treatments.

Finally, consider the controversial aspects of this excursion into the narrative terrain of archaeology. As noted earlier, it is ironic that histories of archaeology produced by "insiders" are generally (but not exclusively) ideographic with only latent analytic potential, while those narratives produced by "outsiders" (at least more recently) are moving to an overtly analytic or nomothetic genre. Historically nomothetic or sociological accounts produce the same relativizing or centrifugal forces in the discipline as do the postprocessualist critiques. This is to be opposed to the centripetal forces by insiders' accounts fostering coherence and uniformity. In one sense, this look at the history of archaeology and its narrative structures relies on a controversial intellectual move similar to the one framing conflicts that archaeology has internally generated over processualist and postprocessualist archaeologies. Steven Shapin (1982:157) has noted that one can either "debate the possibility of the sociology of science, or one [can] do it."[9] Here is the irony: Nomothetic or processual approaches to the history of archaeology result in the same epistemological results as postprocessualist critiques of archaeological assumptions. Because both of these approaches generally seek to explain knowledge in terms of social structures or cultural phenomena operating at various levels, they are seen (in conventional positivist views of science) as discrediting the enterprise.

Archaeology, along with the other human sciences, has variously struggled with science anxiety. This affliction uses a mythical conception of science, which has varied in interesting ways over time (see Embree 1992; Gibbon 1989), and shortchanges the unique properties of archeological craft and theory, and will ultimately be counterproductive for the field. The exchanges in AAA and SAA newsletters of recent years and a history of many attempts to "scientize" archaeology generally rely on a model of science rather undone by numerous science studies (Knorr-Cetina 1983; Latour and Woolgar 1986; Lynch 1993) or in postpositivist philosophy. As Rachel Laudan (1993:1) noted, the "production of biographies, eloges [eulogies], and histories are one strategy to promote science and to secure it a firm institutional footing." Narratives of archaeological progress over several generations have worked in this vein.

My point here is that there are a number of ways to handle the uncertainties of the human sciences. One method is to abjure its "human nature" for a mythic notion of objectivity. Another is to take the tack that some (but not all) historians have taken:

> The past is a resource. When we confront it, interpret it, the past has much to tell us about power, lifestyle, the absolute presuppositions by which people live. . . . No matter how many new facts and hard data we uncover about the past, the job of doing history always comes down to interpretation. Every generation finds itself in history, and finds it must rewrite the history books to account for its priorities, its interpretive strengths and proclivities. . . . Point of view is no pitfall; it's a responsibility. (Olmert 1996:27)

A further challenge for the field emerges when considering the merits of professionalization. Joseph Ben-David (1960:557) noted "professionalization, which necessarily turns scientific research into a monopoly of insiders rather than—as it used to be until well into the nineteenth century—of inspired amateurs (i.e., outsiders), may ultimately endanger its revolutionary character." So, Andrew Christenson's (1989:1) argument that historiography is evidence of disciplinary maturity and professionalization and is necessary for development contains within it the possibility that it is evidence of disciplinary stagnation.

Perhaps a better view is that it is not stagnation, per se, but a kind of consensus in the field's methods, central questions, and objects of study that exist despite the great diversity of theoretical orientation and local, internal controversies about details of chronology and interpretation. In sociological terms, we have the institutionalization or sedimentation (Berger and Luckmann 1967) of archaeology, which leads to the possibility of metarchaeologies, histories and historiographies, and the manipulation of archeological knowledge in and of itself as a source of evidence for abstraction. In a more literary vein, consider White's (1987:20) assertion that "in order to qualify as historical, an event must be susceptible to at least two narratives of its occurrence. Unless at least two versions of the same set of events can be imagined, there is no reason for the historian to take upon him[her]self the authority of giving a true account of what really happened." As regional chronologies become settled, the level of specificity of historical questions will have to increase and the scale of inquiries will decrease. Despite the solidification of chronologies and the relative consensus of accounts, archaeologists have much to keep them busy in making the transformation to understanding not only what happened, but formulating explanations as to *how it happened*. However, these questions are largely of interest to specialists and will likely be of decreasing interest to the public. Thus whether or not analytic or "nomothetic" approaches in and about archaeology, bereft of articulations of historical specificity, will be adequate to the task of a fully contextualized and productive archaeology is an open question. As historian Peter Gay noted, historical narrative without analysis is trivial; historical analysis without narration is incomplete (see White 1987:5).

These observations set off a series of sociologically interesting empirical questions: When, in what forms, and by whom, do fields start articulating their own histories? Certainly, that a small and somewhat scattered generation of students is now writing dissertations *about* archaeology rather than *in* archaeology says several things about the development of the field. It is suggested (Collins 1989) that a relative recession in resources and a growing population has a series of natural consequences for an intellectual community.[10] The field will consolidate, some schools will die out, and increasingly arcane distinctions will be elevated to matters of great importance to maximize originality within a highly constrained intellectual terrain. We should expect to see a lengthening corpus of theoretical works, the emergence of increasingly complex exegetics of classical texts and historical studies, and increasingly abstract metatheoretical work.

Another relevant metatheoretical/sociological question is, "When do new techniques become adopted in relation to prior explanatory frameworks?" In the cases presented here, it requires us to move from simply describing the ways that dating techniques intersect with the formation of chronologies. That is, rather than simply ask about techniques, such as whether archaeomagnetism should be preferred in relation to carbon dating, obsidian hydration, ceramic assemblage dating, and stratigraphy, or dendrochronological evidence prioritized in relation to the historical record, the question becomes, Under what circumstances (historical, political, structural, intellectual) is the advent of a new dating technique likely to be adopted and by whom? What is the key turning point in the standardization and calibration of dating techniques, the point at which they cease to be validated by other methods and become in and of themselves sources of validation? These questions remain to be answered in the future.

Finally, for me, a series of questions emerges from these papers, and the general study of narratives of archaeology, at the intersection of sociology, science studies, history, and archaeology itself: When do social groups become systematic about the study of their origins? When do they achieve a measure of reflexivity? Thinking archaeologically, what are the conditions of the homotaxial moment, present in a number of places throughout history, where people want to dig up the past?[11] This question operates on two levels: When do *disciplines* start a metanarrative or historiographic approach to themselves (whether by way of scholasticism or reflexivity), when do outsiders (such as myself) start constructing historical accounts, and when do *"civilizations"* begin systematic explorations of their past? In that regard, I will close with the idea that the emergence of the critical historical study of archaeology's origins stands as a microcosm of archaeology's emergence as the professionalized inquiry about the origins of society.

Acknowledgments. This chapter first appeared as a presentation at the SAA Annual Meeting, April 2–6, 1997, Nashville, Tennessee. My thanks to Stephen Nash for his forbearance on a paper whose irreverence for archaeological tradition and discourse might be disturbing and for his work as symposium organizer and volume editor.

PART V

Conclusion

CHAPTER 11

Just a Matter of Time?

NORTH AMERICAN ARCHAEOLOGICAL DATING IN THE TWENTY-FIRST CENTURY

Stephen E. Nash
Department of Anthropology
Field Museum of Natural History

During the twentieth century, archaeologists and their scientific colleagues have invested a great deal of time, effort, and therefore money in the development of dating techniques that can illuminate, at various levels of accuracy, precision, and resolution, the temporal relationships contained in the archaeological record. Some techniques, such as tree-ring dating, radiocarbon dating, stratigraphy, and seriation, have been so successful that they are now routinely practiced in archaeological research situations in which they apply. Other techniques, such as archaeomagnetic, obsidian hydration, luminescence dating, and, perhaps most surprisingly, the analysis of historic records, are not applied in archaeological research as often as their proponents suggest is justified. The papers presented herein successfully demonstrate that the many and varied reasons for the underutilization of these techniques often have nothing to do with the techniques' intrinsic limitations. Contingency, personality, academic politics, innocent ignorance, professional biases, and funding restrictions have all taken their toll in restricting the productive application of these techniques. Is it just a matter of time, then, before these techniques are employed in all research situations in which they apply? I think not, and I hope that the histories presented in this volume provide a critical foundation on which archaeologists who are less well versed in the nuances of archaeological dating can better understand how these dating techniques can be productively applied to the interpretation of North American prehistory.

Jim Feathers (this volume) offered a useful heuristic in the consideration of the underutilization of luminescence dating in North American archaeology: Archaeological dating techniques are affected by the vagaries of supply and demand. In keeping with the multidisciplinary nature of archaeological research, all of the dating techniques considered herein, except the ceramic dating (Blinman, this volume), came to archaeology after development and preliminary application in other disciplines, be they astronomy, chemistry, geology, geophysics, or history. This has created a situation in which active collaboration between specialists and archaeologist-practitioners is necessary but not sufficient for the productive utilization of each technique in archaeological research. What is needed is increased collaboration and communication between archaeologist-practitioners and archaeologist-consumers. Unfortunately, as Jeff Eighmy and Jim Feathers note in this volume, there are a number of barriers to such communication, including the four-field approach to anthropological training in the United States, which often precludes literacy in the archaeometric sciences; the low number of archaeologist-practitioners of any given dating technique; the relatively low number of archaeologists literate in the nuances of proper date interpretation; and the vagaries of institutional support for fledgling dating laboratories. All of these are major barriers; none will be ameliorated by wishful thinking.

From the demand side, archaeologists must again recognize that chronology, in the strictest sense, requires a great deal more than the uncritical acceptance of dates returned by a laboratory. All archaeological dates, no matter how they are obtained, must be critically examined not only in light of the intrinsic limitations of the dating technique but also in terms of the archaeological context from which they were derived. Archaeologists' often unrealistic expectations regarding the potential of any dating technique (see Eighmy and Beck and Jones, this volume) must be mitigated by professional participation in, or at least awareness of, all aspects of the dating process. Smiley and Ahlstrom's (1997) analysis of tree-ring and radiocarbon dates within archaeological contexts on Black Mesa provides the best recent example of the successful integration of these various datasets and serves as a goal to which all chronometric analysis should strive.

Jennifer Croissant (this volume) offers a number of penetrating questions. The answers to most of her queries can be determined only through more detailed analyses in the history, sociology, and philosophy of science and are therefore well beyond the scope of this volume, but nevertheless provide food for thought on how dating techniques have affected archaeological research and interpretation. Specifically, one must consider at what point a particular dating technique shifts from being a research object to being a research tool. For tree-ring dating, the point is clearly identifiable: Tree-ring dating became an archaeological research tool in December 1929, when Douglass (1929) published tree-ring dates for some 40 southwestern sites. On the other hand, one could argue that this process was not complete until the end of the Synthesis Project in the 1970s, when North American archaeological tree-ring analysis finally became the purview of one intellectual tradition (Nash, this volume). For other dating techniques, especially obsidian hydration, luminescence, and archaeomagnetism, the threshold is less than clear. Does this mean that these dating techniques require similar synthetic treatments? Certainly, these would be welcome, but it seems to me that such operations are necessary, but not sufficient, conditions for the increased utilization of these techniques. Native American Graves Protection and Repatriation Act regulations have made it more important than ever that archaeologists control the temporal aspects of the archaeological record (Towner, this volume). As we enter the new millennium, archaeologist-consumers must actively participate in the development and application of these techniques if they are to realize their fullest potential. Such realization is not, therefore, just a matter of time. It requires charismatic yet scientifically stringent leadership by dating specialists, increased funding for basic research and archaeologist-practitioner training, standardized date derivation techniques and publication formats, and collaborative critical evaluation of dates within their archaeological contexts. The dating techniques considered herein occupy different moments on their passage to maturation, but by improving our understanding of where these techniques have been, we can learn from the lessons of the past and look to the future with the confidence and enthusiasm that befits a new millennium.

Notes

4: SEVEN DECADES OF ARCHAEOLOGICAL
TREE-RING DATING

1. This situation is perhaps not so surprising, for consultants for the Navajo Nation were all employed by the Laboratory of Tree-Ring Research, and the consultant for the United State Indian Claims Commission was none other than Florence Hawley. Nevertheless, the point remains.

2. The Laboratory of Tree-Ring Research produced two electronic databases that summarize the tree-ring data on 1,300 prehistoric (Robinson and Cameron 1992) and 1,400 historic (Robinson and Towner 1993) sites. These documents do not include a list of the more than 40,000 individual tree-ring dates produced by the Laboratory to date, however.

5: THE INTRODUCTION OF RADIOCARBON DATING

1. There were actually several parts to the project that Ernest Anderson and James Arnold contributed to in different ways and at different times. Anderson, who had begun at Chicago as a Ph.D. student early in 1947 (he had worked at the Manhattan Project at Los Alamos during World War II), tended to concentrate his attention toward making what most investigators thought were extremely recalcitrant solid counting detectors work—at least some of the time. Anderson did not think they were that hard to make work, a view not shared by most of the other pioneering researchers involved in ^{14}C solid carbon counting (Anderson et al. 1951) (E. C. Anderson, personal communication 1996). He also was involved in the measurement of the difference in ^{14}C activity between contemporary ["biomethane"] and fossil carbon ["petromethane"] (Anderson et al. 1947a, 1947b) and finally, undertook a series of ^{14}C measurements on contemporary samples from different latitudes and carbon reservoirs to determine the range in ^{14}C activities in modern samples. This last project constituted the basis of his Ph.D. dissertation, which he filed in late May 1949 (Anderson 1949, 1953). Upon completion of his Ph.D., he left the Chicago radiocarbon project to return to Los Alamos. He spent most of the remainder of his career at Los Alamos. However, he continued to be involved in the development of low-level counting (Anderson and Haynes 1956) and was instrumental in setting up the radiocarbon laboratory at the University of Copenhagen in the early 1950s (Anderson et al. 1953).

Arnold, who arrived in March 1948, returned to work with Libby on the ^{14}C project (he had been at Chicago earlier in a postdoctoral capacity). He tended to concentrate his attention on the measurement of samples, first the samples that comprised the initial "Curve of Knowns" (Arnold and Libby 1949) and then the first set of Chicago unknown-age samples (Arnold and Libby 1950, 1951). He later pioneered the development of liquid scintillation technology for low-level counting (Arnold 1954). He spent most of his illustrious career—he was elected to the National Academy of Sciences in 1964—as Professor of Chemistry at the University of California, San Diego, working in the field of cosmogonic geochemistry.

2. The most critical technical advancement that allowed the development of radiocarbon dating as a practical technique was the use of *anticoincidence* counting strategy. The principles of anticoincidence counting are outlined in Taylor (1987:79–80, Fig 4.7). It allowed the measurement of natural levels of ^{14}C without the need for isotopic enrichment, a requirement that would have made ^{14}C measurements for routine ^{14}C dating purposes prohibitively expensive, and thus the method would have been rendered essentially impractical. It should be noted that although it appears that Libby probably independently conceived of anticoincidence counting, it was later learned that Danish scientists in the 1930s had employed it for low-level counting. Also, it appears that the idea behind anticoincidence counting was familiar to cosmic-ray physicists at the University of Chicago at the time (E. Anderson, personal communication 1996). There is a possibility that Ernest Anderson actually was the first to suggest the idea of anticoincidence counting for radiocarbon measurement in Libby's lab.

3. The actual published "date" was not expressed in "years" but in specific ^{14}C activity as represented in counts per minute per grams of carbon. The first sample (C–1) to be measured was wood from the tomb of the Old Kingdom (Third Dynasty) Egyptian King Djoser [referred to as Zoser in Libby's publications]. A second sample, wood from the tomb of Sneferu (Fourth Dynasty) was later measured and was published along with the Djoser [Zoser] date.

4. The publication date of the first date list in January 1950 was one of the factors that was later considered in making A.D. 1950 the zero reference year in the counting of radiocarbon time. "B.P." is an abbreviation for "radiocarbon years before the present" where "the present" or 0 B.P. is equal to 1950 (Stuiver and Polach 1977).

5. The first Chicago date list included seven determinations that had not appeared in the 1950 booklet and excluded two. One of the excluded dates (C–276) appeared in the second Chicago list (Libby 1951). However, the second excluded date never did reappear in any of the three subsequent Chicago date lists (Libby 1952b, 1954a, 1954b), in any edition of *Radiocarbon Dating* (Libby 1952a, 1955, 1965a), or in any subsequent index of dates (e.g., Deevey et al. 1967). The only still unpublished Chicago ^{14}C value (C–459) is a charcoal sample that was expected to be of Mousterian age (i.e., in excess of 40,000 years B.P.). The average ^{14}C age cited in Arnold and Libby (1950:4) was 973 ± 230 B.P. The comment in the text was that the date was "much too young." An examination of the correspondence files of the Chicago laboratory has determined that the date was withdrawn at the last minute from the galleys of the first Chicago date list at the request of H. J. Movius, the Harvard archaeologist who had obtained the sample. He feared that his relationship with the archaeologists in France who collected the sample would be jeopardized (McBurney 1952:40).

6. More recently, geological evidence combined with additional ^{14}C data points lead to the conclusion that the burned-bone sample used for C–558 did not, in fact, come from the Folsom levels at the Lubbock Lake site (Holliday and

Johnson 1986). If this is correct, the first ¹⁴C age determination actually associated with Folsom materials was obtained much later on charcoal collected at the Lindenmeier site in Colorado. The value on this sample was 10,780 ± 375 B.P. (Haynes and Agogino 1960).

7. However, the first ¹⁴C determinations that were concerned with the Maya correlation problem obtained values from wooden lintels from Tikal that supported the Spinden correlation (Kulp et al. 1951; Libby 1954b). It was not until the late 1950s, when the University of Pennsylvania MASCA Laboratory undertook an extensive, detailed examination of the question, that it was determined that the so-called "presample-growth error" had to be taken into consideration since the dates had been obtained on wooden beams that contained several hundred years of rings. New wood samples were collected at Tikal with due consideration of the problem of "old wood." More than 100 new ¹⁴C determinations were obtained that provided strong, but to some, not conclusive evidence of the validity of the Goodman-Martinez-Thompson (GMT) correlation rather than the Spinden correlation (Ralph 1965; Satterthwaite and Ralph 1960).

8. Interestingly, Libby later stated that his World War II Manhattan Project research focused on inventing a material that would work in a method of gaseous diffusion enrichment of uranium using uranium hexafluoride was "better than my carbon 14 dating" (Libby 1978:37).

9. The beginnings of concern about the ¹⁴C "secular variation" phenomenon in ¹⁴C can be traced back to the studies of Hessel de Vries (1958) and Hans Suess (1961). Libby resisted the notion of serious deviations between ¹⁴C and "real time" until the mid-1960s (Libby 1963).

10. It appears that Redfield's interest grew out of informal cross-disciplinary "seminars" between University of Chicago faculty, including Harold Urey, Harrison Brown, and Libby from the Chemistry Department; members of the Department of Anthropology, including Redfield, Fay-Cooper Cole, Fred Eggan; and Sol Tax, Robert Braidwood from the Oriental Institute; and Donald Collier from the Chicago Natural History Museum. The general topic was "social science's role in the atomic age" (Gregory Marlowe, personal communication 1997).

11. There had been two earlier formal presentations on the ¹⁴C dating method to the archaeological/anthropological community: one by the Dutch paleoanthropologist G. H. R. von Koenigswald in October 1947 to a Viking Fund Supper Conference session and a second by Fred Eggan (University of Chicago) in December 1947 at a meeting of the AAA and SAA in Albuquerque, New Mexico (Gregory Marlowe, personal communication 1997).

12. Actually, the grant was given to both Libby and Harold Urey, who had been Libby's immediate superior at the Manhattan Project at Columbia University and who had been largely responsible for bringing Libby to Chicago at the conclusion of World War II. It has been reported that the first contact that finally resulted in Libby obtaining the support of the Viking Fund was a chance conversation between Urey and von Koenigswald (Libby 1980:1019; Marlowe 1980:1007; cf. Dodds 1973:100). Most of the Viking Fund support was expended in constructing a thermal diffusion column designed to enrich samples. The column was never routinely used for ¹⁴C dating because of the success of the

solid carbon screen-wall counting system. It should be emphasized that if solid carbon counting had not been feasible and if isotopic enrichment of samples had been required, the practicality of ^{14}C dating would have been seriously compromised because of two factors: the cost of producing each date and the lack of precision in knowing what the enrichment factor would be for each sample. The later problem would have increased the error factor that would have been assigned to each sample.

13. Frederick Johnson reports that Libby had made a request for samples but that many who heard him misunderstood the nature of the request. At this point in the development of the method, "known age" materials were needed to test the basic ^{14}C model. In early January 1948, Libby was still not entirely certain that there might not be some fatal defect in his reasoning. Johnson reports that many archaeologists who heard Libby that night apparently failed to appreciate this point (F. Johnson, personal communication 1986) (Marlowe 1980:1010).

Libby's initial interaction with archaeologists might also provide some perspective on a puzzling statement apparently first publicly made by him during his Nobel Prize address in 1960. In his Nobel lecture he stated,

> The research in the development of the dating technique consisted of two stages—the historical and the prehistorical epochs. The first shock Dr. Arnold and I had was when our advisors informed us that history extended back only to 5,000 years. We had thought initially that we would be able to get samples all along the curve back to 30,000 years, put the points in, and then our work would be finished. You read statements in books that such a society or archaeological site is 20,000 years old. We learned rather abruptly that these numbers, these ancient ages, are not known accurately; in fact, it is at about the time of the first dynasty in Egypt that the first historical date of any real certainty has been established. So we had, in the initial stages, the opportunity to check against knowns, principally Egyptian artifacts, and in the second stage we had to go into the great wilderness of prehistory to see whether there were elements of internal consistency which would lead one to believe that the method was sound or not. (Libby 1961a:102; see also Libby 1961b:624)

The facts are that Libby had been informed by Arnold of the approximately early third millennium B.C. historic boundary in the Near East as early as 1946 (J. R. Arnold, personal communication 1997). One explanation may be that up to the time of the Viking Fund dinner, Libby might have assumed that archaeologists from areas other than the Near East could provide well-dated materials earlier than 3000 B.C. Another—and to those who knew Libby personally more likely—explanation is that Libby's 1960 remembrance may have reflected a penchant for dramatizing certain events in his retrospective oral presentations dealing with the development of ^{14}C dating.

14. One early "known-age" sample of wood was supposed to have an age of about 2,000 years. However, the results of this measurement were not reported in print until 1967 (Libby 1967:17). This is because its count rate was essentially the same as that of the contemporary samples measured by Anderson. What had happened was that John Wilson, a highly respected University of Chicago Egyp-

tologist, had been asked to supply a piece of wood allegedly from the Hellenistic period. He apparently did not know that the wood selected had originally been obtained from an antiquities dealer in Egypt. It in no sense was a "known-age" sample. Its ^{14}C activity indicated that it was modern wood, i.e., a fake (Arnold in Marlowe 1980:1012–1013).

15. The initial corpus of ^{14}C data contained age estimates at variance with long-held views of some archaeologists—particularly of the older generation of archaeologists in central and eastern Europe (e.g., Neustupny 1970). The only continuing objection to the *overall* accuracy of the method has been based almost exclusively on quasi-theological grounds most often—but not exclusively (e.g., Cremo and Thompson 1993:764–794)—expressed within a European and American Protestant fundamentalist, young-earth, "creationist" framework (e.g., Brown 1983; Aardsma 1991).

7: Obsidian Hydration Dating, Past and Present

1. The term "absolute" is used by many researchers to refer to methods that yield quantitative results but most of which have degrees of uncertainty attached. Colman et al. (1987:315), in reviewing the situation for Quaternary dating methods, have suggested that the term "absolute" be abandoned altogether and replaced by four categories: numerical-age methods, applied to those that produce results on a ratio scale but that may have uncertainties attached; calibrated-age methods, those in which rates of particular processes must be calibrated by independent chronological control; relative-age methods, those that produce sequences of events; and correlated-age methods, those in which age estimates are produced through correlation (or association) with independently dated events. We use this terminology throughout this paper.

2. Experiments in a hydrothermal environment involve placing the specimens in distilled deionized water within a hydrothermal pressure vessel and then heating them to temperatures of between 150°C and 250°C for a specified length of time. Experiments by Rimstidt and Barnes (1980) and Stevenson, Carpenter, and Scheetz (1989) indicate that distilled deionized water can act as a solvent under temperatures of less than 300°C causing dissolution of the hydrated surface. Stevenson, Carpenter, and Scheetz (1989:195) suggest that use of a vapor environment at 100% relative humidity will prevent extended dissolution "since no water is present to remove a dissolved species."

10: Narrating Archaeology

1. See, for example, Lawrence Stone's discussion of the relationship of narrative history, as a descriptive mode, in contrast to analytic or "scientific history... which would in time produce generalized laws to explain historical change" (Stone 1979:5).

2. See also, for example, Roald Hoffman's (1988) analysis of writing in chemistry; Knorr-Cetina (1983) does a sophisticated analysis of the development of texts in protein chemistry. Gardin (1980) is also classic.

3. See, for example, M. B. Schiffer's (1996) discussion of the relationship

between behavioral and evolutionary archaeologies for a brief review of his model of inferential mechanisms and as an example of the "science anxiety" I present in a later section.

4. A hagiography is a biography of someone under consideration for canonization to sainthood. Whiggish histories are histories that assess prior knowledge in relation to and in support of the status and legitimacy of contemporary knowledge claims. See Rosenberg (1983), Staudenmaier (1985), and Shapin (1982).

5. See, for example, the discussions about a professional "registry" for archaeologists in the *Society for American Archaeology Bulletin* (13(2):2,18; 13(3):6-9, 14–15; 14(2):2; 14(4):14-20; 15(2):20; 15(3):6–14). Licensing has also been discussed in several states (*Society for American Archaeology Bulletin* 15(3):8).

6. Fagette (1996) shies away from any epistemological implications of his study beyond noting that the voluminous data provided by relief archaeology allowed for the establishment of regional chronologies and that the standardization of archaeological reporting allowed for an accumulationist model of science to be enacted.

7. For example, Stein (this volume) positions archaeology much more closely to paleontology and geology.

8. This is similar to the problem with the work of William Rathje's Garbage Project, in that the "hard evidence" of garbage is always given priority over people's accounts of their behavior. Again, we must determine under what circumstances various prioritizations of evidence occur, and, philosophically speaking, when each is legitimate.

9. Preucel's (1991) collection, among numerous other works, describes this debate. In a more recent example, Arnold (1996) made the unfortunately typical maneuver (an anachronistic fallacy to say the least) of comparing the relativism of postprocessualists with the ideological machinations of archeologists during Nazi authority. The critique goes like this: These Nazis "bent" the archeological record and available evidence to support their own agendas framed around a national narrative of superiority, placing facts in the service of ideology. For postpositivists, the conjecture is that facts become facts only when placed into a historically and culturally contingent, and merely locally coherent frame of reference, espousing perceptual (but not ontological) relativism. Arnold (1996) concludes that postpositivists are similar to Nazis. While the causes and implications of this particular collapse of epistemology to politics are beyond the scope of this paper, let me declare here publicly that although I do work within a postpositivist epistemology, I am not a Nazi. See also Star (1995:9-12).

10. Collins is talking about financial resources. It may also be interesting to think about accessible and yet untrammeled sites as scarce resources as well. This is obviously an issue when one sees discussions about limiting digging to professionals, but it also has an impact on the ability of students to formulate original research and, in fact, shapes what it means to be "original."

11. The origins of archaeology in the project of building nation-states is obvious, and well noted. But not every complex civilization or state undertakes archaeology, and it has been institutionalized very differently (or not at all) in the

places it has appeared. Rather than dismiss the Chinese speculations, Thracian collectors, Greek pot hunters, or the fifteenth-century excavations of Nero's quarters as nonscientific and as inferior archaeology, we need a much better socio-archaeological explanation for the interest in those represented in those projects in the first place.

References

Aardsma, G. E.
   1991   *Radiocarbon and the* Genesis *Flood*. Institute for Creation Research. San Diego.

Abel, Leland J.
   1955   *Pottery Types of the Southwest: Wares 5A, 10A, 10B, 12A, San Juan Red Ware, Mesa Verde Gray and White Ware, San Juan White Ware*, edited by Harold S. Colton. Museum of Northern Arizona Ceramic Series 3. Flagstaff.

Abrajano, T. A., J. K. Bates, and C. D. Byers
   1986   Aqueous Corrosion of Natural and Nuclearwaste Glasses. *Journal of Non-Crystalline Solids* 84:251–257.

Ahlstrom, Richard V. N.
   1985   *The Interpretation of Archaeological Tree-Ring Dates*. Ph.D. dissertation, University of Arizona. University Microfilms, Ann Arbor.
   1989   Tree-Ring Dating of Pindi Pueblo. *The Kiva* 54(4):361–384.

Ahlstrom, Richard V. N., David A. Breternitz, and Richard L. Warren
   1985   Archival Excavation: New Tree-Ring Dates from Lowry Ruin. *The Kiva* 51(1):39–42.

Ahlstrom, Richard V. N., Jeffrey S. Dean, and William J. Robinson
   1978   *Tree-Ring Studies of Walpi Pueblo*. University of Arizona Press, Tucson.
   1991   Evaluating Tree-Ring Interpretations at Walpi Pueblo. *American Antiquity* 56:628–644.

Ahlstrom, Richard V. N., Carla R. Van West, and Jeffrey S. Dean
   1995   Environmental and Chronological Factors in the Mesa Verde— Northern Rio Grande Migration. *Journal of Anthropological Archaeology* 14(1):125–142.

Aitken, M. J.
   1961   Measurement of the Magnetic Anomaly. *Archaeometry* 4:28–30.
   1985   *Thermoluminescence Dating*. Academic Press, London.
   1990   *Science-Based Dating in Archaeology*. Longman, London.
   1992   Optical Dating. *Quaternary Science Reviews* 11:127–131.
   1994   Optical Dating: A Non-Specialist Review. *Quaternary Geochronology* 13:503–508.

Aitken, M. J., J. Huxtable, and A. Murray
   1983   Thermoluminescence Dating of Ban Chiang Pottery. *Antiquity* 57:217–218.

Aitken, M. J., M. S. Tite, and S. J. Fleming
   1967   Luminescence Dosimetry. In *Proceedings of the International*

Conference on Luminescence Dosimetry, U.S. Atomic Energy
Commission, pp. 490–501. Stanford.

Aitken, M. J., M. S. Tite, and J. Reid
   1963   Thermoluminescent Dating: Progress Report. *Archaeometry*
          6:65–75.

Aitken, M. J., D. W. Zimmerman, and S. J. Fleming
   1968   Thermoluminescent Dating of Ancient Pottery. *Nature* 219:442–445.

Allsbrook, R. C.
   1995   Limestone, Grog and Shell: An Intemperate View of Pottery Temper
          in the Tennessee Valley. Paper Presented at the 60th Annual Meeting
          of the Society for American Archaeology. Minneapolis.

Ambler, J. Richard
   1985   Northern Kayenta Ceramic Chronology. In *Archaeological
          Investigations Near Rainbow City, Navajo Mountain, Utah*, edited
          by Phil R. Geib, J. Richard Ambler, and Martha M. Callahan, pp.
          28–68. Northern Arizona University Archaeological Report 576.
          Flagstaff.

Ambrose, W. R.
   1976   Intrinsic Hydration Rate Dating of Obsidian. In *Advances in
          Obsidian Glass Studies*, edited by R. E. Taylor, pp. 81–105. Noyes
          Press, Park Ridge, New Jersey.
   1984   Soil Temperature Monitoring at Lake Mungo: Implications for
          Racemisation Dating. *Australian Archaeology* 19:64–74.
   1993   Obsidian Hydration Dating. In *Archaeometry: Current Australasian
          Research*, edited by B. L. Frankhouser and J. R. Bird, pp. 79–84.
          Department of Prehistory, Research School of Pacific Studies, the
          Australian National University, Canberra.

Amsden, Charles Avery
   1931   Black-on-white Ware. In *the Pottery of Pecos, Vol. 1, the Dull Paint
          Wares*, by Alfred Vincent Kidder, pp. 17–72. Papers of the Phillips
          Academy Southwestern Expedition 5. Yale University Press, New
          Haven.

Anderson, E. C.
   1949   *Natural Radiocarbon*. Ph.D. dissertation, University of Chicago.
   1953   The Production and Distribution of Natural Radiocarbon. *Annual
          Review of Nuclear Science* 2:63–89.

Anderson, E. C., J. R. Arnold, and W. F. Libby
   1951   Measurement of Low Level Radiocarbon. The *Review of Scientific
          Instruments* 22:225–230.

Anderson, E. C. and R. N. Hayes
   1956   Recent Advances in Low Level Counting Techniques. *Annual
          Review of Nuclear Science* 6:303–323.

Anderson, E. C., H. Levi, and H. Tauber
   1953   Copenhagen Natural Radiocarbon Measurements, I. *Science*
          118:6–9.

Anderson, E. C., W. F. Libby, S. Weinhouse, A. F. Reid, A. D. Kirshenbaum,
          and A. V. Grosse

1947a Radiocarbon from Cosmic Radiation. *Science* 105:576.
1947b Natural Radiocarbon from Cosmic Radiation. The *Physical Review*
72:931–936.

Anovitz, L. M., J. M. Elam, L. R. Riciputi, and D. R. Cole
1999 The Failure of Obsidian Hydration Dating: Sources, Implications,
and New Directions. *Journal of Archaeological Science*.

Arnold, Bettina
1996 Archaeology as the Mother of Invention: National Mythmaking in
Nazi Germany. Paper presented at the 1996 AAA Annual Meeting,
San Francisco.

Arnold, J. R.
1954 Scintillation Counting of Natural Radiocarbon: I. The Counting
Method. *Science* 119:155–157.
1981 Introduction to Paper 50. In *Willard F. Libby Collected Papers.
Volume 1: Tritium and Radiocarbon* edited by R. Berger and L. M.
Libby, p. 14. Geo Science Analytical, Santa Monica.
1992 The Early Years with Libby at Chicago: A Retrospective. In
Radiocarbon after Four Decades: An Interdisciplinary Perspective,
R. E. Taylor, A. Long, and R. S. Kra, editors, pp. 3–10. Springer-
Verlag, New York.
1996 Interview for Faculty Oral History Archives, University of
California, San Diego. University Library, University of California,
San Diego.

Arnold, J. R. and W. F. Libby
1949 Age Determinations by Radiocarbon Content: Checks with Samples
of Known Age. *Science* 110:678–680.
1950 *Radiocarbon Dates* (September 1, 1950). University of Chicago,
Institute for Nuclear Studies.
1951 Radiocarbon Dates. *Science* 113:111–120.

Asaro, F., H. V. Michel, R. Sidrys, and F. Stross
1978 High-Precision Chemical Characterization of Major Obsidian
Sources in Guatemala. *American Antiquity* 43:436–443.

Ashmore, W. and R. J. Sharer
1996 *Discovering Our Past*. Mayfield Publishing, Mountain View,
California.

Bailey, Garrick A. and Roberta G. Bailey
1986 *A History of the Navajos: The Reservation Years*. School of
American Research Press, Santa Fe.

Baillie, M. G. L.
1982 *Tree-Ring Dating in Archaeology*. University of Chicago Press,
Chicago.
1995 *A Slice Through Time: Dendrochronology and Precision Dating*.
B. T. Batsford, London.

Baldwin, Gordon C.
1938 Basketmaker and Pueblo Sandals. *Southwestern Lore* 4(1):1–6.

Bandelier, Adolph F.
1890–1892 Final Report of Investigations Among the Indians of the

Southwestern United States. J. Wilson, Cambridge.

Bannister, Bryant

1962   The Interpretation of Tree-Ring Dates. *American Antiquity*
        27:508–514.

1963   A Synthesis of Southwestern Dendrochronology. Proposal Submitted
        to the National Science Foundation. Manuscript on file at the
        Laboratory of Tree-Ring Research, University of Arizona, Tucson.

Bannister, Bryant, Jeffrey S. Dean, and Elizabeth A. M. Gell

1966   *Tree-Ring Dates from Arizona E, Chinle—Canyon De Chelly—Red
        Rock Area.* Laboratory of Tree-Ring Research, Tucson.

Bannister, Bryant, Jeffrey S. Dean, and William J. Robinson

1968   *Tree-Ring Dates from Arizona C-D, Eastern Grand Canyon—Tsegi
        Canyon—Kayenta Area.* Laboratory of Tree-Ring Research, Tucson.

1969   Tree-Ring Dates from Utah S-W: Southern Utah Area. Laboratory of
        Tree-Ring Research, Tucson.

Bannister, Bryant, Elizabeth A. M. Gell, and John W. Hannah

1966   *Tree-Ring Dates from Arizona N-Q: Verde—Show Low—St. Johns
        Area.* Laboratory of Tree-Ring Research, Tucson.

Bannister, Bryant, John W. Hannah, and William J. Robinson

1966   *Tree-Ring Dates from Arizona K: Puerco—Wide Ruin—Ganado
        Area.* Laboratory of Tree-Ring Research, Tucson.

1970   *Tree-Ring Dates from New Mexico M, N, S, and Z: Southwestern
        New Mexico Area.* Laboratory of Tree-Ring Research, Tucson.

Bannister, Bryant, and William J. Robinson

1971   *Tree-Ring Dates from Arizona U-W: Gila—Salt Rivers Area.*
        Laboratory of Tree-Ring Research, Tucson.

1986   Archaeology and Dendrochronology. In *Emil W. Haury's Prehistory
        of the American Southwest*, edited by J. Jefferson Reid and David E.
        Doyel, pp. 49–54. University of Arizona Press, Tucson.

Bannister, Bryant, William J. Robinson, and Richard L. Warren

1967   *Tree-Ring Dates from Arizona J: Hopi Mesas Area.* Laboratory of
        Tree-Ring Research, Tucson.

1970   *Tree-Ring Dates from New Mexico A, G-H: Shiprock—Zuni—Mt.
        Taylor Area.* Laboratory of Tree-Ring Research, Tucson.

Basgall, M. E.

1983   *Archaeology of the Forest Service Forty Site (CA-Mno-529), Mono
        County, California.* Submitted to the U.S. Department of the
        Interior, Forest Service, Inyo National Forest, Bishop, California.

1989   Obsidian Acquisition and Use in Prehistoric Central-Eastern
        California: A Preliminary Assessment. In *Current Directions in
        California Obsidian Studies*, edited by R. E. Hughes, pp. 111–126.
        Contributions of the University of California Archaeological
        Research Facility No. 48. Berkeley.

1990   Hydration Dating of Coso Obsidian: Problems and Prospects. Paper
        presented at the 24th Meeting of the Society for California
        Archaeology, Foster City.

1993   *The Archaeology of Nelson Basin and Adjacent Areas, Fort Irwin,*

San Bernardino County, California. Report submitted to the U.S. Army Corps of Engineers, Los Angeles by Far Western Anthropological Research Group, Inc., Davis.

1995 Obsidian Hydration Dating of Early-Holocene Assemblages in the Mojave Desert. *Current Research in the Pleistocene* 12:57–60.

n.d. An Archaeological Approach to the Hydration Dating of Coso Obsidian. Manuscript in possession of C. Beck.

Basgall, M. E. and M. C. Hall

1993 *Archaeology of the Awl Site, CA-SBR-4562, Fort Irwin, San Bernardino County, California.* Submitted to the U.S. Army Corps of Engineers, Los Angeles, by Far Western Anthropological Research Group, Davis.

Basgall, M. E., M. C. Hall, and W. R. Hildebrandt

1988 *The Late Holocene Archaeology of Drinkwater Basin, Fort Irwin, San Bernardino County, California.* Submitted to the U.S. Army Corps of Engineers, Los Angeles, by Far Western Anthropological Research Group, Inc., Davis.

Basgall, M. E. and K. R. McGuire

1988 *The Archaeology of CA-INY-30: Prehistoric Culture Change in the Southern Owens Valley, California.* Submitted to California Department of Transportation, Sacramento, by Far Western Anthropological Research Group, Inc., Davis.

Basgall, M. E. and D. L. True

1985 *Archaeological Investigations in Crowder Canyon, 1973–1984: Excavation at Sites SBR-421B, SBR-421C, SBR-421D, and SBR-713.* Submitted to the California Department of Transportation, Office of Environmental Analysis, Sacramento.

Bates, J. K., T. A. Abrajano, Jr., W. L. Ebert, J. J. Mazer, and T. J. Gerding

1988 Experimental Hydration Studies of Natural and Synthetic Glasses. In *Materials in Art and Archaeology*, edited by E. Sayer, P. Vandiver, J. Druzik, and C. Stevenson. Materials Research Society Symposium Proceedings 123:237.

Batt, C. M.

1997 The British Archaeomagnetic Calibration Curve: An Objective Treatment. *Archaeometry* 39:153–168.

Beals, Ralph L., George W. Brainerd, and Watson Smith

1945 *Archaeological Studies in Northeast Arizona: A Report on the Archaeological Work of the Rainbow Bridge–Monument Valley Expedition.* University of California Publications in American Archaeology and Ethnology 44(1). Berkeley.

Beck, C.

1995 Functional Attributes and Differential Persistence of Great Basin Dart Forms. *Journal of California and Great Basin Anthropology* 17:222–243.

1998 Projectile Points as Valid Chronological Units. In *Unit Issues in Archaeology. Measuring Time, Space, and Material*, edited by A. F. Ramenofsky and A. Steffen, pp. 21–40. University of Utah Press,

Salt Lake City.

1999   Modeling Chronology. In *Models for the Future. Great Basin Anthropology Today*, edited by C. Beck. University of Utah Press, Salt Lake City.

Beck, C. (editor)

1994   *Dating in Exposed and Surface Contexts*. University of New Mexico Press, Albuquerque.

Beck, C. and G. T. Jones

1990   Toolstone Selection and Lithic Technology in Early Great Basin Prehistory. *Journal of Field Archaeology* 17:283–299.

1992   Paleoindian/Archaic Range Shifts in Eastern Nevada. *Current Research in the Pleistocene* 9:1–20.

1994   Dating Surface Assemblages Using Obsidian Hydration. In *Dating in Exposed and Surface Contexts*, edited by C. Beck. University of New Mexico Press, Albuquerque.

1997   The Late Pleistocene Early Holocene Archaeology of the Great Basin. *Journal of World Prehistory* 11:161–236.

Ben-David, Joseph

1960   Roles and Innovations in Medicine. *American Journal of Sociology* 55(6):557–568.

Ben-David, Joseph and Randall Collins

1966   Social Factors in the Origins of a New Science: The Case of Psychology. *American Sociological Review* 31(4):451–569.

Berger, Peter L. and Thomas Luckmann

1967   *The Social Construction of Reality: A Treatise in the Sociology of Knowledge*. Anchor/Doubleday, New York.

Berger, R. and L. M. Libby (editors)

1981   *Willard F. Libby Collected Papers. Volume 1: Tritium and Radiocarbon*. Geoscience Analytical, Santa Monica.

Berry, Michael S.

1982   *Time, Space, and Transition in Anasazi Prehistory*. University of Utah Press, Salt Lake City.

Betancourt, Julio F., Jeffrey S. Dean, and Herbert M. Hull

1986   Prehistoric Long-Distance Transport of Construction Beams, Chaco Canyon, New Mexico. *American Antiquity* 51:370–375.

Bettinger, R. L.

1989   Establishing an Hydration Rate for Fish Springs Obsidian. In *Current Directions in California Obsidian Studies*, edited by R. E. Hughes, pp. 59–68. Contributions of the University of California Archaeological Research Facility No. 48. Berkeley.

Bettinger, R. L., M. G. Delacorte, and R. L. Jackson

1984   Visual Sourcing of Central Eastern California Obsidians. In *Obsidian Studies in the Great Basin*, edited by R. E. Hughes, pp. 63–78. Contributions of the University of California Archaeological Research Facility No. 45. Berkeley.

Bettinger, R. L., J. F. O'Connell, and D. H. Thomas

1991   Projectile Points as Time Markers in the Great Basin. *American*

Antiquity 51:737–747.

Binford, Lewis R.

1964 A Consideration of Archaeological Research Design. *American Antiquity* 29:425–441.

1977 General Introduction. In *For Theory Building in Archaeology*, edited by L. R. Binford, pp. 1–10. Academic Press, New York.

Blake, M., J. E. Clark, B. Voorhies, G. Michaels, M. W. Love, M. E. Pye, A. A. Demarest, and B. Arroyo

1995 Radiocarbon Chronology for the Late Archaic and Formative Periods on the Pacific Coast of Southeastern Mesoamerica. *Ancient Mesoamerica* 6:161–183.

Blinman, Eric

1984 Dating with Neckbands: Calibration of Temporal Variation in Moccasin Gray and Mancos Gray Ceramic Types. In *Dolores Archaeological Program Synthetic Report, 1978–1981*, pp. 128–138. U.S. Department of the Interior, Bureau of Reclamation, Engineering and Research Center, Denver.

1988a *The Interpretation of Ceramic Variability: A Case Study from the Dolores Anasazi*. Ph.D. dissertation, Department of Anthropology, Washington State University, Pullman.

1988b Justification and Procedures for Ceramic Dating. In *Dolores Archaeological Program: Supporting Studies: Additive and Reductive Technologies*, compiled by Eric Blinman, Carl J. Phagan, and Richard H. Wilshusen, pp. 501–544. U.S. Department of the Interior, Bureau of Reclamation, Engineering and Research Center, Denver.

Blitz, J. H.

1993 *Ancient Chiefdoms of the Tombigbee*. University of Alabama Press, Tuscaloosa.

Blume, Stuart S.

1992 *Insight and Industry: On the Dynamics of Technological Change in Medicine*. Massachusetts Institute of Technology Press, Cambridge.

Bonde, Niels

1994 The Dating of the Norwegian Viking Age Ship Burials: A Successful Norwegian-Danish Research Project. In *Saetryk Fra Nationalmuseets Arbejdsmark* 1994:128–148.

Bonde, Niels and Arne E. Christensen

1993 Dendrochronological Dating of the Viking Age Ship Burials at Oseberg, Gokstad, and Tune, Norway. *Antiquity* 67(256):575–583.

Bonfiglioli, G.

1968 Thermoluminescence: What It Can and Cannot Show. In *Thermoluminescence of Geological Materials*, edited by D. J. McDougall, pp. 15–24. Academic Press, London.

Bordes, F.

1961 Mousterian Cultures in France. *Science* 134:803–810.

1968 *The Old Stone Age*. Weidenfeld & Nicholson, London.

1972 *A Tale of Two Caves*. Harper & Rowe, New York.

1978 Typological Variability in the Mousterian Layers at Pech Del'aze II and IV. *Journal of Anthropological Research* 34:181–193.

Bøtter-Jensen, L.
1988 The Automated Risø TL Dating Reader System. *Nuclear Tracks and Radiation Measurements* 14:177–180.

Bøtter-Jensen, L., H. Jungner, and V. Mejdahl
1993 Recent Developments of OSL Techniques for Dating Quartz and Feldspars. *Radiation Protection Dosimetry* 47:643–648.

Bøtter-Jensen, L., N. R. J. Poolton, F. Willumsen, and H. Christiansen
1994 A Compact Design for Monochromatic OSL Measurements in the Wavelength Range 380–1020 Nm. *Radiation Measurements* 23:519–522.

Bouey, P. D. and M. E. Basgall
1984 Trans-Sierran Exchange in Prehistoric California: The Concept of Economic Articulation. In *Obsidian Studies in the Great Basin*, edited by R. E. Hughes, pp. 135–172. Contributions of the University of California Archaeological Research Facility, No. 45. Berkeley.

Bowman, Sheridan
1991 Questions of Chronology. In *Science and the Past*, edited by S. Bowman, pp. 117–140. British Museum Press, London.

Boyle, R.
1691 *Experimenta & Observationes Physicae*. Printed for J. Taylor and J. Wyat, London.

Brady, Lionel F.
1932 Geological Activities of the Museum of Northern Arizona, 1931. *Museum Notes* 4(9):1–4.

Brainerd, George W.
1951 The Place of Chronological Ordering in Archaeological Analysis. *American Antiquity* 16:301–313.

Braun, David P.
1985 Absolute Seriation: A Time Series Approach. In *For Concordance in Archaeological Analysis: Bridging Data Structure, Quantitative Technique, and Theory*, edited by Christopher Carr, pp. 509–539. Westport Publishers, Kansas City.

Breternitz, David A.
1966 *An Appraisal of Tree-Ring Dated Pottery in the Southwest*. Anthropological Papers of the University of Arizona, No. 10. Tucson.

Britton, D. and E. E. Richards
1963 Optical Emission Spectroscopy and the Study of Metallurgy in the European Bronze Age. In *Science and Archaeology*, edited by D. Brothwell and E. Higgs, pp. 603–613. Praeger Publishers, New York.

Bronson, B. and M. C. Han
1972 A Thermoluminescence Series from Thailand. *Antiquity* 46:322–326.

Browman, David L. and Douglas R. Givens
1996 Stratigraphic Excavation: The First "New Archaeology." *American*

Anthropologist 98(1):80–95.

Brown, Gary M.

1998   Old Wood and Early Navajo: A Chronometric Analysis of the
       Dinétah Phase. In *Diné Bikéyah: Papers in Honor of David M.*
       Brugge, edited by Meliha S. Duran and David T. Kirkpatrick, pp.
       39–56. The Archaeological Society of New Mexico No. 24.
       Albuquerque.

Brown, Gregory J. and David F. Muraca

1993   Phasing Stratigraphic Sequences at Colonial Williamsburg. In
       Practices of Archaeological Stratigraphy, edited by Edward C.
       Harris, Marley R. Brown, III, and Gregory J. Brown, pp. 155–166.
       Academic Press, London.

Brown, Marley R., III and Edward C. Harris

1993   Interfaces in Archaeological Stratigraphy. In *Practices of*
       Archaeological Stratigraphy, edited by Edward Harris, Marley R.
       Brown, III, and Gregory J. Brown, pp. 7–20. Academic Press, New
       York.

Brown, R. H.

1983   The Interpretation of Carbon-14 Age Data. In *Origin by Design*,
       H. G. Coffin, pp. 309–329. Review and Harold Publishing
       Association, Washington, D.C.

Brugge, David M.

1983   Navajo Prehistory and History to 1850. In *Southwest*, edited by
       Alfonso Ortiz, pp. 489–501. Handbook of North American Indians,
       Volume 10, W. Sturtevant, general editor. Smithsonian Institution,
       Washington, D.C.

1986   *Tsegai: An Archaeological Ethnohistory of the Chaco Region*. U.S.
       Department of the Interior, National Park Service, Washington, D.C.

Bryan, Kirk

1937   Geology of the Folsom Deposits in New Mexico and Colorado. In
       Early Man, A Symposium, edited by G. G. Maccurdy, pp. 139–152.
       Lippincott, Philadelphia.

Bryan, Kirk and Louis L. Ray

1940   *Geologic Antiquity of the Lindenmeier Site in Colorado.*
       Smithsonian Miscellaneous Collections 99(2). Smithsonian
       Institution, Washington, D.C.

Buchanan, R. A.

1991   Theory and Narrative in the History of Technology. *Technology and*
       Culture 32(2):365–376.

Burlatskaya, S. P. and G. N. Petrova

1961   First Results of a Study of the Geomagnetic Field in the Past by the
       "Archaeomagnetic" Method. *Geomagnetism and Aeronomy*
       1:233–236. English translation.

Burns, Barney T.

1983   *Simulated Anasazi Storage Behavior Using Crop Yields*
       Reconstructed from Tree-Rings: A.D. 652–1968. Ph.D. dissertation,
       University of Arizona. University Microfilms, Ann Arbor.

Burris, Beverly
    1993   *Technocracy at Work*. State University of New York Press, Albany.
Bushnell, G.
    1961   Radiocarbon Dates and New World Chronology. *Antiquity*
           35:286–291.
Butzer, Karl W.
    1964   *Environment and Archaeology: An Introduction to Pleistocene
           Geography*. Aldine Publishing, Chicago.
    1971   *Environment and Archaeology: An Ecological Approach to
           Prehistory*. Aldine-Atherton, Chicago.
Cann, J. R. and C. Renfrew
    1964   The Characterization of Obsidian and Its Application to the
           Mediterranean Region. *Proceedings of the Prehistoric Society*
           30:111–133.
Carlson, R. L.
    1965   *Eighteenth Century Navajo Fortresses of the Gobernador District*.
           Museum Series in Anthropology, Volume 10. University of
           Colorado, Boulder.
Carriveau, G. W. and G. Harbottle
    1983   Van Chiang Pottery: Thermoluminescence Dating Problems.
           Antiquity 58:56–58.
Chapman, Kenneth M.
    1921   What the Potsherds Tell. *Art and Archaeology* 11:39–44.
    1923   Casas Grandes Pottery. *Art and Archaeology* 16:25–34.
Chardon, Roland
    1980   The Linear League in North America. *Annals of the Association for
           American Geographers* 70(2):129–153.
Christenson, Andrew L.
    1986   Projectile Point Size and Projectile Point Aerodynamics: An
           Exploratory Study. *Plains Anthropologist* 31:109–128.
    1988   *The Cultural Sequences of Black Mesa and Tsegi Canyon, Arizona:
           A Comparison Using Mean Ceramic Dating*. Paper Presented at the
           53rd Annual Meeting of the Society for American Archaeology,
           Phoenix.
    1989   *Tracing Archaeology's Past: The Historiography of Archaeology*.
           Southwest Illinois University Press, Carbondale.
    1994   A Test of Mean Ceramic Dating Using Well-Dated Kayenta Anasazi
           Sites. *The Kiva* 59:297–317.
    1995   Nonbuffware Decorated Ceramics and Mean Ceramic Dating. In
           *The Roosevelt Community Development Study, Vol. 2: Ceramic
           Chronology, Technology, and Economics*, edited by James M.
           Heidke and Miriam T. Stark, pp. 85–132. Anthropological Papers
           14. Center for Desert Archaeology, Tucson.
Christenson, Andrew L. and Marilyn J. Bender
    1994   A Method for the Chronological Classification of Black Mesa Sherd
           Assemblages. In *Function and Technology of Anasazi Ceramics from
           Black Mesa, Arizona*, edited by Marion F. Smith, Jr., pp. 223–236.

Center for Archaeological Investigations, Occasional Paper No. 15. Southern Illinois University, Carbondale.

Clark, D. L.
1961 *The Application of the Obsidian Dating Method to the Archaeology of Central California.* Ph.D. dissertation, Stanford University, California.
1964 Archaeological Chronology in California and the Obsidian Hydration Method. In *University of California Archaeological Survey Report 1963–1964*, pp. 143–211. Berkeley.

Clark, J. D.
1979 Radiocarbon Dating and African Archaeology. In *Radiocarbon Dating*, edited by R. Berger and H. E. Suess, pp. 7–31. University of California Press, Berkeley
1984 Foreword. In *Radiocarbon User's Handbook*, by R. Gillespie. Oxonian Rewley Press, Oxford.

Clark, W.
1964 *The Field Notes of Captain William Clark, 1803–1805.* Yale University Press, New Haven.

Cleland, J. H.
1990 *Sugarload Archaeological District Cultural Resources Management Plan.* Submitted to the Environmental Branch, Naval Air Station, China Lake, California.

Colcutt, S. N.
1987 Archaeostratigraphy: A Geoarchaeologist's Viewpoint. *Stratigraphica Archaeologica* 2:11–18.

Cole, Fay-Cooper
1934 *Dendrochronology in the Mississippi Valley.* Committee on State Archaeological Surveys, Division of Anthropology and Psychology, National Research Council, Circular Series No. 16. Ann Arbor, Michigan.

Collins, Randall
1989 Toward a Theory of Intellectual Change: The Social Causes of Philosophies. *Science, Technology, and Human Values* 14(2):107–140.

Colman, S. M., K. L. Pierce, and P. W. Birkeland
1987 Suggested Terminology for Quaternary Dating Methods. *Quaternary Research* 28:314–319.

Colton, Harold S.
1932 Sunset Crater: The Effect of a Volcanic Eruption on an Ancient Pueblo People. *The Geographical Review* 32:582–590.
1945 Sunset Crater. *Plateau* 18:7–14.
1946 *The Sinagua.* Museum of Northern Arizona Bulletin No. 17. Flagstaff.
1952 *Pottery Types of the Arizona Strip and Adjacent Areas in Utah and Nevada.* Museum of Northern Arizona Ceramic Series 1. Flagstaff.
1953 *Potsherds: An Introduction to the Study of Prehistoric Southwestern Ceramics and Their Use in Historic Reconstruction.* Museum of

Northern Arizona Bulletin 25. Flagstaff.

1955   *Pottery Types of the Southwest: Wares 8A, 8B, 9A, 9B, Tusayan
        Gray and White Ware, Little Colorado Gray and White Ware.*
        Museum of Northern Arizona Ceramic Series 3. Flagstaff.

1956   *Pottery Types of the Southwest: Wares 5A, 5B, 6A, 6B, 7A, 7B, 7C,
        San Juan Red Ware, Tsegi Orange Ware, Homolovi Orange Ware,
        Winslow Orange Ware, Awatovi Yellow Ware, Jeddito Yellow Ware,
        Sichomovi Red Ware.* Museum of Northern Arizona Ceramic Series
        3C. Flagstaff.

1958   *Pottery Types of the Southwest: Wares 14, 15, 16, 17, 18. Revised
        Description: Alameda Brown Ware, Tizon Brown Ware, Lower
        Colorado Buff Ware, Prescott Gray Ware, San Francisco Mt. Gray
        Ware.* Museum of Northern Arizona Ceramic Series 3D. Flagstaff.

1960   *Black Sand: Prehistory in Northern Arizona.* University of New
        Mexico Press, Albuquerque.

Colton, Harold S. and Lyndon L. Hargrave

1937   *Handbook of Northern Arizona Pottery Wares.* Museum of
        Northern Arizona Bulletin 11. Flagstaff.

Conkey, Margaret W. and Sarah H. Williams

1991   Original Narratives: The Political Economy of Gender in
        Archaeology. In *Gender at the Crossroads: Feminist Anthropology
        in the Postmodern Era,* edited by Micaela di Leondardo, pp.
        102–138. University of California Press, Berkeley.

Conkin, Barbara M. and James E. Conkin

1984   *Stratigraphy: Foundations and Concepts.* Van Nostrand Reinhold,
        New York.

Cook, R. M. and J. C. Belshé

1958   Archaeomagnetism: A Preliminary Report from Britain. *Antiquity*
        32:167–178.

Cornelius, Oliver Frasier

1938   Basketmaker Sandals (?). *Southwestern Lore* 3(4):74–78.

Cox, J. R. and E. Blinman

1997   NSEP Archaeomagnetic Dating: Procedures, Results, and
        Interpretations. In *Pipeline Archaeology 1990–1993: The El Paso
        Natural Gas North System Expansion Project, New Mexico and
        Arizona,* Vol. 12, edited by T. M. Kerns, pp. 19.1–19.56. Western
        Cultural Resources Management, Farmington.

Crawford, G. W., D. G. Smith, and V. E. Bowyer

1997   Dating the Entry of Corn (*Zea Mays*) into the Lower Great Lakes
        Region. *American Antiquity* 62:112–119.

Cremeens, David L. and John P. Hart

1995   On Chronostratigraphy, Pedostratigraphy, and Archaeological
        Context. In *Pedological Perspectives in Archaeological Research,*
        edited by Mary E. Collins, Brian J. Carter, Bruce G. Gladfelter, and
        Randal J. Southard, pp. 15–33. Soil Science Society of America,
        Special Publication 44, Madison.

Cremo, M. A. and R. L. Thompson

1993   *Forbidden Archaeology.* Bhaktivedanta Institute, San Diego.
Crown, Patricia L.
1991   Evaluating the Construction Sequence and Population of Pot Creek
        Pueblo, Northern New Mexico. *American Antiquity* 56(2):291–314.
Cummings, Byron
1936   Prehistoric Pottery of the Southwest. *The Kiva* 1(2):1–8.
Daniel, Glyn E.
1950   *A Hundred Years of Archaeology.* Duckworth, London.
1967   *The Origins and Growth of Archaeology.* Crowell, New York.
1975   *A Hundred and Fifty Years of Archaeology.* Duckworth, Cambridge,
        England.
1976   *A Hundred and Fifty Years of Archaeology.* Harvard University
        Press, Cambridge.
Daniels, Farrington, Charles A. Boyd, and Donald F. Saunders
1953   Thermoluminescence as a Research Tool. *Science* 117:343–349.
Dark, K. R.
1995   *Theoretical Archaeology.* Duckworth, London.
Davidson, D. A. and M. L. Shackley
1976   *Geoarchaeology.* Westview Press, Boulder.
Deal, Michael
1985   Household Pottery Disposal in the Maya Highlands: An
        Ethnoarchaeological Interpretation. *Journal of Anthropological
        Archaeology* 4:243–291.
Dean, Dennis R.
1992   *James Hutton and the History of Geology.* Cornell University Press,
        Ithaca, New York.
Dean, Jeffrey S.
1969a   Dendrochronology and Archaeological Analysis: A Possible Ute
        Example from Southwestern Colorado. *Southwestern Lore*
        35(3):29–41.
1969b   *Chronological Analysis of Tsegi Phase Sites in Northeastern
        Arizona.* Papers of the Laboratory of Tree-Ring Research, No. 3.
        University of Arizona, Tucson.
1970   Aspects of Tsegi Phase Social Organization: A Trial Reconstruction.
        In *Reconstructing Prehistoric Pueblo Societies,* edited by W. A.
        Longacre, pp. 140–174. University of New Mexico Press,
        Albuquerque.
1975   Tree-Ring Dates from Colorado W: Durango Area. Laboratory of
        Tree-Ring Research, Tucson.
1978   Independent Dating in Archaeological Analysis. In *Advances in
        Archaeological Method and Theory,* Vol. 1, edited by M. B. Schiffer,
        pp. 223–255. Academic Press, New York.
1985   Review of Time, Space, and Transition in Anasazi Prehistory by
        Michael S. Berry, University of Utah Press, Salt Lake City. *American
        Antiquity* 50:704–705.
1988   A Model of Anasazi Behavioral Adaptation. In *The Anasazi in a
        Changing Environment,* edited by George J. Gumerman, pp.

119–167. Cambridge University Press, Cambridge, England.

1991   Thoughts on Hohokam Chronology. In *Exploring the Hohokam: Prehistoric Desert Peoples of the American Southwest*, edited by George J. Gumerman, pp. 61–149. An Amerind Foundation Publication, University of New Mexico Press, Albuquerque.

1996a   Dendrochronology and the Study of Human Behavior. In Tree-Rings, Environment, and Humanity, edited by J. S. Dean, D. M. Meko, and T. W. Swetnam. *Radiocarbon* 1996:461–469.

1996b   Behavioral Sources of Error in Archaeological Tree-Ring Dating: Navajo and Pueblo Wood Use. In Tree-Rings, Environment, and Humanity, edited by J. S. Dean, D. M. Meko, and T. W. Swetnam. *Radiocarbon* 1996:497–503.

1997   Dendrochronology. In *Chronometric Dating in Archaeology*, edited by R. E. Taylor, and M. J. Aitken, pp. 31–64. Plenum Press, New York.

Dean, Jeffrey S., William H. Doelle, and Janet D. Orcutt

1994   Adaptive Stress: Environment and Demography. In *Themes in Southwestern Prehistory*, edited by George J. Gumerman, pp. 53–86. School of American Research, Santa Fe.

Dean, Jeffrey S., Robert C. Euler, George J. Gumerman, Fred Plog, Richard H. Hevly, and Thor V. N. Karlstrom

1985   Human Behavior, Demography, and Paleoenvironment on the Colorado Plateau. *American Antiquity* 50:537–554.

Dean, Jeffrey S. and William A. Robinson

1977   *Dendroclimatic Variability in the American Southwest, A.D. 680–1970*. Laboratory of Tree-Ring Research, Tucson.

Dean, Jeffrey S. and Scott C. Russell

1978   Navajo Wood Use Behavior. Ms. on file at the Laboratory of Tree-Ring Research, University of Arizona, Tucson.

Dean, Jeffrey S. and Richard L. Warren

1983   Dendrochronology. In *The Architecture and Dendrochronology of Chetro Ketl*, edited by S. H. Lekson, pp. 105–240. Reports of the Chaco Center 6. U.S. Department of the Interior, National Park Service, Albuquerque.

Deaver, W. L. and R. S. Ciolek-Torrello

1995   Early Formative Period Chronology for the Tucson Basin. *The Kiva* 60:481–529.

De Barros, Phillip L. F.

1982   The Effects of Variable Site Occupation Span on the Results of Frequency Seriation. *American Antiquity* 47:291–315.

Debenham, N. C. and M. J. Aitken

1984   Thermoluminescence of Stalagmitic Calcite. *Archaeometry* 26:155–170.

Deevey, E. S., Jr., R. F. Flint, and I. Rouse

1967   *Radiocarbon Measurements: Comprehensive Index, 1950–1965*. Yale University, New Haven.

de Vries, H.

1958   Variations in Concentration of Radiocarbon with Time and Location on Earth. *Proceedings, Nederlandsche Akademie Van Wetenschappen* Series B 61:1

Dillehay, Tom D.

1989   *Monte Verde, A Pleistocene Settlement in Chile: A Palaeoenvironment and Site Context*, Vol. 1. Smithsonian Series in Archaeological Inquiry. Smithsonian Institution Press, Washington, D. C.

1997   *Monte Verde, A Pleistocene Settlement in Chile: The Archaeological Context and Interpretation*, Vol. 2. Smithsonian Series in Archaeological Inquiry. Smithsonian Institution Press, Washington D.C.

Dittert, Alfred E., Jr. and Stewart Peckham

1998   Foreword. In *Prehistoric Ceramics of the Puerco Valley, Arizona: The 1995 Chambers-Sanders Trust Lands Ceramic Conference*, edited by Kelley Hays-Gilpin and Eric Van Hartesveldt. Museum of Northern Arizona Ceramic Series No. 7. Flagstaff.

Dixon, Roland B.

1913   Some Aspects of North American Archaeology. *American Anthropologist* 15(4):549–573.

Dodds, J. W.

1973   *The Several Lives of Paul Fejos*. Wenner-Gren Foundation, New York.

Donaldson, B. R. and J. R. Welch

1991   Western Apache Dwellings and Their Archaeological Correlates. In *Mogollon V*, edited by P. Beckett, pp. 93–105. COAS Publishing, Las Cruces.

Doremus, R. H.

1975   Interdiffusion of Hydrogen and Alkalai Ions in a Glass Surface. *Journal of Non-Crystalline Solids* 19:137–144.

Douglass, Andrew Ellicott

1929   The Secret of the Southwest Solved by Talkative Tree-Rings. *National Geographic Magazine* 56(6):736–770.

1935   *Dating Pueblo Bonito and Other Ruins of the Southwest*. National Geographic Society Contributed Technical Papers, Pueblo Bonito Series, Number 1. Washington, D.C.

1936   The Central Pueblo Chronology. *Tree-Ring Bulletin* 2(4):29–34.

1938   Southwestern Dated Ruins: V. *Tree-Ring Bulletin* 5(2):10–13.

1939   Notes on Beam Dating by Sap-Heart Contact. *Tree-Ring Bulletin* 6(1):3–6.

Downum, Christian S.

1988   *One Grand History: A Critical Review of Flagstaff Archaeology, 1951–1988*. Ph.D. dissertation, Department of Anthropology, University of Arizona. Tucson.

Drews, M. and R. G. Elston

1983   *An Archaeological Investigation of Drilling Locations and Power Plant Site in the Coso Known Geothermal Resource Area, China Lake Naval Weapons Center*. Submitted to the Environmental Branch, Naval Air Weapons Station, China Lake, California.

DuBois, R. L.

1975   Secular Variation in Southwestern U.S.A. as Suggested by
       Archaeomagnetic Results. In *Proceedings of the Takesi Nagata
       Conference: Magnetic Fields, Past and Present*, edited by R. M.
       Fisher, M. Fuller, V. A. Schmidt, and P. J. Wasilewski, pp. 133–144.
       Goddard Space Flight Center, Greenbelt, Maryland.

1989   Archaeomagnetic Results from Southwest United States and
       Mesoamerica, and Comparison with Some Other Areas. *Physics of
       the Earth and Planetary Interiors* 56:18–33.

DuBois, R. L. and N. Watanabe

1965   Preliminary Results of Investigations Made to Study the Use of
       Indian Pottery to Determine the Paleointensity of the Geomagnetic
       Field for the United States A.D. 600–1400. *Journal of Geomagnetism
       and Geoelectricity* 17:417–423.

Duff, Andrew I.

1996   Ceramic Micro-Seriation: Types or Attributes? *American Antiquity*
       61:89–101.

Dunnell, Robert C.

1970   Seriation Method and Its Evaluation. *American Antiquity*
       35:305–319.

1986   Five Decades of American Archaeology. In *American Archaeology
       Past and Future*, edited by David J. Meltzer, Donald D. Fowler, and
       Jeremy L. Sabloff, pp. 23–49. Smithsonian Institution Press,
       Washington, D.C.

1992   The Notion Site. In *Space, Time and Archaeological Landscapes*,
       edited by J. Rossignol and L. Wandsnider, pp. 21–41. Plenum Press,
       New York.

Dunnell, R. C. and M. L. Readhead

1988   The Relation of Dating and Chronology: Comments on Chatters
       and Hoover (1986) and Butler and Stein (1988). *Quaternary
       Research* 30:232–233.

Dykeman, Douglas D. and Jeffrey T. Wharton

1994   The Morris 1 Land Use Study: An Alternative Data Recovery Plan
       for Site LA 11196, LA 83529, and LA 88766 In *Williams Services
       Unit 29–7 Gas Gathering System, Rio Arriba County, New Mexico*.
       Ms. on file, NNAD, Farmington.

Ebert, W. L., R. F. Hoburg, and J. K. Bates

1991   The Sorption of Water on Obsidian and a Nuclear Waste Glass.
       Physics and Chemistry of Glasses 32:133–137.

Eckstein, D., T. Wazny, J. Bauch, and P. Klein

1986   New Evidence for the Dendrochronological Dating of Netherlandish
       Paintings. *Nature* 320:465–466.

Eighmy, J. L.

1980   Archaeomagnetists Agree on Reporting Procedure. *Society for
       Archaeological Science Newsletter* 4:1–2.

1991   Archaeomagnetism: New Data on the South-West U.S.A. Master
       Virtual Geomagnetic Pole Curve. *Archaeometry* 33:201–213.

Eighmy, J. L. and L. B. Davis
   1997   Archaeomagnetometry of Early-Holocene Alder Complex Roasting
          Pits, Barton Gulch, Montana. *Current Research in the Pleistocene*
          14:22–24.
Eighmy, J. L. and J. H. Hathaway
   1987   Contemporary Archaeomagnetic Results and the Accuracy of
          Archaeomagnetic Dates. *Geoarchaeology* 2:49–61.
Eighmy, J. L., J. H. Hathaway, and S. Counce
   1987   *Independently Dated Virtual Geomagnetic Poles: The C.S.U.*
          Archaeometric Data Base. Colorado State University Archaeometric
          Laboratory, Technical Series, No. 1. Fort Collins.
Eighmy, J. L., J. H. Hathaway, and A. E. Kane
   1990   The Dolores Modification: Final Results. In *Archaeomagnetic*
          Dating, edited by J. L. Eighmy and R. S. Sternberg, pp. 226–236.
          University of Arizona Press, Tucson.
Eighmy, J. L. and J. B. Howard
   1991   Direct Dating of Prehistoric Canal Sediments Using
          Archaeomagnetism. *American Antiquity* 56:88–102.
Eighmy, J. L. and P. Y. Klein
   1988   *1988 Additions to the List of Independently Dated Virtual*
          Geomagnetic Poles and the South-West Master Curve. Colorado
          State University Archaeometric Laboratory, Technical Series, No. 4.
          Fort Collins.
   1990   *1990 Additions to the List of Independently Dated Virtual*
          Geomagnetic Poles and the South-West Master Curve. Colorado
          State University Archaeometric Laboratory, Technical Series, No 5.
          Fort Collins.
Eighmy, J. L. and R. H. McGuire
   1989   Dating the Hohokam Phase Sequence: An Analysis of
          Archaeomagnetic Dates. *Journal of Field Archaeology* 16:215–231.
Eighmy, J. L. and D. R. Mitchell
   1994   Archaeomagnetic Dating at Pueblo Grande. *Journal of*
          Archaeological Research 21:445–453.
Eighmy, J. L. and R. S. Sternberg
   1990   *Archaeomagnetic Dating.* University of Arizona Press, Tucson.
Eighmy, J. L., R. S. Sternberg, and R. F. Butler
   1980   Archaeomagnetic Dating in the American Southwest. *American*
          Antiquity 45:507–517.
Eighmy, J. L., R. S. Taylor, and P. Y. Klein
   1993   Archaeomagnetic Dating on the Great Plains. *Plains Anthropologist*
          38(142):21–50.
Elston, R. G. and C. D. Zeier
   1984   *The Sugarload Obsidian Quarry.* Naval Weapons Center
          Administrative Publication 313. China Lake, California.
Embree, Lester
   1989   Contacting the Theoretical Archaeologists. In *Tracing Archaeology's*
          Past: The Historiography of Archaeology, edited by A. L.

Christenson, pp. 62–74. Southwest Illinois University Press, Carbondale.

Embree, Lester (editor)

1992   *Metaarchaeology: Reflections by Archaeologists and Philosophers.* Kluwer Academic Publishers, Dordrecht.

Engelkemeir et al.

1949   The Half-life of Radiocarbon (C^{14}). *Physical Review 7.*

Ericson, J. E.

1975   New Results in Obsidian Hydration Dating. *World Archaeology* 7:151–159.

1977a   *Evolution of Prehistoric Exchange Systems: Results of Obsidian Dating and Tracing.* Ph.D. dissertation, University of California, Los Angeles.

1977b   Egalitarian Exchange Systems in California: A Preliminary View. In *Exchange Systems in Prehistory,* edited by T. K. Earle and J. E. Ericson, pp. 129–148. Academic Press, New York.

1978   Obsidian Hydration Dating in California. *Society for California Archaeology, Occasional Papers in Method and Theory in California Archaeology* 2:43–52.

1981   *Exchange and Production Systems in California Prehistory.* British Archaeological Reports, International Series 110. Oxford, England.

1982   Production for Obsidian Exchange in California. In *Contexts for Prehistoric Exchange,* edited by J. E. Ericson and T. K. Earle, pp. 129–148. Academic Press, New York.

1989   Toward Flow-Specific Obsidian Hydration Rates: Coso Volcanic Field, Inyo County, California. In *Current Directions in California Obsidian Studies,* edited by R. E. Hughes, pp. 13–22. Contributions of the University of California Archaeological Research Facility No. 48. Berkeley.

Ericson, J. E. and R. Berger

1976   Physics and Chemistry of the Hydration Process in Obsidian II: Experiments and Measurements. In *Advances in Obsidian Glass Studies. Archaeological and Geochemical Perspectives,* edited by R. E. Taylor, pp. 46–62. Noyes Press, Park Ridge, New Jersey.

Ericson, J. E., T. A. Hagan, and C. W. Chesterman

1976   Prehistoric Obsidian in California II: Geologic and Geographic Aspects. In *Advances in Obsidian Glass Studies. Archaeological and Geochemical Prospectives,* edited by R. E. Taylor, pp. 218–239. Noyes Press, Park Ridge, New Jersey.

Ericson, J. E. and J. Kimberlin

1977   Obsidian Sources, Chemical Characterization and Hydration Rates in West Mexico. *Archaeometry* 19:157–166.

Ericson. J. E., H. C. Koerper, C. E. Drover, and P. E. Langenwalter, II

1989   Hydration Dating and Obsidian Exchange in Prehistoric Orange County. *Pacific Coast Archaeological Society Quarterly* 25(2):45–60.

Ericson, J. E., J. D. MacKenzie, and R. Berger

1976 Physics and Chemistry of the Hydration Process in Obsidian I: Theoretical Implications. In *Advances in Obsidian Glass Studies. Archaeological and Geochemical Perspectives*, edited by R. E. Taylor, pp. 25–45. Noyes Press, Park Ridge, New Jersey.

Ericson, J. E. and C. W. Meighan

1984 Boundaries, Alliance, and Exchange in California. In *Exploring the Limits: Frontiers and Boundaries in Prehistory*, edited by S. P. Deatley and F. J. Findlow. British Archaeological Reports, International Series 223. Oxford, England.

Espinosa, J. Manuel

1988 The Pueblo Indian Revolt of 1696 and the Franciscan Missions in New Mexico. University of Oklahoma Press, Norman.

Evans, C. and B. J. Meggers

1960 A New Dating Method Using Obsidian: Part II, An Archaeological Evaluation of the Method. *American Antiquity* 25:523–537.

Fagan, Brian

1975 *In the Beginning*. Little Brown, Boston.

1988 *In the Beginning*. Scott, Foresman, Glenview, Illinois.

Fagette, Paul

1996 *Digging for Dollars: American Archaeology and the New Deal*. University of New Mexico Press, Albuquerque.

Farrand, William R.

1975 Analysis of the Abri Pataud Sediments. In *Excavation of the Abri Pataud, Les Eyzies (Dordogne)*, edited by H. L. Movius, Jr., pp. 27–66. American School of Prehistoric Research, Bulletin 30. Peabody Museum, Harvard University, Cambridge.

1984a Stratigraphic Classification: Living Within the Law. *Quarterly Review of Archaeology* 5:1.

1984b More on Stratigraphic Practice. *Quarterly Review of Archaeology* 5:3.

1993 Discontinuity in the Stratigraphic Record: Snapshots from Franchthi Cave. In *Formation Processes in Archaeological Context*, edited by Paul Goldberg, David T. Nash, and Michael D. Petraglia, pp. 85–96. Monographs in World Archaeology No. 17. Prehistory Press, Madison.

Faul, H. and C. Faul

1983 *It Began with a Stone: A History of Geology from the Stone Age to the Age of Plate Tectonics*. John Wiley, New York.

Feathers, J. K.

1997a The Application of Luminescence Dating in American Archaeology. *Journal of Archaeological Method and Theory* 4:1–66.

1997b Luminescence Dating of Early Mounds in Northeast Louisiana. *Quaternary Geochronology* 16:333–340.

Feathers, J. K. and D. Rhode

1997 Luminescence Dating of Protohistoric Pottery from the Great Basin. *Geoarchaeology* 13:287–308.

Ferring, C. Reid

1986   Rates of Fluvial Sedimentation: Implications for Archaeological Variability. *Geoarchaeology: An International Journal* 1:259–274.

Fetterman, Jerry
1996   Radiocarbon and Tree-Ring Dating at Early Navajo Sites: Examples from the Aztec Area. In *The Archaeology of Navajo Origins*, edited by R. H. Towner, pp. 71–82. University of Utah Press, Salt Lake City.

Fewkes, J. Walter
1904   Two Summers' Work in Pueblo Ruins. In *22nd Annual Report of the Bureau of American Ethnology for the Years 1900–1901*, pp. 4–195. Smithsonian Institution, Washington, D.C.

1919   Designs on Prehistoric Hopi Pottery. In *33rd Annual Report of the Bureau of American Ethnology 1911–1912*, pp. 207–284. (Reprinted in 1973 by Dover Publications, New York.)

1923   *Designs on Prehistoric Pottery from the Mimbres Valley, New Mexico.* Smithsonian Miscellaneous Collections 74, No. 6. Washington, D.C. (Reprinted in 1989, in *The Mimbres: Art and Archaeology*, J. Walter Fewkes with an introduction by J. J. Brody. Avanyu Publishing, Albuquerque.)

Findlow, F. J., V. C. Bennett, J. E. Ericson, and S. P. De Atley
1975   A New Obsidian Hydration Rate for Certain Obsidians in the American Southwest. *American Antiquity* 40:344–348.

Fish, Paul R.
1976   Replication Studies in Ceramic Classification. *Pottery Southwest* 3(4):4–6.

Fleck, Ludwik
1979   *Genesis and Development of a Scientific Fact*, trans. and edited by Thaddeus J. Treun and Robert K. Merton. University of Chicago Press, Chicago.

Fleming, S. J.
1966   Study of Thermoluminescence of Crystalline Extracts from Pottery. *Archaeometry* 9:170–173.

1970   Thermoluminescent Dating: Refinement of the Quartz Inclusion Method. *Archaeometry* 12:133–145.

1978   Thermoluminescent Dating: MASCA Date-List I, Quotation of Results. *MASCA Journal* 1:14–15.

1979   Thermoluminescence Techniques in Archaeology. Clarendon Press, Oxford.

Flenniken, J. J. and A. W. Raymond
1986   Morphological Projectile Point Typology: Replication Experimentation and Technological Analysis. *American Antiquity* 51:603–614.

Flenniken, J. J. and P. J. Wilke
1989   Typology, Technology, and Chronology of Great Basin Dart Points. *American Anthropologist* 91:149–158.

Fletcher, J. M.
1986   Dating of Art-Historical Artifacts. *Nature* 320:466.

Forbes, Jack D.
1960   *Apache, Navajo, and Spaniard*. University of Oklahoma Press, Norman.

Ford, James A.
1962   *A Quantitative Method for Deriving Cultural Chronology*. Technical Manual I. Pan American Union, Washington, D.C.

Franklin, A. D., W. F. Hornyak, and A. A. Tschirgi
1988   Thermoluminescence Dating of Tertiary Period Calcite. *Quaternary Science Reviews* 7:361–365.

Fremlin, J. H. and S. Srirath
1964   Thermoluminescent Dating: Examples of Non-Uniformity of Luminescence. *Archaeometry* 7:58–62.

Friedman, Irving
1976   Calculation of Obsidian Hydration Rates from Temperature Measurements. In *Advances in Obsidian Glass Studies. Archaeological and Geochemical Perspectives*, edited by R. E. Taylor, pp. 173–180. Noyes Press, Park Ridge, New Jersey.

Friedman, Irving and C. Evans
1968   Obsidian Dating Revisited. *Science* 152:813–814.

Friedman, Irving and W. D. Long
1976   Hydration Rate of Obsidian. *Science* 191:347–352.

Friedman, Irving and D. R. Norton
1981   Ground Temperature Measurements. Part III, Ground Temperatures in and near Yellowstone National Park. In *USGS Professional Paper* 1203, pp. 23–39. U.S. Government Printing Office, Washington, D.C.

Friedman, Irving and J. Obradovich
1981   Obsidian Hydration Dating of Volcanic Events. *Quaternary Research* 16:37–41.

Friedman, Irving and Robert L. Smith
1958   Deuterium Content of Water in Some Volcanic Glasses. *Geochemica et Cosmochimica Acta* 15:218–228.
1960   A New Dating Method Using Obsidian: Part I. The Development of the Technique. *American Antiquity* 25:476–522.

Friedman, Irving, Robert L. Smith, and D. Clark
1970   Obsidian Dating. In *Science in Archaeology*, edited by D. Brothwell and E. Higgs, pp. 62–75. Praeger, New York.

Friedman, Irving, Robert L. Smith, and W. D. Long
1966   Hydration of Natural Glass and Formation of Perlite. *Geological Society of America Bulletin* 77:323–328.

Friedman, Irving and F. W. Trembour
1978   Obsidian: The Dating Stone. *American Scientist* 66:44–51.

Friedman, Irving, F. W. Trembour, and R. E. Hughes
1997   Obsidian Hydration Dating. In *Chronometric Dating in Archaeology*, edited by R. E. Taylor and M. J. Aitken, pp. 297–321. Plenum Press, New York.

Friedman, Irving, F. W. Trembour, F. L. Smith, and G. I. Smith

1994   Is Obsidian Hydration Dating Affected by Relative Humidity?
       Quaternary Research 41:185–190.
Fritts, Harold C.
1976   *Tree-Rings and Climate*. Academic Press, London.
Fung, Christopher
1996   Mesoamerican and the Maya: Narrative on the Southeast Frontier.
       Paper Presented at the 1996 AAA Annual Meeting, San Francisco.
Galison, Peter
1987   *How Experiments End*. University of Chicago Press, Chicago.
Gamio, Manuel
1913   Arqueologia de Atzcapotzalco, D. F., Mexico. In *Proceedings, 18th
       International Congress of Americanists*, pp. 180–187. London.
Gardin, Jean-Claude
1980   *Archaeological Constructs: An Aspect of Theoretical Archaeology*.
       Cambridge University Press, Cambridge.
Garlick, G. F. J. and A. F. Gibson
1948   The Electron Trap Mechanism of Luminescence in Sulfide and
       Silicate Phosphors. *Proceedings of the Physics Society* 60:574–590.
Gasche, H. and O. Tunca
1983   Guide to Archaeostratigraphic Classification and Terminology:
       Definitions and Principles. *Journal of Field Archaeology*
       10:325–335.
Gell, Alfred
1992   *The Anthropology of Time: Cultural Constructions of Temporal
       Maps and Images*. Berg Publishing, Oxford.
Gero, Joan M.
1996   Reflexive Field Narratives: Knowing What We Do. Paper Presented
       at the 1996 AAA Annual Meeting, San Francisco.
Gibbon, Guy
1989   *Explanation in Archaeology*. Basil Blackwell. Oxford.
Gibson, J. L.
1994   Before Their Time? Early Mounds in the Lower Mississippi Valley.
       Southeastern Archaeology 13:162–186.
Giddings, James Louis, Jr.
1941   *Dendrochronology of Northern Alaska*. University of Arizona
       Bulletin 7(4). Laboratory of Tree-Ring Research Bulletin No. 1.
       Tucson.
1954   Tree-Ring Dating in the American Arctic. *Tree-Ring Bulletin*
       20(3/4):23–25.
1962   Development of Tree-Ring Dating as an Archaeological Aid. In *Tree-
       Growth*, edited by T. T. Kozlowski, pp. 119–130. Ronald Press,
       New York.
Gieryn, Thomas E. and Anne E. Figert
1990   Ingredients for a Theory of Science in Society. In *Theories of Science
       in Society*, edited by Susan E. Cozzens and Thomas F. Gieryn, pp.
       67–97. Indiana University Press, Bloomington.
Gifford-Gonzalez, Diane

1993   You Can Hide, But You Can't Run: Representations of Women's
Work in Illustrations of Paleolithic Life, *Visual Anthropology
Review* 9:23–41.

Gilreath, A. J., M. E. Basgall, and M. C. Hall

1988   *Compendium of Chronologically Indicative Data from Fort Irwin
Archaeological Sites, San Bernardino County, California.* Submitted
to the U.S. Army Corps of Engineers, Los Angeles, by Far Western
Anthropological Research Group, Davis.

Gilreath, A. J., and W. R. Hildebrandt

1997   *Prehistoric Use of the Coso Volcanic Field.* Contributions of the
University of California Research Facility No. 56. Berkeley.

Gittins, G. O.

1984   *Radiocarbon Chronometry and Archaeological Thought.* Ph.D. dissertation, University of California, Los Angeles.

Gladfelter, Bruce G.

1977   Geoarchaeology: The Geomorphologist and Archaeology. *American
Antiquity* 42:519–538.

1981   Developments and Directions in Geoarchaeology. *Advances in
Archaeological Method and Theory* 4:344–364.

Gladwin, Harold S.

1940a   Methods and Instruments for Use in Measuring Tree-Rings.
Medallion Paper No. 27. Gila Pueblo, Globe, Arizona.

1940b   Tree-Ring Analysis: Methods of Correlation. Medallion Paper No.
28. Gila Pueblo, Globe, Arizona.

1943   *A Review and Analysis of the Flagstaff Culture.* Medallion Paper
No. 31. Gila Pueblo, Globe, Arizona.

1944   *Tree-Ring Analysis: Problems of Dating I: The Medicine Valley
Sites.* Medallion Paper No. 32. Gila Pueblo, Globe, Arizona.

1945   *The Chaco Branch: Excavations at White Mound in the Red Mesa
Valley.* Medallion Paper No. 33. Gila Pueblo, Globe, Arizona.

1946   *Tree-Ring Analysis: Problems of Dating II. The Tusayan Ruin.*
Medallion Paper No. 36. Gila Pueblo, Globe, Arizona.

1947   *Tree-Ring Analysis: Tree-Rings and Droughts. Medallion Paper No.
37.* Gila Pueblo, Globe, Arizona.

1948   Excavations at Snaketown: Reviews and Conclusions. Medallion
Paper No. 38. Gila Pueblo, Globe, Arizona.

Gladwin, Harold S., Emil W. Haury, E. B. Sayles, and Nora Gladwin

1938   *Excavations at Snaketown: Material Culture.* Medallion Paper No.
25. Gila Pueblo, Globe, Arizona. (Reprinted in 1965 by the
University of Arizona Press, Tucson.)

Gladwin, Winifred, and Harold S. Gladwin

1928   *The Use of Potsherds in an Archaeological Survey.* Gila Pueblo
Medallion Paper No. 2. Gila Pueblo, Globe, Arizona.

1934   *A Method for Designation of Cultures and Their Variations.* Gila
Pueblo Medallion Paper No. 15. Gila Pueblo, Globe, Arizona.

Goetze, Christine E., and Barbara J. Mills

1993   Ceramic Chronometry. In *Interpretation of Ceramic Artifacts*, by

Barbara J. Mills, Christine E. Goetze, and María Nieves Zedeño, pp. 87–150. Across the Colorado Plateau: Anthropological Studies for the Transwestern Pipeline Expansion Project, Volume XVI. Office of Contract Archaeology and Maxwell Museum of Anthropology, University of New Mexico, Albuquerque.

Goff, Joell and Lori Stephens Reed
   1998   Introduction and Analytical Methods. In *Exploring Ceramic Production, Distribution, and Exchange in the Southern Chuska Valley: Analytical Results from the El Paso Natural Gas North System Expansion Project*, by Lori Stephens Reed, Joell Goff, and Kathy Niles Hensler, pp. 1.1–1.26. Pipeline Archaeology 1990–1993: The El Paso Natural Gas North System Expansion Project, New Mexico and Arizona, Vol. XI, Book 1. Western Cultural Resource Management, Inc., Farmington, New Mexico.

Gordus, A. A., G. A. Wright, and J. B. Griffin
   1968   Obsidian Sources Characterized by Neutron Activation Analysis. *Science* 161:382–384.

Gose, Wulf A.
   1993   Archaeomagnetic Dating of Burned Features. In *Data Recovery at Justiceburg Reservoir (Lake Alan Henry), Garza and Kent Counties, Texas: Phase III, Season 2*, by D. K. Boyd, S. A. Tomka, and K. W. Kibler, pp. 329–337. Report of Investigations, No. 88. Prewitt and Associates, Inc., Austin, Texas.

Gottschalk, Louis
   1955   *Understanding History: A Primer of Historical Method.* Alfred A. Knopf, New York.

Graham, Loren, Wolf Lepenies, and Peter Weingart (editors)
   1983   *Functions and Uses of Disciplinary Histories.* D. Reidel, Dordrecht, Holland.

Graves, Michael W.
   1982   Anomalous Tree-Ring Dates and the Sequence of Room Construction at Canyon Creek Ruin, Arizona. *The Kiva* 47:107–131.
   1983   Growth and Aggregation at Canyon Creek Ruin: Implications for Evolutionary Change in East-Central Arizona. *American Antiquity* 48:290–315.
   1991   Estimating Ring Loss on Tree-Ring Specimens from East-Central Arizona: Implications for Prehistoric Growth at Grasshopper Ruin. *Journal of Quantitative Anthropology* 3:83–115.

Grayson, Donald. K.
   1983   *The Establishment of Human Antiquity.* Academic Press, New York.

Green, R. D.
   1964   Sources, Ages, and Exploitation of New Zealand Obsidian. *New Zealand Archaeological Association Newsletter* 73:134–143.

Griffin, J. B.
   1949 C^{14} Dates. *American Antiquity* 15:80.

Griffin, J. B., A. A. Gordus, and G. A. Wright

1969   Identification of the Sources of Hopewellian Obsidian in the Middle West. *American Antiquity* 34:1–14.

Grögler, V. N, F. G. Houtermans, and H. Stauffer
1960   Über die Datierung von Keramik und Ziegel Durch Thermolumineszenz. *Helvetica Physics Acta* 33:595–596.

Gumerman, G. J. and D. A. Phillips, Jr.
1978   Archaeology Beyond Anthropology. *American Antiquity* 43:184–191.

Gunnerson, James H.
1969   Apache Archaeology in Northeastern New Mexico. *American Antiquity* 34:23–39.
1987   *Archaeology of the High Plains.* Cultural Resource Series Number 19. Bureau of Land Management. Denver.

Gunnerson, James H. and Dolores A. Gunnerson
1988   *Ethnohistory of the High Plains.* U.S. Department of the Interior, Bureau of Land Management Cultural Resource Series No. 26. Colorado State Office, Denver.

Guthe, Carl E.
1927   A Method of Ceramic Description. *Papers of the Michigan Academy of Science, Art, and Letters* 8:23–29. Ann Arbor.

Hall, E. T., Jr.
1951   Southwest Dated Ruins VI. *Tree-Ring Bulletin* 17:26–28.

Hall, Martin
1990   Hidden History: Iron Age Archaeology in Southern Africa. In *History of African Archaeology*, edited by Peter Robertshaw, pp. 59–77. Heinemann, Portsmouth, New Hampshire; J. Currey, London.

Hall, M. C.
1983   *Late Holocene Hunter-Gatherers and Volcanism in the Long Valley–Mono Basin Region: Prehistoric Culture Change in the Eastern Sierra Nevada.* Ph.D. dissertation, University of California, Riverside.
1984   Obsidian, Paleoeconomy, and Volcanism in the Eastern Sierra Nevada. Paper Presented at the 18th Biennial Meeting of the Great Basin Anthropological Conference, Pocatello, Idaho.
1993   *Archaeology of Seven Prehistoric Sites in the Tiefort Basin, Fort Irwin, San Bernadino County, California.* Submitted to the U.S. Army Corps of Engineers, Los Angeles, by Far Western Anthropological Research Group, Davis, California.

Hall, M. C. and M. E. Basgall
1994   Casa Diablo Obsidian in California and Great Basin Prehistory. Paper Presented at the 24th Biennial Meeting of the Great Basin Anthropological Conference, Elko, Nevada.

Hall, M. C. and R. J. Jackson
1989   Obsidian Hydration Rates in California. In *Current Directions in California Obsidian Studies*, edited by R. E. Hughes, pp. 31–58. Contributions of the University of California Archaeological

Research Facility No. 48. Berkeley.

Haller, W.

1963   Concentration-Dependent Diffusion Coefficient of Water in Glass. *Physics and Chemistry of Glasses* 4:217–220.

Halley, Edmund

1692   An Account of the Cause of the Change of the Variation of the Magnetic Needle; with an Hypothesis of the Structure of the Internal Part of the Earth. *Philosophical Transactions of the Royal Society of London* 17:563–578.

Hammond, Norman

1993   Matrices and Maya Archaeology. In *Practices of Archaeological Stratigraphy*, edited by Edward C. Harris, Marley R. Brown, III, and Gregory J. Brown, pp. 139–152. Academic Press, London.

Hampel, J. H.

1984   Technical Considerations in X-ray Fluorescence Analysis of Obsidian. In *Obsidian Studies in the Great Basin*, edited by R. E. Hughes, pp. 21–25. Contributions of the University of California Archaeological Research Facility No. 45. Berkeley.

Han, Mark C.

1975   Effects of Alpha and X-ray Doses and Annealing Temperatures upon Pottery Dating by Thermoluminescence. *MASCA Newsletter* 11:1–3.

Hancock, Patricia M.

1997   Dendrochronology Dates in the Dinétah. Paper Presented at the 5th Fruitland Conference, Farmington, New Mexico.

Hannaford, Charles A.

1993   Prehistoric Communities in the La Plata Valley. Paper Presented at the 1993 Anasazi Symposium, Farmington, New Mexico.

Hargrave, Lyndon L.

1932   *Guide to Forty Pottery Types from the Hopi Country and the San Francisco Mountains, Arizona*. Museum of Northern Arizona Bulletin 1. Flagstaff.

1935   Concerning the Names of Southwestern Pottery Types. *Southwestern Lore* 1(3):17–23.

Harrill, Bruce G. and C. D. Breternitz

1976   Chronology and Cultural Activity in Johnson Canyon Cliff Dwellings: Interpretations from Tree-Ring Data. *Journal of Field Archaeology* 3:375–390.

Harris, Edward. C.

1975   The Stratigraphic Sequence: A Question of Time. *World Archaeology* 7:109–121.

1977   Units of Archaeological Stratification. *Norwegian Archaeological Review* 10:84–94.

1979   *Principles of Archaeological Stratigraphy*. Academic Press, London.

1989   *Principles of Archaeological Stratigraphy*, 2nd ed. Academic Press, New York.

Harris, Edward C., Marley R. Brown, III, and Gregory J. Brown

1993   Practices of Archaeological Stratigraphy. Academic Press, London.

Hassan, Fekri A.

1978   Sediments in Archaeology: Methods and Implications for Paleoenvironmental and Cultural Analysis. *Journal of Field Archaeology* 5:197–213.

1979   Geoarchaeology: The Geologist and Archaeology. *American Antiquity* 44:267–270.

Hathaway, J. H.

1990   Firing Temperature and Time as Variables Affecting the Quality of Archaeomagnetic Results. In *Archaeomagnetic Dating*, edited by J. L. Eighmy and R. S. Sternberg, pp. 158–166. University of Arizona Press, Tucson.

Hathaway, J. H. and G. J. Krause

1990   The Sun Compass Versus the Magnetic Compass in Archaeomagnetic Sample Collection. In *Archaeomagnetic Dating*, edited by J. L. Eighmy and R. S. Sternberg, pp. 139–147. University of Arizona Press, Tucson.

Hathaway, J. H., G. P. Smith, and G. J. Krause

1990   Variation in Soil Texture and Its Effect on Archaeomagnetic Sample Quality. In *Archaeomagnetic Dating*, edited by J. L. Eighmy and R. S. Sternberg, pp. 168–177. University of Arizona Press, Tucson.

Haury, Emil W.

1930   *A Sequence of Decorated Redware from Silver Creek Drainage.* Museum of Northern Arizona Museum Notes 2(11). Flagstaff.

1931   Showlow and Pinedale Ruins. In *Recently Dated Pueblo Ruins in Arizona,* by Emil W. Haury and Lyndon L. Hargrave, pp. 4–79. Smithsonian Miscellaneous Collections 82(11). Smithsonian Institution, Washington, D.C.

1934   *The Canyon Creek Ruin and the Cliff Dwellings of the Sierra Ancha.* Medallion Paper No. 14. Gila Pueblo, Globe, Arizona.

1935   Tree-Rings: The Archaeologist's Time-Piece. *American Antiquity* 1:98–108.

1936   *Some Southwestern Pottery Types, Series IV.* Medallion Paper No. 14. Gila Pueblo, Globe, Arizona.

1938   Southwestern Dated Ruins: II. *Tree-Ring Bulletin* 4(3):3–4.

1976   *The Hohokam: Desert Farmers and Craftsmen.* University of Arizona Press, Tucson.

1988   Gila Pueblo Archaeological Foundation: A History and Some Personal Notes. *The Kiva* 54:1–77.

Hawley, Florence M.

1938   Southwestern Dated Ruins: IV. *Tree-Ring Bulletin* 5(1):6–7.

Haynes, C. Vance, Jr.

1964   *The Geologist's Role in Pleistocene Paleoecology and Archaeology in the Reconstruction of Past Environments*, edited by James J. Hester and James Schoenwetter, pp. 61–64. Publication of the Fort Burgwin Research Center, No. 3. Taos.

1990   The Antevs-Bryan Years and the Legacy for Paleoindian Geochronology. In *Establishment of a Geologic Framework for*

Paleoanthropology, edited by L. F. Laporte, pp. 55–68. Geological Society of America Special Paper 242. Boulder.

Haynes, C. Vance, Jr. and G. Agogino
   1960   *Geological Significance of a New Radiocarbon Date from the Lindenmeier Site*. The Denver Museum of Natural History Proceedings, No. 9. Denver Museum of Natural History, Denver.

Hays-Gilpin, Kelley Ann and Eric Van Hartesveldt (editors)
   1998   *Prehistoric Ceramics of the Puerco Valley, Arizona: The 1995 Chambers-Sanders Trust Lands Ceramic Conference*. Museum of Northern Arizona Ceramic Series No. 7. Flagstaff.

Heidke, James
   1995   Overview of the Ceramic Collection. In *The Roosevelt Community Development Study, Vol. 2: Ceramic Chronology, Technology, and Economics*, edited by James M. Heidke and Miriam T. Stark, pp. 7–18. Anthropological Papers 14. Center for Desert Archaeology, Tucson.

Heizer, Robert F.
   1949   *A Guide to Archaeological Field Methods*. National Press, Palo Alto.

Hendricks, R. and J. P. Wilson
   1996   *The Navajos in 1705: Roque de Madrid's Campaign Journal*. University of New Mexico Press, Albuquerque.

Herz, N. and E. G. Garrison
   1997   *Geological Methods for Archaeology*. Oxford University Press, London.

Hester, James J.
   1962   *Early Navajo Migrations and Acculturation in the Southwest*. Museum of New Mexico Papers in Anthropology, Vol. 6. Museum of New Mexico Press, Santa Fe.

Hester, Thomas R., Robert Heizer, and John Graham
   1975   *Field Methods in Archaeology*. Mayfield Publishing, Palo Alto.

Hewett, Edgar Lee
   1930   *Ancient Life in the Southwest*. Bobbs-Merrill, Indianapolis.

Hill, James N.
   1970a   *Prehistoric Social Organization in the American Southwest*. School of American Research Press, Santa Fe.
   1970b   *Broken K. Pueblo: Prehistoric Social Organization in the American Southwest*. Anthropological Papers of the University of Arizona No. 18, Tucson.

Hill, W. W.
   1940   Some Navajo Culture Changes During Two Centuries. *Smithsonian Miscellaneous Collections* 100:395–415.

Hirschauer, Stefan
   1991   The Manufacture of Bodies in Surgery. *Social Studies of Science* 21:279–319.

Hodge, Frederick W.
   1924   Pottery of Hawikuh. *Indian Notes* 1:8–15. Museum of the American Indian, Heye Foundation. New York.

Hoffmann, Roald
    1988   Under the Surface of a Chemistry Article. *Angewandte Chemie*
            27:1593–1602.
Hogan, Patrick
    1989   Dinétah: A Reevaluation of Pre-Revolt Navajo Occupation in
            Northwestern New Mexico. *Journal of Anthropological Research*
            45:53–56.
    1991   Navajo-Pueblo Interaction During the Gobernador Phase: A
            Reassessment of the Evidence. In *Rethinking Navajo Pueblitos.*
            Cultural Resources Series, Vol. 8. U.S. Department of the Interior,
            New Mexico Bureau of Land Management, Albuquerque.
Hole, Frank and Mary Shaw
    1967   *Computer Analysis of Chronological Seriation.* Rice University
            Studies 53(3). Houston, Texas.
Holliday, Vance T.
    1997   *Paleoindian Geoarchaeology of the Southern High Plains.* University
            of Texas Press, Austin, Texas.
Holliday, V. T. and E. Johnson
    1986   Re-Evaluation of the First Radiocarbon Age of the Folsom Culture.
            American Antiquity 51:332–338.
Holmes, William H.
    1878   Report on the Ancient Ruins of Southwestern Colorado, Examined
            During the Summers of 1875 and 1876. In *United States Geological
            and Geographical Survey of the Territories for 1876, 10th Annual
            Report*, pp. 383–408. United States Geological and Geographical
            Survey, Washington, D.C.
    1886   *Pottery of the Ancient Pueblos.* Bureau of American Ethnology,
            Annual Report 4:257–360. Washington D. C.
    1903   *Aboriginal Pottery of the Eastern United States.* Bureau of American
            Ethnology, 20th Annual Report. Washington D. C.
Howard, Edgar B.
    1935   Evidence of Early Man in North America. *The Museum Journal,
            University of Pennsylvania Museum* 24:61–175.
    1943   The Finley Site: Discovery of Yuma Points, in situ, near Eden,
            Wyoming. *American Antiquity* 8:224–234.
Hrdlička, Aleš
    1912   *Early Man in South America.* Bureau of American Ethnology
            Bulletin 52. Washington, D.C.
Huber, B. and V. Giertz
    1969   Our 1000 Year Oak Chronology. *Conference Report to the Austrian
            Academy of Science* 178:32–42.
Hughes, R. E.
    1982   Age and Exploitation of Obsidian from the Medicine Lake,
            Highland, California. *Journal of Archaeological Science* 9:173–185.
    1984   Obsidian Studies in the Great Basin: Problems and Prospects. In
            Obsidian Studies in the Great Basin, edited by R. E. Hughes, pp.
            1–19. Contributions of the University of California Archaeological

Research Facility No. 45. Berkeley.

1986 *Diachronic Variability in Obsidian Procurement Patterns in Northeast California and Southcentral Oregon.* University of California Publications in Anthropology No. 17. Berkeley.

1988 The Coso Volcanic Field Reexamined: Implications for Obsidian Sourcing and Hydration Dating Research. *Geoarchaeology: An International Journal* 3:253–265.

1989 A New Look at Mono Basin Obsidians. In *Current Directions in California Obsidian Studies,* edited by R. E. Hughes, pp. 1–12. Contributions of the University of California Archaeological Research Facility No. 48. Berkeley.

1992 Northern California Obsidian Studies: Some Thoughts and Observations of the First Two Decades. *Proceedings of the Society for California Archaeology* 5:113–122.

1994 Intrasource Chemical Variability of Artifact-Quality Obsidian from the Casa Diablo Area, California. *Journal of Archaeological Science* 21:263–271.

Hughes, R. E. and R. L. Smith

1993 Archaeology, Geology, and Geochemistry in Obsidian Provenance Studies. In *The Effects of Scale in Archaeological and Geological Perspectives,* edited by J. K. Stein and A. R. Binse, pp. 79–91. Geological Society of America Special Papers, No. 283. Washington, D.C.

Hull, K. L.

1996 Time, Temperature, and Rate of Hydration: A Consideration of Casa Diablo Obsidian in Western Great Basin Archaeology. Paper presented at the 25th Biennial Meeting of the Great Basin Anthropological Conference, Kings Beach, California.

Huxtable, J., M. J. Aitken, and J. C. Weber

1972 Thermoluminescent Dating of Baked Clay Balls of the Poverty Point Culture. *Archaeometry* 14:269–275.

Ichikawa, Yoneta

1965 Dating of Ancient Ceramics by Thermoluminescence. *Bulletin of the Institute of Chemical Research, Kyoto University* 43:1–6.

Ikeya, M.

1978 Electron Spin Resonance as a Method of Dating. *Archaeometry* 20:147–158.

Jack, R. N.

1976 Prehistoric Obsidian in California I: Geochemical Aspects. In *Advances in Obsidian Glass Studies. Archaeological and Geochemical Perspectives,* edited by R. E. Taylor, pp. 183–217. Noyes Press, Park Ridge, New Jersey.

Jack, R. N. and I. S. E. Carmichael

1969 *The Chemical "Fingerprinting" of Acid Volcanic Rocks.* California Division of Mines and Geology Special Report 100:17–32. Sacramento.

Jack, R. N. and R. F. Heizer

1968 *"Fingerprinting" of Some Mesoamerican Obsidians*. Contributions of the University of California Archaeological Research Facility No. 5. Berkeley.

Jackson, R. L.

1984a Current Problems in Obsidian Hydration Analysis. In *Obsidian Studies in the Great Basin*, edited by R. E. Hughes, pp. 103–115. Contributions of the University of California Archaeological Research Facility No. 45. Berkeley.

1984b Obsidian Hydration: Application in the Western Great Basin. In *Obsidian Studies in the Great Basin*, edited by R. E. Hughes, pp. 173–192. Contributions of the University of California Archaeological Research Facility No. 45. Berkeley.

1990 Standardizing Microscope Calibration. *International Association for Obsidian Studies Newsletter* 3:12.

Jackson, T. L.

1984 A Reassessment of Obsidian Production Analysis for the Bodie Hills and Casa Diablo Quarry Areas. In *Obsidian Studies in the Great Basin*, edited by R. E. Hughes, pp. 117–134. Contributions of the University of California Archaeological Research Facility No. 45. Berkeley.

1986 *Late Prehistoric Obsidian Exchange in Central California*. Ph.D. dissertation, Department of Anthropology, Stanford.

1988 Amending Models of Trans-Sierran Obsidian Tool Production and Exchange. *Journal of California and Great Basin Anthropology* 10:62–72.

1989 Late Prehistoric Obsidian Production and Exchange in the North Coast Ranges, California. In *Current Directions in California Obsidian Studies*, edited by R. E. Hughes, pp. 79–94. Contributions of the University of California Archaeological Research Facility No. 48. Berkeley.

Jackson, T. L. and J. E. Ericson

1994 Prehistoric Exchange Systems in California. In *Prehistoric Exchange Systems in North America*, edited by T. Baugh and J. E. Ericson, pp. 385–415. Plenum Press, New York.

Jeançon, Jean A.

1924 Pottery of the Pagosa-Piedra Region. *Colorado Magazine* 1:260–276, 301–307.

Jenkins, N. J.

1981 *Gainsville Lake Area Ceramic Descriptions and Chronology*. Report of Investigations 12. Office of Archaeological Research, University of Alabama, Tuscaloosa.

Johnson, Eileen

1995 *Ancient Peoples and Landscapes*. Museum of Texas Tech University, Lubbock.

Johnson, F.

1951 Introduction. In *Radiocarbon Dating, Memoirs of the Society for American Archaeology* 8:1–3. (*American Antiquity* 17:1–3.)

1965   The Impact of Radiocarbon Dating upon Archeology. In *Proceedings of the 6th International Conference on Radiocarbon and Tritium Dating*, edited by R. M. Chatters and E. A. Olson, pp. 762–784. Clearinghouse for Federal Scientific and Technical Information, Springfield, Virginia.

Johnson, L.
1969   Obsidian Hydration Rate for the Klamath Basin of California and Oregon. *Science* 165:1354–1356.

Jones, G. T. and C. Beck
1990   An Obsidian Hydration Chronology of Late Pleistocene–Early Holocene Surface Assemblages from Butte Valley, Nevada. *Journal of California and Great Basin Anthropology* 12:84–100.
1992   Chronological Resolution in Distributional Archaeology. In *Place, Time, and Archaeological Landscapes*, edited by L. Wandsnider and J. Rossignol, pp. 167–192. Plenum Press, New York.

Jones, M., P. J. Sheppard, and D. G. Sutton
1997   Soil Temperature and Obsidian Hydration Dating: A Clarification of Variables Affecting Accuracy. *Journal of Archaeological Science* 24:505–516.

Jones, M., D. G. Sutton, G. Jones, and C. McLeod
1995   Measuring Soil Temperatures for Obsidian Hydration Dating in Northern New Zealand. *Archaeology in New Zealand* 38:9–16.

Joukowsky, Martha
1980   *A Complete Manual of Field Archaeology: Tools and Techniques of Field Work for Archaeologists*. Prentice-Hall, Englewood Cliffs, New Jersey.

Judd, Neil M.
1968   *Men Met Along the Trail: Adventures in Archaeology*. University of Oklahoma Press, Norman.

Katsui, Y. and Y. Kondo
1965   Dating of Stone Implements Using Hydration Layer of Obsidian. *Japanese Journal of Geology and Geography* 46:46–60.
1976   Variation in Obsidian Hydration Rates for Hokkaido, Northern Japan. In *Advances in Obsidian Glass Studies. Archaeological and Geochemical Properties*, edited by R. E. Taylor, pp. 120–140. Noyes Press, Park Ridge, New Jersey.

Kean, W., S. Ahler, M. Fowler, and D. Wolfman
1997   Archaeomagnetic Record from Modoc Rock Shelter, Illinois, for the Time Range of 6200–8900 B.P. *Geoarchaeology* 12:93–115.

Kehoe, Alice B.
1992   The Paradigmatic Vision of Archaeology: Archaeology as Bourgeois Science. In *Rediscovering Our Past: Essays on the History of American Archaeology*, edited by Jonathan Reyman, pp. 3–14. Avebury Press, Aldershot.

Kelley, J. H. and R. F. Williamson
1996   The Position of Archaeology Within Anthropology: A Canadian Historical Perspective. *American Antiquity* 61:5–20.

Kennedy, G. C. and L. Knopff
  1960 Dating by Thermoluminescence. *Archaeology* 13:147–148.
Kenyon, Kathleen M.
  1952 *Beginning in Archaeology*. Phoenix House, London.
Keur, D. L.
  1944 A Chapter in Navajo-Pueblo Relations. *American Antiquity* 10:75–86.
Kidder, Alfred Vincent
  1915 Pottery of the Pajarito Plateau and of Some Adjacent Regions in New Mexico. *Memoirs of the American Anthropological Association* 2:407–462. Menasha, Wisconsin.
  1920 Ruins of the Historic Period in the Upper San Juan Valley, New Mexico. *American Anthropologist* 22:322–329.
  1924 *An Introduction to the Study of Southwestern Archaeology*. Phillips Academy, Andover.
  1927 The Museum's Expedition to Cañon de Chelly and Canyon del Muerto, Arizona. *Natural History* 27:203–209.
  1936 Speculations on New World Prehistory. In *Essays in Anthropology Presented to A. L. Kroeber in Celebration of His Sixtieth Birthday, June 11, 1936*, edited by Robert H. Lowie, pp. 143–152. University of California Press, Berkeley.
  1958 *Pecos, New Mexico: Archaeological Notes*. Papers of the Robert S. Peabody Foundation for Archaeology, No. 5. Andover.
Kimberlin, J.
  1976 Obsidian Hydration Rate Determination on Chemically Characterized Samples. In *Advances in Obsidian Glass Studies. Archaeological and Geochemical Perspectives*, edited by R. E. Taylor, pp. 63–80. Noyes Press, Park Ridge, New Jersey.
Kintigh, Keith W.
  1985 *Settlement, Subsistence, and Society in Late Zuni Prehistory*. Anthropological Papers of the University of Arizona 44. Tucson.
Kluckhohn, Clyde
  1939 The Place of Theory in Anthropological Studies. *The Philosophy of Science* 6:328–344.
Knorr-Cetina, Karin
  1983 *The Manufacture of Knowledge*. Pergamon Press, Oxford.
Koerper, H. C., J. E. Ericson, C. E. Drover, and P. E. Langenwalter, II
  1986 Obsidian Exchange in Prehistoric Orange County. *Pacific Coast Archaeological Society Quarterly* 22:33–69.
Kohler, Timothy A. and Eric Blinman
  1987 Solving Mixture Problems in Archaeology: Analysis of Ceramic Materials for Dating and Demographic Reconstruction. *Journal of Anthropological Archaeology* 6:1–28.
Kojo, Y.
  1991 The Reliability of Thermoluminescence Dating: A Pilot Experiment. *Geoarchaeology* 6:367–374.
Korff, S. A. and W. E. Danforth

1939   Neutron Measurements with Boron-Trifluoride Counters. *Physical Review* 55:980.

Kornmeier, C. M. and S. R. Sutton
1985   Thermoluminescence Dating Results for Ten Ceramics from Site 23BU10. Manuscript on file, Midwest Archaeological Center, National Park Service, Lincoln, Nebraska.

Kroeber, Alfred
1916a   Zuni Culture Sequences. *Proceedings of the National Academy of Sciences* 2:42–45.
1916b   Zuni Potsherds. *Anthropological Papers of the American Museum of Natural History* 28:1–37.

Kulp, J. L., H. W. Feely, and L. E. Tryon
1951   Lamont Natural Radiocarbon Measurements, I. *Science* 114:565–568.

LaBelle, J. M. and J. L. Eighmy
1995   *Additions to the List of Independently Dated Virtual Geomagnetic Poles and the South-West Master Curve.* Colorado State University Archaeometric Laboratory, Technical Series, No. 7. Fort Collins.
1997   Additional Archaeomagnetic Data on the U.S. South-West Master Geomagnetic Pole Curve. *Archaeometry* 39:431–439.

Ladd, Edmund
1998   Zuni the Day the Men in Metal Arrived. In *The Coronado Expedition to Tierra Nueva: The 1540–1542 Route Across the Southwest*, edited by R. F. Flint and S. C. Flint, pp. 225–234. University Press of Colorado, Niwot.

Landau, Misia
1984   Human Evolution as Narrative. *American Scientist* 72:262–268.

Lange, Richard C. and Barbara A. Murphy
1990   A Discussion of Collection Factors Affecting the Quality of Archaeomagnetic Results. In *Archaeomagnetic Dating*, edited by Jeffrey L. Eighmy and Robert S. Sternberg, pp. 65–80. University of Arizona Press, Tucson.

Latour, Bruno and Steve Woolgar
1986   *Laboratory Life: The (Social) Construction of Scientific Facts.* Princeton University Press, Princeton.

Laufer, Berthold
1913   Remarks. *American Anthropologist* 15:573–577.

Laursen, T. and W. A. Lanford
1978   Hydration of Obsidian. *Nature* 276:153–156.

Laudan, Rachel
1993   Histories of Sciences and Their Uses: A Review to 1913. *History of Science* 31:1–34.

Laville, Henri
1976   Deposits in Calcareous Rock Shelters: Analytical Methods and Climatic Interpretation. In *Geoarchaeology: Earth Science and the Past*, edited by D. A. Davidson and M. L. Shackley, pp. 137–155. Westview, Boulder.

Laville, Henri and Jean-Philippe Rigaud
   1973   The Perigordian V Industries in Perigord: Typological Variations,
          Stratigraphy and Relative Chronology. *World Archaeology*
          4:330–338.
Laville, Henri, Jean-Philippe Rigaud, and James Sackett
   1980   *Rock Shelters of the Perigord: Geological Stratigraphy and
          Archaeological Succession.* Academic Press, New York.
Law, John
   1991   Theory and Narrative in the History of Technology: Response.
          Technology and Culture 32:377–394.
Layton, T. N.
   1973   Temporal Ordering of Surface-Collected Obsidian Artifacts by
          Hydration Measurement. *Archaeometry* 15:129–132.
Leach, B. F. and G. E. Hamel
   1984   The Influence of Archaeological Soil Temperatures on Obsidian
          Dating in New Zealand. *New Zealand Journal of Science*
          27:399–408.
Leach, B. F. and H. Naylor
   1981   Dating New Zealand Obsidians by Resonant Nuclear Reactions.
          New Zealand Journal of Archaeology 3:33–49.
Leblanc, Steven A.
   1975   Micro-Seriation: A Method for Fine Chronologic Differentiation.
          American Antiquity 40:22–38.
Lee, R. R.
   1969   Chemical Temperature Integration. *Journal of Applied Meteorology*
          8:423–430.
Lee, R. R., D. A. Leech, T. A. Tombrello, J. E. Ericson, and I. Friedman
   1974   Obsidian Hydration Profile Measurements Using a Nuclear Reaction
          Technique. *Nature* 250:44–47.
Levy, Paul W.
   1968   A Brief Survey of Radiation Effects Applicable to Geology Problems.
          In *Thermoluminescence of Geological Materials*, edited by D. J.
          McDougall, pp. 25–38. Academic Press, New York.
Lewis-Beck, Michael S.
   1980   *Applied Regression: An Introduction.* Sage University Papers,
          Beverly Hills.
Libby, W. F.
   1946   Atmospheric Helium Three and Radiocarbon from Cosmic
          Radiation. *Physical Review* 69:671–672.
   1951   Radiocarbon Dates II. *Science* 114:291–296.
   1952a *Radiocarbon Dating.* University of Chicago Press, Chicago.
   1952b Chicago Radiocarbon Dates III. *Science* 116:673–681.
   1954a Chicago Radiocarbon Dates IV. *Science* 119:135–140.
   1954b Chicago Radiocarbon Dates V. *Science* 120:733–742.
   1955   *Radiocarbon Dating,* 2nd ed. University of Chicago Press, Chicago.
   1961a Radiocarbon Dating. Nobel Lecture, December 12, 1960. *Les Prix
          Nobel En 1960*, pp. 95–112. Nobel Foundation, Stockholm.

1961b   Radiocarbon Dating. *Science* 133:621–629.

1963   Accuracy of Radiocarbon Dates. *Science* 140:278–280. (*Antiquity* 37:213–218.)

1965a   *Radiocarbon Dating*, 2nd ed. (First Phoenix ed.) University of Chicago Press, Chicago.

1965b   Natural Radiocarbon and Tritium in Retrospect and Prospect. *Proceedings of the Sixth International Conference on Radiocarbon and Tritium Dating*, compiled by R. M. Chatters and E. A. Olson, pp. 745–751. Clearinghouse for Federal Scientific and Technical Information, Springfield, Virginia.

1967   History of Radiocarbon Dating. In *Radioactive Dating and Methods of Low Level Counting*, pp. 3–25. International Atomic Energy Agency, Vienna.

1970a   Radiocarbon Dating. *Philosophical Transactions of the Royal Society of London* 269A:1–10.

1970b   Ruminations on Radiocarbon Dating. In *Radiocarbon Variations and Absolute Chronology*, edited by I. U. Olsson, pp. 629–640. Almqvist and Wiksell, Stockholm.

1973   Radiocarbon Dating, Memories and Hopes. In *Proceedings of the 8th International Radiocarbon Conference*, compiled by T. A. Rafter and T. Grant-Taylor, pp. xxvii–xliii. Royal Society of New Zealand, Wellington.

1978   Nobel Laureate Willard F. Libby Interviewed by Mary Terrall. Oral History Program 1983, University of California, Los Angeles.

1979a   Radiocarbon Dating in the Future: Thirty Years After Inception. *Environment International* 2:205–207.

1979b   Interview with W. F. Libby, April 12, 1979. On file at the Center for the History of Physics, American Institute of Physics.

1980   Archaeology and Radiocarbon Dating. *Radiocarbon* 22:1017–1020.

1982   Nuclear Dating: An Historical Perspective. In *Nuclear and Chemical Dating Techniques Interpreting the Environmental Record*, edited by L. A. Currie, pp. 1–4. American Chemical Society, Washington, D.C.

Libby, W. F., E. C. Anderson, and J. R. Arnold

1949   Age Determination by Radiocarbon Content: World Wide Assay of Natural Radiocarbon. *Science* 109:227–228.

Liese, W.

1978   Bruno Huber: The Pioneer of European Dendrochronology. *BAR International Series* 51:1–10.

Lillios, Katina

1996   Anthropological and Archeological Narratives of Social Collapse: Contradictions Between Theory and Practice. Paper Presented at the 1996 AAA Annual Meeting, San Francisco.

Linick, T. W., P. E. Damon, D. J. Donahue, and A. J. T. Jull

1989   Accelerator Mass Spectrometry: The New Revolution in Radiocarbon Dating. *Quaternary International* 1:1–6.

Longacre, William A.

1966   Changing Patterns of Social Integration: A Prehistoric Example from the American Southwest. *American Anthropologist* 68:94–102.

1968   Some Aspects of Prehistoric Society in East-Central Arizona. In *New Perspectives in Archaeology*, edited by S. A. Binford and L. R. Binford, pp. 89–102. Aldine Publishing, Chicago.

Loofs, H. H. E.
1974   Thermoluminescence Dates from Thailand: Comments. *Antiquity* 48:58–62.

Love, Michael W.
1993   Ceramic Chronology and Chronometric Dating. *Ancient Mesoamerica* 4:17–29.

Lumley, Henri de
1975   Cultural Evolution in France in Its Paleoecological Setting During the Middle Pleistocene. In *After the Australopithecines*, edited by K. W. Butzer and G. L. Isaac, pp. 745–808. Mouton, The Hague.

Lund, S. P.
1996   A Comparison of Holocene Paleomagnetic Secular Variation Records from North America. *Journal of Geophysical Research* 101(B4):8007–8024.

Lyell, Charles
1837   *Principles of Geology*. James Kay, Jun. and Brother, Philadelphia.

Lyman, R. Lee, Michael J. O'Brien, and Robert C. Dunnell
1997   *The Rise and Fall of Culture History*. Plenum Press, New York.

Lyman, R. Lee, Steve Wolverton, and Michael J. O'Brien
1998   Seriation, Superposition, and Interdigitation: A History of Americanist Graphic Depictions of Culture Change. *American Antiquity* 63:239–261.

Lynch, Michael
1993   *Scientific Practice and Ordinary Action: Ethnomethodology and Social Studies of Science*. Cambridge University Press, New York.

Lyon, Edwin
1996   *A New Deal for Southeastern Archaeology*. University of Alabama Press, Tuscaloosa.

Lyotard, Jean François
1984   *The Postmodern Condition: A Report on Knowledge*. University of Minnesota Press, Minneapolis.

Mandel, Rolfe
1999   *Geoarchaeological Research in the Great Plains: A Historical Perspective*. University of Oklahoma Press, Norman.

Marlowe, G.
1980   W. F. Libby and the Archaeologists, 1946–1948. *Radiocarbon* 22:1005–1014.
1999   Year One: Radiocarbon Dating and American Archaeology, 1947–1948. *American Antiquity* 64:9–32.

Marquardt, William H.
1978   Advances in Archaeological Seriation. In *Advances in Archaeological Method and Theory*, Vol. 1, edited by Michael B. Schiffer, pp. 257–314. Academic Press, New York.

Marshall, Michael P.

1991   The Pueblito as a Site Complex: Archaeological Investigations in the Dinétah District. In *Rethinking Navajo Pueblitos*, by Patrick Hogan and Michael P. Marshall, pp. 1–282. Cultural Resources Series No. 8. New Mexico Bureau of Land Management, Farmington.

1995   A Chapter in Early Navajo History: Late Gobernador Phase Pueblito Sites of the Dinétah District. Office of Contract Archaeology, University of New Mexico Report No. 185–469B, Albuquerque.

Martin, Paul S.

1971   The Revolution in Archaeology. *American Antiquity* 36:1–8.

MASCA Newsletter

1965   Dating Pottery by Thermoluminescence. *MASCA Newsletter* 3:2.

Matson, R. G. and William D. Lipe

1977   Seriation of Pueblo Ceramic Assemblages from Cedar Mesa, SE Utah. Manuscript in possession of Eric Blinman.

Maurer, C. and B. A. Purdy

1986   Thermoluminescence of Heat-Altered Florida Chert. In *Proceedings of the 24th International Archaeometry Symposium*, edited by J. S. Olin and M. J. Blackman, pp. 473–476. Smithsonian Institution Press.

May, S. R. and R. F. Butler

1986   North American Jurassic Apparent Polar Wander: Implications for Plate Motion, Paleogeography and Cordilleran Tectonics. *Journal of Geophysical Research* 91(B11):519–544.

Mazer, J. J., J. K. Bates, C. M. Stevenson, and J. P. Bradley

1992   Obsidians and Tektites: Natural Analogues for Water Diffusion in Nuclear Waste Glass. *Materials Research Society Symposium Proceedings* 257:513–520.

Mazer, J. J., C. M. Stevenson, W. L. Ebert, and J. K. Bates

1991   The Experimental Hydration of Obsidian as a Function of Relative Humidity and Temperature. *American Antiquity* 56:504–513.

McBurney, C. B. M.

1952   Radiocarbon Dating Results from the Old World. *Antiquity* 26:35–40.

McCook, Stuart

1996   "It May Be Truth, But It Is Not Evidence": Paul Du Chaillu and the Legitimation of Evidence in the Field Sciences. *Osiris* 11:177–197.

McGrail, B. P., L. R. Perderson, D. M. Strachan, R. C. Ewing, and L. S. Cordell

1988   Obsidian Hydration Dating—Field, Laboratory, and Modeling Results. In *Materials Research Society Symposium Proceedings* 123:237–244.

McGregor, John C.

1936   Dating the Eruption of Sunset Crater, Arizona. *American Antiquity* 2:15–26.

1938a   Southwestern Dated Ruins: III. *Tree-Ring Bulletin* 4(4):6.

1938b   *How Some Important Northern Arizona Pottery Types Were Dated.*

Museum of Northern Arizona Bulletin No. 18. Flagstaff.

McGuire, K. R., A. P. Garfinkel, and M. E. Basgall

1982 *Archaeological Investigations in the El Paso Mountains of the Western Mojave Desert: The Bickel and Last Chance Sites, CA-KER-250, -261.* Submitted to the Department of the Interior, Bureau of Land Management, California Desert District, Ridgecrest, California.

McKeever, S. W. S.

1985 *Thermoluminescence of Solids.* Cambridge University Press, Cambridge.

McKeever, S. W. S. and R. Chen

1997 Luminescence Models. *Radiation Measurements* 27:625–661.

McKern, W. C.

1939 The Midwestern Taxonomic Method as an Aid to Archaeological Culture Study. *American Antiquity* 4:301–313.

McNitt, Frank

1972 *Navajo Wars, Military Campaigns, Slave Raids, and Reprisals.* University of New Mexico Press, Albuquerque.

McNutt, Charles H.

1973 On the Methodological Validity of Frequency Seriation. *American Antiquity* 38:45–60.

Meighan, C. W.

1970 Obsidian Hydration Rates. *Science* 170:99–100.

1976 Empirical Determination of Obsidian Hydration Rates from Archaeological Evidence. In *Advances in Obsidian Glass Studies. Archaeological and Geochemical Perspectives*, edited by R. E. Taylor, pp. 106–119. Noyes Press, Park Ridge, New Jersey.

1978 Obsidian Dating of the Malibu Site. In *Obsidian Dates II: A Compendium of the Obsidian Hydration Determinations Made at the U. C. L. A. Obsidian Hydration Laboratory*, edited by C. W. Meighan and P. I. Vanderhoeven, pp. 158–161. University of California Institute of Archaeology Monograph 6. Los Angeles.

1981 The Little Lake Site, Pinto Points, and Obsidian Hydration Dating in the Great Basin. *Journal of California and Great Basin Anthropology* 3:200–214.

1983 Obsidian Dating in California. *American Antiquity* 48:600–609.

1984 Overview of Great Basin Obsidian Studies. In *Obsidian Studies in the Great Basin*, edited by R. E. Hughes, pp. 225–230. Contributions of the University of California Archaeological Research Facility No. 45. Berkeley.

Meighan, C. W., L. J. Foote, and P. V. Aiello

1968a Obsidian Dating in West Mexican Archaeology. *Science* 160:1069–1075.

1968b Obsidian Dating Revisited. *Science* 162:814.

Meighan, C. W. and C. V. Haynes

1970 The Borax Lake Site Revisited. *Science* 167:1213–1221.

Mejdahl, V.

1969   Thermoluminescence Dating of Ancient Danish Ceramics. *Archaeometry* 11:95–104.

1983   Feldspar Inclusion Dating of Ceramics and Burnt Stone. *PACT* 9:351–364.

1988   The Plateau Method for Dating Partially Bleached Sediments by Thermoluminescence. *Quaternary Science Reviews* 7:347–348.

Mejdahl, V. and L. Bøtter-Jensen

1994   Luminescence Dating of Archaeological Materials Using a New Technique Based on Single Aliquot Measurements. *Quaternary Geochronology* 13:551–554.

Meltzer, David J.

1983   The Antiquity of Man and the Development of American Archaeology. *Advances in Archaeological Method and Theory* 6:1–51.

1985   North American Archaeology and Archaeologists: 1879–1934. *American Antiquity* 50:241–260.

Mera, Harry P.

1931   *Chupadero Black-on-white*. Laboratory of Anthropology Technical Series, Bulletin 1. Santa Fe.

1934   *Observations on the Archaeology of the Petrified Forest National Monument*. Laboratory of Anthropology, Technical Series, Bulletin 7. Santa Fe.

1935   *Ceramic Clues to the Prehistory of North Central New Mexico*. Laboratory of Anthropology Technical Series, Bulletin 8. Santa Fe.

Mercier, N., H. Valladas, and G. Valladas

1995   Flint Thermoluminescence Dates from the CFR Laboratory at Gif: Contributions to the Study of the Chronology of the Middle Paleolithic. *Quaternary Science Reviews* 14:351–364.

Merrill, R. S.

1947   *A Progress Report on the Dating of Archaeological Sites by Means of Radioactive Elements*. Duplicated Report, October 20, 1947.

1948   Progress Report on the Dating of Archaeological Sites by Means of Radioactive Elements. *American Antiquity* 13:281–286.

Merton, Robert

1973   *The Sociology of Science: Theoretical and Empirical Investigations*, edited by N. Storer. University of Chicago Press, Chicago.

Michab, M., J. K. Feathers, J.-L. Joron, N. Mercier, J.-L. Reyss, M. Selo, H. Valladas, G. Valladas, and A. Roosevelt

1998   New Dates for the Brazilian Paleoindian Cave-Site of Pedra Pintada. *Quaternary Science Reviews* 17:1041–1046.

Michels, J. W.

1965   *Lithic Serial Chronology Through Obsidian Hydration Dating*. Ph.D. dissertation, University of California, Los Angeles.

1967   Archaeology and Dating by Hydration of Obsidian. *Science* 158:211–214.

1969   Testing Stratigraphy and Artifact Re-Use Through Obsidian Hydration Dating. *American Antiquity* 34:15–22.

1971 The Colonial Obsidian Industry of the Valley of Mexico. In *Science in Archaeology*, edited by R. H. Brill, pp. 251–271. Massachusetts Institute of Technology Press, Cambridge.

1973 *Dating Methods in Archaeology*. Seminar Press, New York.

1981 *The Hydration Rate Constants for Batza Tena Obsidian, the North Slope of Alaska*. MOLAB Technical Report No. 1. State College, Pennsylvania.

1982 *The Hydration Rate Constants for the Casa Diablo Obsidian, Mammoth Junction Area of Mono County, California*. MOLAB Technical Report No. 6. State College, Pennsylvania.

1983 *The Hydration Rate Constants for Coso (Sugarloaf) Obsidian at Archaeological Sites in the China Lake Area of California*. MOLAB Technical Report No. 23. State College, Pennsylvania.

Michels, J. W. and C. Bebrich

1971 Obsidian Hydration Dating. In *Dating Techniques for the Archaeologist*, edited by H. N. Michael and E. K. Ralph, pp. 164–221. Massachusetts Institute of Technology Press, Cambridge.

Michels, J. W. and I. S. T. Tsong

1980 Obsidian Hydration Dating: A Coming of Age. In *Advances in Archaeological Method and Theory*, edited by M. B. Schiffer, Vol. 3, pp. 405–444. Academic Press, New York.

Michels, J. W., I. S. T. Tsong, and G. A. Smith

1983 Experimentally Derived Hydration Rates in Obsidian Dating. *Archaeometry* 25:107–117.

Mistovich, T. S.

1988 Early Mississippian in the Black Warrior Valley: The Pace of Transition. *Southeastern Archaeology* 7:21–38.

Moorehead, Warren K.

1928 *The Cahokia Mounds*. University of Illinois Bulletin 26. Urbana.

Morozov, G. V.

1968 The Relative Dating of Quaternary Ukranian Sediments by the Thermoluminescence Method. *8th International Quaternary Association Congress, Paris*, pp. 167. U.S. Geological Survey Library, Washington, D. C.

Morris, Earl H.

1936 Archaeological Background of Dates in Early Arizona Chronology. *Tree-Ring Bulletin* 2(4):34–36.

1939 *Archaeological Studies in the La Plata District, Southwestern Colorado and Northwestern New Mexico*. Carnegie Institution of Washington 519:1–298. Washington, D.C.

Moser, Stephanie

1996 Visual Representation in Archaeology: Depicting the Missing Link in Human Origins. In *Picturing Knowledge: Historical and Philosophical Problems Concerning the Use of Art in Science*, edited by Brian S. Biagre, pp. 184–214. University of Toronto Press, Toronto, Canada.

Muller, R. A.

1977 Radioisotope Dating with a Cyclotron. *Science* 196:489–494.

Mullins, Nicholas C.
  1972   The Development of A Scientific Specialty: The Phage Group and
          the Origins of Molecular Biology. *Minerva* 19:52–82.
Nash, Stephen E.
  1997a   *A History of Archaeological Tree-Ring Dating: 1914–1945.* Ph.D.
          dissertation, University of Arizona. University Microfilms, Ann
          Arbor.
  1997b   Archaeological Cutting Date Estimation and the Interpretation of
          Estimated Tree-Ring Dates. *American Antiquity* 62:260–272.
  1998   Time for Collaboration: A. E. Douglass, Archaeologists, and the
          Establishment of Tree-Ring Dating in the American Southwest.
          Journal of the Southwest 40:261–305.
  1999   *Time, Trees, and Prehistory: Archaeological Tree-Ring Dating and
          the Development of North American Archaeology 1914–1950.*
          University of Utah Press, Salt Lake City.
Neff, Hector and Barbara Arroyo
  1996   The Evolution of Early Formative Ceramic Traditions in Pacific
          Coastal Southern Mesoamerica. Proceedings of the 1996 Chacmool
          Conference, Calgary, Alberta.
Nelson, F. W., Jr.
  1984   X-ray Fluorescence Analysis of Some Western North American
          Obsidians. In *Obsidian Studies in the Great Basin*, edited by R. E.
          Hughes, p. 62. Contributions of the University of California
          Archaeological Research Facility No. 45. Berkeley.
Nelson, F. W., Jr., K. K. Nielson, N. F. Mangelson, M. W. Hill, and R. T.
      Matheny
  1977   Preliminary Studies of the Trace Element Composition of Obsidian
          Artifacts from Northern Campeche, Mexico. *American Antiquity*
          42:209–225.
Nelson, Nels C.
  1914   Pueblo Ruins of the Galisteo Basin, New Mexico. *Anthropological
          Papers of the American Museum of Natural History* 15.
  1916   Chronology of the Tano Ruins, New Mexico. *American
          Anthropologist* 18:159–180.
  1918   Chronology in Florida. *Anthropological Papers of the American
          Museum of Natural History* 22(Pt. 2):75–103.
Neustupny, E.
  1970   The Accuracy of Radiocarbon Dating. In *Radiocarbon: Variations
          and Absolute Chronology*, edited by I. U. Olsson, pp. 23–34.
          Almqvist and Wiksell, Stockholm.
Newman, J. R. and R. L. Nielsen
  1985   Initial Notes on the X-ray Fluorescence Sourcing of Northern New
          Mexico Obsidians. *Journal of Field Archaeology* 12:377–383.
Nichols, Robert F. and Thomas P. Harlan
  1967   Archaeological Tree-Ring Dates from Wetherill Mesa. *Tree-Ring
          Bulletin* 28(1–4):13–40.

Nichols, Robert F., and D. G. Smith
  1965   Evidence of Prehistoric Cultivation of Douglas-Fir Trees at Mesa
         Verde. In *Contributions of the Wetherill Mesa Archaeological
         Project*, edited by D. Osborne, pp. 57–64. Memoirs of the Society
         for American Archaeology 19.
Nixon, Richard M.
  1978   *The Memoirs of Richard M. Nixon.* Grosset and Dunlap, New York.
Noel Hume, Ivor
  1969   *Historical Archaeology.* Knopf, New York.
  1970   *James Geddy and Sons: Colonial Craftsmen.* Colonial Williamsburg
         Archaeological Series No. 5, Williamsburg, Virginia.
Norton, D. R. and I. Friedman
  1981   Ground Temperature Measurements. Part I, Pallman Technique.
         USGS Professional Paper 1203:1–11. U.S. Government Printing
         Office, Washington, D.C.
Olmert, Michael
  1996   *Milton's Teeth and Ovid's Umbrella: Curiouser and Curiouser
         Adventures in History.* Touchstone/Simon & Schuster, New York.
Olmstead, F. H., I. Friedman, and D. R. Norton
  1981   Ground Temperature Measurements. Part II, Evaluation of the
         Pallman Technique in Two Geothermal Areas of West-Central
         Nevada. *USGS Professional Paper* 1203:13–21. U.S. Government
         Printing Office, Washington, D.C.
Olsson, I. U. (editor)
  1970   *Radiocarbon Variations and Absolute Chronology.* Almqvist and
         Wiksell, Stockholm.
Orcutt, Janet D.
  1986   Settlement Behavior Modeling Synthesis. In *Dolores Archaeological
         Program: Final Synthetic Report*, compiled by David A. Breternitz,
         Christine K. Robinson, and G. Timothy Gross, pp. 539–576. U.S.
         Department of the Interior, Bureau of Reclamation, Engineering and
         Research Center, Denver.
Orcutt, Janet D., Eric Blinman, and Timothy A. Kohler
  1990   Explanations of Population Aggregation in the Mesa Verde Region
         Prior to A.D. 900. In *Perspectives on Southwestern Prehistory*, edited
         by Paul E. Minnis and Charles L. Redman, pp. 196–212. Westview
         Press, Boulder.
Origer, T. M. and B. P. Wickstrom
  1982   The Use of Hydration Measurements to Date Obsidian Materials
         from Sonoma County, California. *Journal of California and Great
         Basin Anthropology* 4:123–131.
Osborne, Douglas and Robert F. Nichols
  1967   Introduction. The Dendrochronology of the Wetherill Mesa Project.
         Tree-Ring Bulletin 28(1–4):3–6.
Peacock, Evan
  1995   Text Excavations at an Upland Mississippian Site in Oktibbeha

County, Mississippi. *Mississippi Archaeology* 30:1–20.

Peacock, Evan and Janet Rafferty

1995 Settlement Pattern Continuity and Change in the Mississippi Black Prairie: A Response to Johnson. *Southeastern Archaeology* 15:249–253.

Petrie, W. M. Flinders

1899 Sequences in Prehistoric Remains. *Journal of the Royal Anthropological Institute* 29:295–301.

Phillips, John

1978 Memoirs of William Smith / John Phillips. Reprint of 1844 ed. Arno Press, New York.

Phillips, Philip, James A. Ford, and James B. Griffin

1951 *Archaeological Survey in the Lower Mississippi Valley, 1940–1947.* Papers of the Peabody Museum of Archeology and Ethnology No. 25. Harvard University, Cambridge.

Piggott, S.

1959 *Approach to Archaeology.* A. and C. Black, London.

Plog, Fred T.

1973 Diachronic Anthropology. In *Research and Theory in Current Archeology*, edited by Charles L. Redman, pp. 181–196. Wiley, New York.

Plog, Stephen

1980 *Stylistic Variation in Prehistoric Ceramics: Design Analysis in the American Southwest.* Cambridge University Press, New York.

1995 Paradigms and Pottery. In *Ceramic Production in the American Southwest*, edited by Barbara J. Mills and Patricia L. Crown, pp. 268–280. University of Arizona Press, Tucson.

1997 *Ancient Peoples of the American Southwest.* Thames and Hudson, London.

Plog, Stephen and Jeffrey L. Hantman

1986 Multiple Regression as a Dating Method in the American Southwest. In *Spatial Organization and Exchange: Archaeological Survey on Northern Black Mesa*, edited by Stephen Plog, pp. 87–113. Southern Illinois University Press, Carbondale.

Polach, D. (compiler)

1988 *Radiocarbon Dating Literature, the First 21 Years, 1947–1968.* London, Academic Press.

Powers, M. A. and B. P. Johnson

1987 *Defensive Sites of Dinétah.* Cultural Resources Series, Vol. 2. U.S. Department of the Interior, New Mexico Bureau of Land Management, Albuquerque.

Prescott, J. R. and G. B. Robertson

1997 Sediment Dating by Luminescence: A Review. *Radiation Measurements* 27:893–922.

Preucel, Robert (editor)

1991 *Processual and Postprocessual Archaeologies: Multiple Ways of Knowing the Past.* Occasional Paper No. 10. Southern Illinois

University at Carbondale.

Purdy, B. A.

1985   Prehistoric Technologies and Problems Related to
       Thermoluminescent Dating of Heated Cherts. In *Indians, Colonists,*
       and Slaves—Essays in Memory of Charles H. Fairbanks. Florida
       Journal of Anthropology, Special Publication No. 4, Gainesville.

Pyddoke, E.

1961   *Stratification for the Archaeologist*. Phoenix House, London.

Ralph, Elizabeth K.

1965   Review of Radiocarbon Dates from Tikal and the Maya Calendar
       Correlation Problem. *American Antiquity* 30:421–427.

Ralph, Elizabeth K. and Mark C. Han

1966   Dating of Pottery by Thermoluminescence. *Nature* 210:245–247.

1968   Progress in Thermoluminescent Dating of Pottery. In
       Thermoluminescence of Geological Materials, edited by D. J.
       McDougall, pp. 379–388. Academic Press, London.

1969   Potential of Thermoluminescence in Supplementing Radiocarbon
       Dating. *World Archaeology* 1:157–169.

1971   Potential of Thermoluminescence Dating. In *Science and*
       Archaeology, edited by R. H. Brill, pp. 244–250. Massachusetts
       Institute of Technology Press, Cambridge.

Randall, J. T. and M. H. F. Wilkins

1945   Phosphorescence and Electron Traps. *Proceedings of the Royal*
       Society of London A 184:366–407.

Rapp, George, Jr.

1975   The Archaeological Field Staff: The Geologist. *Journal of Field*
       Archaeology 2:229–237.

1992   A Partnership. *Society for Archaeological Science Bulletin* 15(4):2–4.

Rapp, George, Jr. and Christopher L. Hill

1998   *Geoarchaeology: The Earth-Science Approach to Archaeological*
       Interpretation. Yale University Press, New Haven.

Rathje, William and Michael B. Schiffer

1982   *Archaeology*. Harcourt Brace Jovanovich, New York.

Reed, A. D. and J. C. Horn

1990   Early Navajo Occupation of the American Southwest:
       Reexamination of the Dinétah Phase. *The Kiva* 55:283–300.

Reed, L. S. and P. F. Reed

1996   Reexamining Gobernador Polychrome: Toward a New
       Understanding of the Early Navajo Chronological Sequence in
       Northwestern New Mexico. In *The Archaeology of Navajo Origins*,
       edited by R. H. Towner, pp. 83–108. University of Utah Press, Salt
       Lake City.

Rees-Jones, J., S. J. B. Hall, and W. J. Rink

1997   A Laboratory Inter-Comparison of Quartz Optically Stimulated
       Luminescence (OSL) Results, *Quaternary Geochronology*
       16:275–280.

Reeve, Frank D.

1958   Navaho-Spanish Wars, 1680–1720. *New Mexico Historical Review*
        33:204–231.

1959   The Navaho-Spanish Peace: 1720's–1770's. *New Mexico Historical
        Review* 34:9–40.

Reeves, R. D. and G. K. Ward

1976   Characterization Studies of New Zealand Obsidians: Toward a
        Regional Prehistory. In *Advances in Obsidian Glass Studies.
        Archaeological and Geochemical Prospectives*, edited by R. E.
        Taylor, pp. 259–287. Noyes Press, Park Ridge, New Jersey.

Reid, J. Jefferson, Barbara Klie Montgomery, and María Nieves Zedeño

1995   Refinements in Dating Late Cibola White Ware. *The Kiva* 61:31–44.

Reiser, Stanley Joel

1978   Medicine and the Reign of Technology. Cambridge University Press,
        New York.

Renaud, Etienne

1928   Evolution of Population and Dwellings in the Indian Southwest. *El
        Palacio* 26(5):75–86.

Renfrew, C.

1973   *Before Civilization: The Radiocarbon Revolution and Prehistoric
        Europe*. Alfred A. Knopf, New York.

1976   Archaeology and the Earth Sciences. In *Geoarchaeology: Earth
        Science and the Past*, edited by D. A. Davidson and M. L. Shackley,
        pp. 1–5. Westview Press, Boulder.

Renfrew, C., J. E. Dixon, and J. R. Cann

1965   Obsidian in the Aegean. *Annual of the British School of
        Archaeology at Athens* 60:225–249.

1966   Obsidian and Early Cultural Contact in the Near East. *Proceedings
        of the Prehistoric Society* 32:30–72.

Reyman, Jonathan E. (editor)

1992   *Rediscovering Our Past: Essays on the History of American
        Archaeology*. Avebury Press, Aldershot.

Rhode, D.

1994a   Obsidian Studies at Yucca Mountain, Nevada: Sourcing and
        Regional Chronological Development. Poster Presented at the 59th
        Annual Meeting of the Society for American Archaeology, Anaheim,
        California.

1994b   Direct Dating of Brown Ware Ceramics Using Thermoluminescence
        and Its Relation to the Numic Spread. In *Across the West: Human
        Population Movement and Expansion of the Numa*, edited by D. B.
        Madsen and D. Rhode, pp. 124–132. University of Utah Press, Salt
        Lake City.

Rice, P. M.

1987   *Pottery Analysis: A Sourcebook*. University of Chicago Press,
        Chicago.

Ridings, R.

1991   Obsidian Hydration Dating: The Effects of Mean Exponential
        Ground Temperature and Depth of Artifact Recovery. *Journal of*

Field Archaeology 18:77–85.

1996 Where in the World Does Obsidian Hydration Dating Work? *American Antiquity* 61:136–148.

Rigaud, Jean-Philippe

1989 From the Middle to the Upper Paleolithic: Transition or Convergence? In *The Emergence of Modern Humans*, edited by E. Trinkaus, pp. 142–153. Cambridge University Press, New York.

Rigaud, Jean-Philippe, Thierry Ge, and Jan F. Simek

1995 Mousterian Fires from Grotte XVI (Dordogne, France). *Antiquity* 60:902–912.

Rimstidt, J. D. and H. L. Barnes

1980 The Kinetics of Silica-Water Reactions. *Geochimica et Cosmochimica Acta* 44:1683–1699.

Roberts, Frank H. H., Jr.

1935a *A Folsom Complex: Preliminary Report on Investigations at the Lindenmeier Site in Northern Colorado.* Smithsonian Miscellaneous Collections 94(4). Smithsonian Institution, Washington, D.C.

1935b A Summary of Southwestern Archaeology. *American Anthropologist* 37:1–35.

1937 Archaeology in the Southwest. *American Antiquity* 3:3–33.

1951 Radiocarbon Dates and Early Man. In *Radiocarbon Dating*, assembled by F. Johnson, pp. 20–22. Society for American Archaeology Memoirs 8. (*American Antiquity* 17 (1) pt2: 20–22.)

Roberts, R. G.

1997 Luminescence Dating in Archaeology: From Origins to Optical. *Radiation Measurements* 27:819–892.

Roberts, R. G., R. Jones, N. A. Spooner, M. J. Head, A. S. Murray, and M. A. Smith

1994 The Human Colonization of Australia: Optical Dates of 53,000 and 60,000 Years Bracket Human Arrival at Deaf Adder Gorge, Northern Territory. *Quaternary Science Reviews* 13:575–583.

Robertshaw, Peter (editor)

1990 *A History of African Archaeology.* Heinemann, Porstmouth, New Hampshire; J. Currey, London.

Robinson, William J.

1967 *Tree-Ring Materials as a Basis for Cultural Interpretation.* Ph.D. dissertation, University of Arizona. University Microfilms, Ann Arbor.

1976 Tree-Ring Dating and Archaeology in the American Southwest. *Tree-Ring Bulletin* 36(1):9–20.

1985 A Construction Sequence for Hubbell Trading Post and Residence. *The Kiva* 50:219–236.

1990 Tree-Ring Studies of the Pueblo de Acoma. *Historical Archaeology* 24:99–106.

Robinson, William J. and Catherine M. Cameron

1992 *A Directory of Tree-Ring Dated Prehistoric Sites.* Laboratory of Tree-Ring Research, University of Arizona, Tucson.

Robinson, William J., John W. Hannah, and Bruce G. Harrill

1972   *Tree-Ring Dates from New Mexico I, O, U: Central Rio Grande Area.* Laboratory of Tree-Ring Research, Tucson.

Robinson, William J. and Bruce G. Harrill

1974   *Tree-Ring Dates from Colorado V: Mesa Verde Area.* Laboratory of Tree-Ring Research, Tucson.

Robinson, William J., Bruce G. Harrill, and Richard L. Warren

1973   *Tree-Ring Dates from New Mexico J-K, P, V: Santa Fe, Pecos, and Lincoln Area.* Laboratory of Tree-Ring Research, Tucson.

1974   *Tree-Ring Dates from New Mexico B: Chaco-Gobernador Area.* Laboratory of Tree-Ring Research, Tucson.

1975   *Tree-Ring Dates from Arizona H-I, Flagstaff Area.* Laboratory of Tree-Ring Research, Tucson.

Robinson, William J. and Ronald H. Towner

1993   *A Directory of Tree-Ring Dated Native American Sites.* Laboratory of Tree-Ring Research, University of Arizona, Tucson.

Robinson, William J. and Richard L. Warren

1971   *Tree-Ring Dates from New Mexico C-D: Northern Rio Grande Area.* Laboratory of Tree-Ring Research, Tucson.

Robinson, W. S.

1951   A Method for Chronologically Ordering Archaeological Deposits. *American Antiquity* 16:293–301.

Rocek, T. R.

1995   *Navajo Multi-Household Social Units.* University of Arizona Press, Tucson.

Roquet, J.

1954   Sur les Rémanences Magnétique des Oxydes de Fer et Leur Intérêt en Géomagnétisme. *Annales de Géophysique* 10:226–247.

Rosenberg, Charles

1983   Science in American Society: A Generation of Historical Debate. *Isis* 74:356–367.

Ross, C. S. and R. L. Smith

1955   Water and Other Volatiles in Volcanic Glasses. *American Mineralogist* 40:1071–1089.

Rossignol, J. and L. Wandsnider (editors)

1992   *Space, Time and Archaeological Landscapes.* Plenum Press, New York.

Rouse, Irving

1955   On the Correlation of Phases of Culture. *American Anthropologist* 57:713–722.

Rozanski, K., W. Stichler, R. Gonfiantini, E. M. Scott, R. P. Beukens, B. Kromer, and J. Van Der Plicht

1992   The IAEA ^{14}C Intercomparison Exercise 1990. *Radiocarbon* 34:506–519.

Rudwick, Martin J. S.

1976   *The Meaning of Fossils: Episodes in the History of Paleontology,* 2nd rev. ed. Science History Publications, New York.

Russell, S. C.

1983   *The Navajo History and Archaeology of East Central Black Mesa.* Navajo Nation Papers in Anthropology, No. 21. Window Rock, Arizona.

Russo, M.

1994   A Brief Introduction to the Study of Archaic Mounds in the Southeast. *Southeastern Archaeology* 13:89–93.

Salvador, A.

1994   *International Stratigraphic Guide: A Guide to Stratigraphic Classification, Terminology, and Procedure,* 2ⁿᵈ edition. The Geological Society of America, Boulder, Colorado.

Sapir, Edward

1916   *Time Perspective in Aboriginal American Culture: A Study in Method.* Geological Survey of Canada, Anthropological Series, No. 13. Ottawa.

Satterthwaite, L. and Elizabeth K. Ralph

1960   New Radiocarbon Dates and the Maya Correlation Problem. *American Antiquity* 26:165–184.

Schaafsma, Curtis F.

1996   Ethnic Identity and Protohistoric Sites in Northwestern New Mexico: Implications for Reconstructions of Navajo and Ute History. In *The Archaeology of Navajo Origins,* edited by R. H. Towner, pp. 19–46. University of Utah Press, Salt Lake City.

Schaafsma, P. and Curtis F. Schaafsma

1996   Daniel Wolfman 1939–1994. *American Antiquity* 61:291–294.

Scheetz, B. E., and C. M. Stevenson

1988   The Role of Resolution and Sample Preparation in Hydration Rim Measurement: Implications for Experimentally Determined Hydration Rates. *American Antiquity* 53:110–117.

Schiffer, Michael Brian

1972   Archaeological Context and Systemic Context. *American Antiquity* 37:156–165.

1976   *Behavioral Archaeology.* Academic Press, New York.

1996   Some Relationships Between Behavioral and Evolutionary Archaeologies. *American Antiquity* 61:643–662.

Schmidt, E. F.

1928   Time-Relations of Prehistoric Pottery Types in Southern Arizona. *Anthropological Papers of the American Museum of Natural History* 30:247–302.

Schliemann, Heinrich

1875   *Troy and Its Remains.* J. Murray, London.

Schneer, C. J.

1969   *Toward a History of Geology.* Massachusetts Institute of Technology Press, Cambridge.

Schroedl, Alan R. and Eric Blinman

1989   Dating and Site Chronologies. In *Kayenta Anasazi Archeology and Navajo Ethnohistory on the Northwestern Shonto Plateau: The N-16 Project,* edited and compiled by Alan R. Schroedl, pp. 53–87.

Report Submitted to the Bureau of Indian Affairs, Navajo Area Office (Contract No. NOO C 1420 9847). P-III Associates, Inc., Salt Lake City.

Schulman, Edmund

1956 *Dendroclimatic Changes in Semi-Arid America*. University of Arizona Press, Tucson.

Scranton, Philip

1991 Theory and Narrative in the History of Technology: Comment. *Technology and Culture* 32:385–393.

Sears, Derek W. G.

1988 Thermoluminescence of Meteorites: Shedding Light on the Cosmos. *Nuclear Tracks and Radiation Measurements* 14:5–17.

Seeley, Mary-Ann

1975 Thermoluminescent Dating in Its Application to Archaeology: A Review. *Journal of Archaeological Science* 2:17–43.

Sellards, E. H.

1952 *Early Man in America*. University of Texas Press, Austin, Texas.

Sesler, Leslie and Tim Hovezak

1996 Navajo Settlement Patterns Within the Fruitland Project Area. Paper presented at the 4th Annual Fruitland Conference, Farmington.

1998 Frances Mesa Navajo Settlement Patterns. Ms. in possession of Ronald Towner.

Shackley, S. (editor)

1996 Method and Theory in Volcanic Glass Studies. Plenum Press, London.

Shafer, Robert (editor)

1980 *A Guide to Historical Method*, 3rd ed. Dorsey Press, Homewood, Illinois.

Shanks, Michael and Christopher Tilley

1987 *Social Theory and Archaeology*. University of New Mexico Press, Albuquerque.

1992 *Reconstructing Archaeology: Theory and Practice*, 2nd ed. Routledge, London.

Shapin, Steven

1982 History of Science and Its Sociological Reconstructions. *History of Science* 20(3):157–211.

1996 *A Social History of Truth: Civility and Science in Seventeenth-Century England*. University of Chicago Press, Chicago.

Sharer, Robert J. and Wendy Ashmore

1979 *Fundamentals of Archaeology*. Benjamin/Cummings Publishing, Menlo Park, California.

1993 *Archaeology: Discovering Our Past*. Mayfield, Mountain View, California.

Shaw, T.

1970 The Use of Stratigraphical Concepts in Archaeology. In *Stratigraphy: An Interdisciplinary Symposium*, edited by S. G. H. Daniels and S. J. Freeth, pp. 16–28. Institute of African Studies, University of Ibadan, Occasional Paper No. 19. Ibadan, Nigeria.

Shepard, Anna O.
 1936 The Technology of Pecos Pottery. In *The Pottery of Pecos*, Vol. 2, by Alfred Vincent Kidder, pp. 389–587. Phillips Academy, Yale University Press, New Haven.

Shott, M. J.
 1993 Spears, Darts, and Arrows: Late Woodland Hunting Techniques in the Upper Ohio Valley. *American Antiquity* 58:425–443.

Silver, Brian L.
 1998 *The Ascent of Science*. Oxford University Press, New York.

Singer, C. A. and J. E. Ericson
 1977 Quarry Analysis at Bodie Hills, Mono County, California: A Case Study. In *Exchanges Systems in Prehistory*, edited by T. K. Earle and J. E. Ericson, pp. 171–190. Academic Press, New York.

Sinopoli, Carla M.
 1991 Approaches to Archaeological Ceramics. Plenum Press, New York.

Skinner, C. E. and K. J. Tremaine (editors)
 1993 *Obsidian: An Interdisciplinary Bibliography*. International Association for Obsidian Studies Occasional Paper No. 1 Department of Anthropology, San Jose State University, San Jose, Calif.

Smiley, Francis E. and Richard V. N. Ahlstrom
 1997 *Archaeological Chronometry: Radiocarbon and Tree-Ring Dating, Models, and Applications from Black Mesa, Arizona*. Southern Illinois University at Carbondale Center for Archaeological Investigations Occasional Paper No. 16. Carbondale.

Smiley, Terah L.
 1951 *A Summary of Tree-Ring Dates from Some Southwestern Archaeological Sites*. University of Arizona Bulletin No. 5. Tucson.

Smiley, Terah L., Stanley A. Stubbs, and Bryant Bannister
 1953 *A Foundation for the Dating of Some Late Archaeological Sites in the Rio Grande Area, New Mexico*. Laboratory of Tree-Ring Research Bulletin No. 6. Tucson.

Smith, G. P.
 1990 Cube Size and Refiring as Factors That Influence Archaeomagnetic Results. In *Archaeomagnetic Dating*, edited by J. L. Eighmy and R. S. Sternberg, pp. 148–157. University of Arizona Press, Tucson.

Smith, I. E. M., G. K. Ward, and W. R. Ambrose
 1977 Geographic Distribution and the Characterization of Volcanic Glasses in Oceania. *Archaeology and Physical Anthropology in Oceania* 12:173–201.

Smith, Watson
 1971 *Painted Ceramics of the Western Mound at Awatovi*. Papers of the Peabody Museum of Archaeology and Ethnology 38. Harvard University, Cambridge.

Sokal, Robert R. and F. James Rohlf
 1969 *Biometry: The Principles and Practice of Statistics in Biological Research*. W. H. Freeman and Company, San Francisco.

South, Stanley

1972 Evolution and Horizon as Revealed in Ceramic Analysis in Historical Archaeology. *The Conference on Historic Site Archaeology Papers* 6:71–116. Institute of Archeology and Anthropology, University of South Carolina, Columbia. (Revised and Reprinted in 1977 in *Method and Theory in Historical Archaeology*, by Stanley South, pp. 201–235. Academic Press, New York.)

Spaulding, Albert C.

1958 The Significance of Differences Between Radiocarbon Dates. *American Antiquity* 23:309–311.

1960 Statistical Description and Comparison of Artifact Assemblages. In *The Application of Quantitative Methods in Archaeology*, edited by Robert F. Heizer and Sherburne F. Cook, pp. 60–92. Viking Fund Publications in Anthropology, No. 28. Wenner-Gren Foundation for Anthropological Research, New York.

Spier, Leslie C.

1917a Zuni Chronology. *Proceedings of the National Academy of Sciences* 3:280–283.

1917b An Outline for a Chronology of Zuni Ruins. *Anthropological Papers of the American Museum of Natural History* 18:207–331.

1931 N. C. Nelson's Stratigraphic Technique in the Reconstruction of Prehistoric Sequences in Southwestern America. In *Methods in Social Science: A Case Book*, edited by Stuart A. Rice, pp. 275–283. University of Chicago Press, Chicago.

Stafford, Barbara Maria

1991 *Body Criticism: Imaging the Unseen in Enlightenment Art and Medicine*. Massachusetts Institute of Technology Press, Cambridge.

Stahle, David

1979 Tree-Ring Dating of Historic Buildings in Arkansas. *Tree-Ring Bulletin* 39:1–28.

Stahle, David, Edward R. Cook, and James W. C. White

1985 Tree-Ring Dating of Baldcypress and the Potential for Millennia-Long Chronologies in the Southeast. *American Antiquity* 50:796–802.

Stahle, David and D. Wolfman

1985 The Potential for Archaeological Tree-Ring Dating in Eastern North America. In *Advances in Archaeological Method and Theory*, Vol. 8, edited by M. B. Schiffer, pp. 279–302. Academic Press, New York.

Stallings, W. S., Jr.

1931 *El Paso Polychrome*. Laboratory of Anthropology, Technical Series, Bulletin 3. Santa Fe.

1933 A Tree-Ring Chronology for the Rio Grande Drainage in Northern New Mexico. *Proceedings of the National Academy of Sciences* 19:803–806.

1936 Letter to Benjamin F. Betts of the Housing Research Project of Purdue University, Dated 25 April 1936. Folder 89CO3.001.1A-B 1930s. Laboratory of Anthropology Archives, Santa Fe.

1937   Southwestern Dated Ruins: I. *Tree-Ring Bulletin* 4(2):3–5.

1940   Using Heartwood to Estimate Sapwood. Manuscript on file,
        Laboratory of Tree-Ring Research, Tucson.

Star, Susan Leigh

1995   *Ecologies of Knowledge: Work and Politics in Science and
        Technology.* State University of New York Press, Albany.

Staudenmaier, John M.

1985   *Technology's Storytellers: Reweaving the Human Fabric.*
        Massachusetts Institute of Technology Press, Cambridge.

Stein, Julie K.

1987   Deposits for Archaeologists. In *Advances in Archaeological Method
        and Theory*, Volume 11, edited by M. B. Schiffer, pp. 337–393.
        Academic Press, Orlando.

1990   Archaeological Stratigraphy. In *Archaeological Geology of North
        America*, edited by Norman P. Lasca and Jack Donahue, pp.
        513–523. Geological Society of America, Centennial Special Vol. 4.
        Boulder.

1992   Interpreting Stratification of a Shell Midden. In *Deciphering a Shell
        Midden*, edited by Julie K. Stein, pp. 71–93. Academic Press, San
        Diego.

1993   Scale in Archaeology, Geosciences, and Geoarchaeology. In *Effects
        of Scale on Archaeological and Geoscientific Perspectives*, edited by
        Julie K. Stein and Angela R. Linse, pp. 1–10. Geological Society of
        America, Special Paper 283. Boulder.

1996   Geoarchaeology and Archaeostratigraphy: View from a Northwest
        Coast Shell Midden. In *Case Studies in Environmental Archaeology*,
        edited by Elizabeth J. Reitz, Lee A. Newson, and Sylvia J. Scudder,
        pp. 35–54. Plenum Press, New York.

Stein, Julie K., Kimberly D. Kombacher, and Jason L. Tyler

1992   British Camp Shell Midden Stratigraphy. In *Deciphering a Shell
        Midden*, edited by Julie K. Stein, pp. 95–134. Academic Press, San
        Diego.

Stein, Julie K. and Angela R. Linse (editors)

1993   *Effects of Scale on Archaeological and Geoscientific Perspectives.*
        Geological Society of America, Special Paper 283. Boulder.

Steno, Nicolaus

1968   *The Prodromus of Nicolaus Steno's Dissertation Concerning a Solid
        Body Enclosed by Process of Nature Within a Solid.* (English version
        with introduction and explanatory notes by John Garrett Winter.)
        Hafner Publishing, New York.

Steponaitis, Vincas P.

1983   *Ceramics, Chronology, and Community Patterns: An Archaeological
        Study at Moundville.* Academic Press, New York.

Sternberg, R. S.

1982   *Archaeomagnetic Secular Variation of Direction and Paleointensity
        in the American Southwest.* Ph.D. dissertation, University of
        Arizona. University Microfilms, Ann Arbor.

1989   Secular Variation of Archaeomagnetic Direction in the American Southwest A.D. 750–1425. *Journal of Geophysical Research* 94:527–547.

1996   Daniel Wolfman: 1939–1994. *Society for Archaeological Science Bulletin* 19(3/4):5–6.

1997   Archaeomagnetic Dating. In *Chronometric and Allied Dating in Archaeology*, edited by R. E. Taylor and M. Aitken. Plenum Press, New York.

Sternberg, R. S., R. C. Lange, B. A. Murphy, W. L. Deaver, and L. S. Teague

1991   Archaeomagnetic Dating at Las Colinas, Arizona, USA. In *Archaeometry '90*, edited by E. Pernicka and G. A. Wagner, pp. 597–606. Birkhäuser Verlag, Basel.

Sternberg, R. S. and R. H. McGuire

1990a Techniques for Constructing Secular Variation Curves and for Interpreting Archaeomagnetic Dates. In *Archaeomagnetic Dating*, edited by J. L. Eighmy and R. S. Sternberg, pp. 109–134. University of Arizona Press, Tucson.

1990b Archaeomagnetic Secular Variation in the American South-West, A.D. 700–1450. In *Archaeomagnetic Dating*, edited by J. L. Eighmy and R. S. Sternberg, pp. 199–225. University of Arizona Press, Tucson.

Stevenson, C. M., J. K. Bates, T. A. Abrajano, and B. E. Scheetz

1989   Obsidian and Basaltic Glass Dating Require Significant Revision of High Temperature Rate Development Methods. *Society for Archaeological Science Bulletin* 12:3–5.

Stevenson, C. M., J. Carpenter, and B. E. Scheetz

1989   Recent Advances in the Experimental Determination and Application of Hydration Rates. *Archaeometry* 31:193–206.

Stevenson, C. M., E. Knaus, J. J. Mazer, and J. K. Bates

1993   Homogeneity of Water Content in Obsidian from the Coso Volcanic Field: Implications for Obsidian Hydration Dating. *Geoarchaeology* 8:371–384.

Stevenson, C. M., J. J. Mazer, and B. E. Scheetz

1998   Laboratory Obsidian Hydration Rates: Theory, Method, and Application. In *Archaeological Obsidian Studies: Method and Theory*, edited by M. S. Shackley, pp. 181-204. Advances in Archaeological and Museum Science Vol. 3. Plenum Press, New York.

Stevenson, C. M. and B. E. Scheetz

1989   Induced Hydration Rate Development of Obsidian from the Coso Volcanic Field: A Comparison of Experimental Procedures. In *Current Directions in California Obsidian Studies*, edited by R. E. Hughes, pp. 23–30. Contributions of the University of California Archaeological Research Facility No. 48. Berkeley.

Stevenson, C. M., P. J. Sheppard, and D. G. Sutton

1996   Advances in the Hydration Dating of New Zealand Obsidian. *Journal of Archaeological Science* 23:233–242.

Steward, Julian

1937   Ecological Aspects of Southwestern Society. *Anthropos* 32:87–104.
Stokes, Marvin A. and Terah L. Smiley
   1963   Tree-Ring Dates from the Navajo Land Claim, I: The Northern
            Sector. *Tree-Ring Bulletin* 25(3–4):8–18.
   1964   Tree-Ring Dates from the Navajo Land Claim, II: The Western
            Sector. *Tree-Ring Bulletin* 26(1–4):13–27.
   1966   Tree-Ring Dates from the Navajo Land Claim, III: The Southern
            Sector. *Tree-Ring Bulletin* 27(3–4):12–15.
   1968   *An Introduction to Tree-Ring Dating.* University of Chicago Press,
            Chicago.
   1969   Tree-Ring Dates from the Navajo Land Claim, IV: The Eastern
            Sector. *Tree-Ring Bulletin* 29(1–2):2–14.
   1996   *An Introduction to Tree-Ring Dating.* University of Arizona Press,
            Tucson.
Stokes, Stephen
   1992   Optical Dating of Independently Dated Late Quaternary Eolian
            Deposits from the Southern High Plains. *Current Research in the
            Pleistocene* 9:125–129.
Stone, Lawrence
   1979   The Revival of Narrative: Reflections on a New Old History. *Past
            and Present* 85:3–24.
Stross, F. H., H. R. Bowman, H. V. Michel, F. Asaro, and N. Hammond
   1978   Mayan Obsidian: Source Correlation for Southern Belize Artifacts.
            Archaeometry 20:89–93.
Stross, F. H., T. R. Hester, R. F. Heizer, and R. N. Jack
   1976   Chemical and Archaeological Studies of Mesoamerican Obsidians.
            In *Advances in Obsidian Glass Studies. Archaeological and
            Geochemical Perspectives*, edited by R. E. Taylor, pp. 240–258.
            Noyes Press, Park Ridge, New Jersey.
Stross, F. H., J. R. Weaver, G. E. Wyld, R. F. Heizer, and J. A. Graham
   1968   *Analysis of American Obsidians by X-ray Fluorescence and Neutron
            Activation Analysis.* Contributions of the University of California
            Research Facility No. 5. Berkeley.
Stucki, Barbara R.
   1993   Three-Dimensional Assessment of Activity Areas in a Shell Midden:
            An Example from the Hoko River Rockshelter, State of Washington.
            In *Practices of Archaeological Stratigraphy*, edited by Edward C.
            Harris, Marley R. Brown, III, and Gregory J. Brown, pp. 122–138.
            Academic Press, London.
Stuiver, M. and H. A. Polach
   1977   Discussion: Reporting of [14]C Data. *Radiocarbon* 19:355–363.
Suess, H. E.
   1961   Secular Changes in the Concentration of Atmospheric Radiocarbon.
            In *Problems Related to Interplanetary Matter*, pp. 90–95. Nuclear
            Science Series Report No. 33, Publication 845. National Academy of
            Sciences–National Research Council, Washington, D.C.
Sullivan, Alan P., III, Matthew E. Becher, and Christian E. Downum

1995   Tusayan White Ware Chronology: New Archaeological and Dendrochronological Evidence. *The Kiva* 61:175–188.

Sutton, S. R.

1985   TL Measurements on Shock-Metamorphosed Sandstone and Dolomite from Meteor Crater, Arizona. *Journal of Geophysical Research* 9:3683–3700.

Tarling, D. H.

1983   *Paleomagnetism: Principles and Applications in Geology, Geophysics and Archaeology.* Chapman and Hall, London.

1991   Archaeomagnetism and Paleomagnetism. In *Scientific Dating Methods*, edited by H. Y. Göksu, M. Oberhofer, and D. Regulla, pp. 217–250. Kluwer, Dordrecht.

Taylor, R. E.

1978   Radiocarbon Dating: An Archaeological Perspective. In *Archaeological Chemistry II*, edited by G. F. Carter, pp. 33–69. Advances in Chemistry Series, No. 171. American Chemical Society, Washington.

1985   The Beginnings of Radiocarbon Dating. In American Antiquity: An Historical Perspective. *American Antiquity* 50:309–325.

1987   *Radiocarbon Dating an Archaeological Perspective.* Academic Press, San Diego.

1996   Radiocarbon Dating: The Continuing Revolution. *Evolutionary Anthropology* 4:169–181.

1997   Radiocarbon Dating. In *Chronometric Dating in Archaeology*, edited by R. E. Taylor and M. J. Aitken, pp. 63–96. Plenum Press, New York.

Taylor, R. E. and Martin J. Aitken (editors)

1997   *Chronometric Dating in Archaeology.* Plenum Press, New York.

Taylor, R. E., M. Stuiver, and P. J. Reimer

1996   Development and Extension of the Calibration of the Radiocarbon Time Scale: Archaeological Applications. *Quaternary Geochronology* 15:665–668.

Taylor, Walter W.

1948   A Study of Archaeology. *American Anthropologist* 50(3), Part 2.

1958   *Two Archaeological Studies in Northern Arizona: The Pueblo Ecology Study: Hail and Farewell, and A Brief Survey Through the Grand Canyon of the Colorado River.* Museum of Northern Arizona Bulletin No. 30. Northern Arizona Society of Science and Art, Flagstaff.

Thellier, E. and O. Thellier

1951   Magnétisme Terrestre: Sur la Directioni du Champ Magnétique Terrestre, Retrouvée sur des Parois de Fours des Époques Punique et Romaine, à Carthage. *Comptes Redus des Seances de l'Academie des Sciences* 233:1476–1479.

Thomas, David Hurst

1978   The Awful Truth About Statistics in Archaeology. *American Antiquity* 43:231–244.

1981 How to Classify the Projectile Points from Monitor Valley, Nevada. *Journal of California and Great Basin Anthropology* 3:7–43.

1986a *Refiguring Anthropology: First Principles of Probability and Statistics.* Waveland Press, Prospect Heights, Illinois.

1986b Points on Points: A Reply to Flenniken and Raymond. *American Antiquity* 51:619–627.

1989 *Archaeology.* Holt, Rinehart and Winston, Fort Worth.

Tite, M. S.

1966 Thermoluminescent Dating of Ancient Ceramics: A Reassessment. *Archaeometry* 9:155–169.

Tite, M. S. and J. Waine

1962 Thermoluminescence Dating: A Re-Appraisal. *Archaeometry* 5:53–79.

Towner, Ronald H.

1996 The Pueblito Phenomenon: A New Perspective on Post-Revolt Navajo Culture. In *The Archaeology of Navajo Origins*, edited by R. H. Towner, pp. 149–170. University of Utah Press, Salt Lake City.

1997 *The Dendrochronology of the Navajo Pueblitos of Dinétah.* Ph.D. dissertation, Department of Anthropology, University of Arizona, Tucson. University Microfilms, Ann Arbor.

Towner, Ronald H. and Jeffrey S. Dean

1992 LA 2298: The Oldest Pueblito Revisited. *The Kiva* 59:315–331.

Tremaine, K. J.

1989 *Obsidian as a Time Keeper: An Investigation in Absolute and Relative Dating.* Master's thesis, Department of Anthropology, Sonoma State University. Rohnert Park, California.

1991 A Relative Dating Approach for Bodie Hills and Casa Diablo Obsidian Derived from Accelerated Hydration Experiments. In *Archaeological Evaluation of CA-Mno-2456, -2488, and -564, Near Bridgeport, Mono County, California.* Ms. on file at California Archaeological Inventory, NW Information Center.

Tremaine, K. J. and D. A. Frederickson

1988 Induced Obsidian Hydration Experiments: An Investigation in Relative Dating. *Materials Research Society Symposium Proceedings* 123:271–278.

Trembour, F. W. and I. Friedman

1984 Obsidian Hydration Dating and Field Site Temperature. In *Obsidian Studies in the Great Basin*, edited by R. E. Hughes, pp. 79–90. Contributions of the University of California Archaeological Research Facility No. 45. Berkeley.

Trembour, F. W., I. Friedman, F. J. Jurceka, and F. L. Smith

1986 A Simple Device for Integrating Temperature, Relative Humidity or Salinity over Time. *Journal of Atmospheric and Oceanic Technology* 3:186–190.

Trembour, F. W., F. L. Smith, and I. Friedman

1988 Diffusion Cells for Integrating Temperature and Humidity over Long

Periods of Time. *Materials Research Society Symposium Proceedings* 123:245–251.

Trigger, Bruce G.

  1978   *Time and Tradition: Essays in Archaeological Interpretation.* Columbia University Press, New York.

  1989   A History of Archaeological Thought. Cambridge University Press, Cambridge.

Tsong, I. S. T., C. A. Houser, N. A. Yusef, R. F. Messico, and W. B. White

  1978   Obsidian Hydration Profile Measured by Sputter-Induced Optical Emission. *Science* 201:339–441.

Tsong, I. S. T., G. A. Smith, J. W. Michels, A. L. Wintenberg, P. D. Miller, and C. D. Moak

  1981   Dating Obsidian Artifacts by Depth-Profiling of Artificially Hydrated Surface Layers. *Journal of Nuclear Instruments and Methods* 191:403–407.

Turner, R. C., J. M. Radley, and W. V. Mayneord

  1958   The Alpha-Ray Activity of Human Tissues. *British Journal of Radiology* 31:397–402.

Vaillant, George C.

  1927   *The Chronological Significance of Maya Ceramics.* Ph.D. dissertation, Harvard University, Cambridge.

Vansina, Jan

  1985   *Oral Tradition as History.* University of Wisconsin Press, Madison.

Van West, Carla R.

  1990   *Modeling Prehistoric Climatic Variability and Agricultural Production in Southwestern Colorado.* Ph.D. dissertation, Washington State University. University Microfilms, Ann Arbor.

Varien, Mark D. and Barbara J. Mills

  1997   Accumulations Research: Problems and Prospects of Estimating Site Occupation Span. *Journal of Archaeological Method and Theory* 4:141–191.

Villa, Paola

  1983   *Terra Amata and the Middle Pleistocene Archaeological Record of Southern France.* U.C. Publications in Anthropology, Vol. 13. University of California Press, Berkeley.

Wallace, Henry D.

  1986   Decorated Ceramics: Introduction, Methods, and Rincon Phase Seriation. In *Archaeological Investigations at the West Branch Site: Early and Middle Rincon Occupation in the Southern Tucson Basin,* by F. W. Huntington, pp. 127–164. Anthropological Papers No. 5. Institute for American Research, Tucson.

Warren, C. N. (editor)

  1990   *Archaeological Investigations at Nelson Wash, Fort Irwin, California.* Submitted to the National Park Service, Western Region, by Dames & Moore, San Diego.

Watanabe, N.

  1959   The Direction of Remnant Magnetization of Baked Earth and Its

Application to Chronology for Anthropology and Archaeology in Japan. *Journal of the Faculty of Science, University of Tokyo* 2:1–188.

Watanabe, N. and R. L. DuBois
1965 Some Results of an Archaeomagnetic Study on the Secular Variation in the Southwest of North America. *Journal of Geomagnetism and Geoelectricity* 17:395–397.

Waters, Michael R.
1992 Principles of Geoarchaeology: A North American Perspective. University of Arizona Press, Tucson.

Weaver, Kenneth F.
1967 Magnetic Clues Help Date the Past. *National Geographic* May 1967:696–701.

Webb, G. E.
1983 *Tree-Rings and Telescopes: The Scientific Career of A. E. Douglass.* University of Arizona Press, Tucson.

Webb, W. S. and D. L. DeJarnette
1942 *An Archaeological Survey of Pickwick Basin in the Adjacent Portions of Alabama, Mississippi, and Tennessee.* Bureau of American Ethnology Bulletin No. 129. Smithsonian Institution, Washington, D.C.

Welch, P. D.
1994 The Occupational History of the Bessimer Site. *Southeastern Archaeology* 13:1–26.

Wheat, Jo Ben
1967 A Paleo-Indian Bison Kill. *Scientific American* 216:43–52.

Wheeler, Sir Mortimer
1954 *Archaeology from the Earth.* Oxford University Press, London.

White, Hayden
1987 *The Content of the Form: Narrative Discourse and Historical Representation.* Johns Hopkins University Press, Baltimore.

Wilcox, David R.
1981 The Entry of the Athabaskans into the American Southwest: The Problem Today. In *The Protohistoric Period in the American Southwest, A.D. 1450–1700*, edited by D. R. Wilcox and W. B. Masse, pp. 213–256. Arizona State University Anthropological Research Papers No. 24. Tempe.

Wilcox, David R. and W. Bruce Masse (editors)
1981 *The Protohistoric Period in the American Southwest, A.D. 1450–1700.* Arizona State University Anthropological Research Papers No. 24. Tempe.

Willey, Gordon R.
1953 Prehistoric Settlement Patterns in the Viru Valley, Peru. *Bulletin of American Ethnology* 155.
1985 Some Continuing Problems in New World Culture History. *American Antiquity* 50:351–363.

Willey, Gordon R. and P. Phillips

1958   *Method and Theory in American Archaeology.* University of Chicago Press, Chicago.

Willey, Gordon R. and Jeremy A. Sabloff

1980   *A History of American Archaeology,* 2ⁿᵈ ed. W. H. Freeman and Company, San Francisco.

1993   *A History of American Archaeology,* 3ʳᵈ ed. W. H. Freeman, New York.

Williams, Stephen

1991   *Fantastic Archaeology: The Wild Side of North American Archaeology.* University of Pennsylvania Press, Philadelphia.

Wilson, C. Dean

1995   A Reexamination of the Recent Dating of Reserve Black-on-white. Paper Presented at the Mogollon Conference, Silver City, New Mexico.

Wilson, C. Dean and Eric Blinman

1994   Early Anasazi Ceramics and the Basketmaker Transition. In *Proceedings of the Anasazi Symposium 1991,* compiled by Art Hutchinson and Jack E. Smith, pp. 199–211. Mesa Verde Museum Association. Mesa Verde, Colorado.

Wilson, C. Dean, Eric Blinman, and James M. Skibo

1997   Resources and Technology: Ceramic Traditions and Cultural Boundaries in the Highlands of the Southwestern United States. Paper Presented at the Conference on Ceramic Technology and Production, British Museum, London.

Wilson, C. Dean, Eric Blinman, James M. Skibo, and Michael Brian Schiffer

1996   Designing of Southwestern Pottery: A Technological and Experimental Approach. In *Interpreting Southwestern Diversity: Underlying Principles and Overarching Patterns,* edited by Paul R. Fish and J. Jefferson Reid, pp. 249–256. Arizona State University Anthropological Research Papers No. 48. Tempe.

Windes, Thomas C.

1977   Typology and Technology of Anasazi Ceramics. In *Settlement and Subsistence Along the Lower Chaco River: The CGP Survey,* edited by Charles A. Reher, pp. 279–370. University of New Mexico Press, Albuquerque.

1987   *Investigations at the Pueblo Alto Complex, Chaco Canyon,* Vol. I. Chaco Canyon Studies, National Park Service, U.S. Department of the Interior, Santa Fe.

Winter, John

1971   Thermoluminescent Dating of Pottery. In *Dating Techniques for the Archaeologist,* edited by Henry N. Michael and Elizabeth K. Ralph, pp. 118–151. The Massachusetts Institute of Technology Press, Cambridge.

Wintle, Ann G.

1996   Archaeologically-Relevant Dating Techniques for the Next Century: Small, Hot, and Identified by Acronyms. *Journal of Archaeological Science* 23:123–138.

Wintle, Ann G., and D. J. Huntley.
  1979   Thermoluminescence Dating of a Deep-Sea Ocean Core. *Nature*
         279:710–712.
  1980   Thermoluminescence Dating of Ocean Sediments. *Canadian Journal
         of Earth Sciences* 17:348–360.
Wissler, Clark
  1917   The New Archaeology. *American Museum Journal* 17(2):100–101.2
Wolfman, D.
  1973   *A Re-Evaluation of Mesoamerican Chronology: A.D. 1–1200*. Ph.D.
         dissertation, University of Colorado. University Microfilms, Ann
         Arbor.
  1978   An Inundated Archaeomagnetic Sample. In *The Mechanical and
         Chemical Effects of Inundation at Abiquiu Reservoir*, edited by C. F.
         Schaafsma, Appendix I. School of American Research, Santa Fe.
  1990a Archaeomagnetic Dating in Arkansas and Border Areas of Adjacent
         States - II. In *Archaeomagnetic Dating*, edited by J. L. Eighmy and
         R. S. Sternberg, pp. 237–260. University of Arizona Press, Tucson.
  1990b Mesoamerican Chronology and Archaeomagnetic Dating. In
         Archaeomagnetic Dating, edited by J. L. Eighmy and R. S.
         Sternberg, pp. 261–308. University of Arizona Press, Tucson.
  1990c Retrospect and Prospect. In *Archaeomagnetic Dating*, edited by J. L.
         Eighmy and R. S. Sternberg, pp. 313–364. University of Arizona
         Press, Tucson.
Wolfman, D. and R. E. Dodson
  1986   *Los Resultados Arqueomagnéticos de las Muestras Recogidas en El
         Péru en 1983*. Submitted to the Instituto Nacional de Cultura, Lima,
         Peru.
  1987   *Los Resultados Arqueomagnéticos de las Muestras Recogidas en El
         México en 1982*. Submitted to Departamento de Monumentos
         Prehispanicos, Instituto Nacional de Antropología e Historia,
         Mexico City.
Wood, W. Raymond
  1990   Ethnohistory and Historical Method. In *Archaeological Method and
         Theory*, Vol. 2, edited by Michael B. Schiffer. Academic Press, New
         York.
Woodbury, Richard B.
  1960a Nels C. Nelson and Chronological Archaeology. *American Antiquity*
         25:400–401.
  1960b Nelson's Stratigraphy. *American Antiquity* 26:98–99.
Wroth, William
  1982   *Christian Images in Hispanic New Mexico: The Taylor Museum
         Collection of Santos*. Taylor Museum of the Colorado Fine Arts
         Center, Colorado Springs.
Zeier, C. D.
  1989   Obsidian Hydration Studies at 35-JA-107: A Study of Alternate
         Methods and Interpretations (Abstract). *Northwest Anthropological
         Research Notes* 22:217.

Zeller, Edward J.

 1968   Geological Age Determination by Thermoluminescence. In *Thermoluminescence of Geological Materials*, edited by D. J. McDougall, pp. 311–327. Academic Press, London.

Zimmerman, D. W.

 1967   Thermoluminescence from Fine Grains from Ancient Pottery. *Archaeometry* 10:26–28.

 1971   Thermoluminescent Dating Using Fine Grains from Pottery. *Archaeometry* 13:29–52.

Zuckerman, Harriet

 1988   The Sociology of Science. In *Handbook of Sociology*, edited by Neil Smelser, pp. 511–574. Sage Publications, Newbury Park, California.

Acknowledgments

I would like to thank Jeffrey S. Dean, C. Vance Haynes, Arthur J. Jelinek, Art McWilliams, Barbara Mills, J. Jefferson Reid, Michael B. Schiffer, and María Nieves Zedeño, for their suggestions regarding potential contributors to this volume. I would also like to thank Richard V. N. Ahlstrom, Dena Dincauze, and an anonymous reviewer for comments on prior drafts of this volume and on the 1997 symposium. The concept for and existence of this volume remain my burden to carry or cause to celebrate; only time will tell.

Contributors

Charlotte Beck
Department of Anthropology
Hamilton College
Clinton, New York

Eric Blinman
Museum of New Mexico
Office of Archaeological Studies
Santa Fe, New Mexico

Jennifer L. Croissant
Program on Culture, Science, Technology, and Society
The University of Arizona
Tucson, Arizona

Jeffrey S. Dean
Laboratory of Tree-Ring Research
The University of Arizona
Tucson, Arizona

Jeffrey L. Eighmy
Department of Anthropology
Colorado State University
Fort Collins, Colorado

James K. Feathers
Department of Anthropology
The University of Washington
Seattle, Washington

George T. Jones
Department of Anthropology
Hamilton College
Clinton, New York

Stephen E. Nash
Department of Anthropology
Field Museum of Natural History
Chicago, Illinois

Julie K. Stein
Department of Anthropology
The University of Washington
Seattle, Washington

R.E. Taylor
Department of Anthropology
The University of California
Riverside, California

Ronald H. Towner
Laboratory of Tree-Ring Research
The University of Arizona
Tucson, Arizona

Index